PRAISE FOR

THE LEADING MAN

"*The Leading Man* is both practical and soulful. Like Stephen Covey, Dale Carnegie, and Deepak Chopra, Greg Dinkin is a gifted teacher, though his sharp edge and laugh-out-loud humor will make you forget this is a how-to book. Kudos to Dinkin for giving us a safe space to get to know ourselves as well as a blueprint so we can all live as leading men."

—Michael Parness, author of *Rule the Freakin' Markets*

"Greg Dinkin has written a book for men who wouldn't be caught dead reading a self-help book. There's no flowery language, no new-age mumbo jumbo, and no vague conceptual BS. Just straightforward guidance from a guy who's been to his own personal hell and back—and figured out what it takes to live well. If you're ready for success, start reading immediately."

—Doug Sundheim, author of *Taking Smart Risks*

"Greg Dinkin is able to communicate the *hows* of life as well as the *whys*. His poker wins give him street cred, his yoga practice gives him heart, and his financial and literary know-how appeals to the brainiest of audiences. Funny, honest, and credible, Dinkin has created a workable and worthwhile map for men to navigate, even if they're not lost. The women in their lives will applaud them for developing that most sought-after quality—intimacy—and, if they're smart, will join them on the journey by answering the same seven questions."

—Amelia Catone, University Academic and Career Advisor

"At last, an accessible book on personal development for men who want answers and can't stand dogma. *The Leading Man* provides the guidance to figure out who you are and what makes you tick. You'll have all the tools you need to develop habits and belief systems that create health, wealth, balance, clarity, and fulfillment."

> —Peter T. Fornatale, *NY Times* bestselling coauthor (with Chris Jericho) of *Undisputed*

ALSO BY GREG DINKIN

Amarillo Slim In a World Full of Fat People (in collaboration with Amarillo Slim Preston)

The Finance Doctor (as Dr. Dink, with Frank R. Scatoni)

The Poker MBA: Winning in Business No Matter What Cards You're Dealt

Watch Greg's TEDTalk and other training videos at www.gregdinkin.com

THE LEADING MAN

---

7 EMPOWERING QUESTIONS
TO BREAK FREE AND
FIND YOUR OWN WINNING WAY

Greg Dinkin

All advice in this book is intended to guide you to explore your personal needs and what suits you best. This book is not intended to provide medical or healthcare advice and should not be treated as such. Just as I emphasize that I can't give you the answers, I can't possibly tell you what medical practices and/or philosophies, workouts, or diets are best for you. To that end, I strongly encourage you to obtain the advice of your healthcare practitioner before beginning a new healthcare regime, diet, exercise plan, or physical activity. Likewise, without knowing you personally, I would be remiss to recommend any juice fast or detoxification programs. Please do not delay seeking medical advice, disregard medical advice, or discontinue medical treatment because of information provided in this book.

Note: This is a work of nonfiction, though creative license was taken and some of the names have been changed. See page 249 for further clarification.

Author photograph by Jamie Sutherland
Front jacket designed by Mike Wierzenski
Back jacket designed by carterdesignworks
"Dinkin's 7 Empowering Questions" designed by Katie Osborn

For bulk orders, contact gregdinkin@gmail.com.

ISBN: 978-0692217665

"None but ourselves can free our minds."
—Bob Marley

For my godson, LRM:
When I stepped up to lead you, you led me. I love you.

TABLE OF CONTENTS

Preface:	*An Inside-Out Approach to Your Movie*	1
Introduction:	*Man Up With 7 Empowering Questions*	9
Question One:	Why Ask?	21
Question Two:	What Is My Ideal Day?	51
Question Three:	Who Am I?	69
Question Four:	Where Am I Now?	93
Question Five:	How Do Thoughts Propel Me?	123
Question Six:	Which Tools Uniquely Suit Me?	159
Question Seven:	What Habits Produce Effective Results?	187
Commencement:	Your Most Powerful Question	211
Appendix:	*Your Answers, Your Map*	231
Acknowledgments and Tools for Leading Writers		239
Clarification of Creative License		249
Leading Movies, Shows, and Books		251
The Dream Team		255
Dinkin's 7 Empowering Questions		259
About the Author		260

AN INSIDE-OUT APPROACH TO YOUR MOVIE

"The trick is to realize that you're always doing what you want to do. Always. Nobody's making you do anything. Once you get that, you see that you're free and that life is really just a series of choices."

—Jeff Daniels' character in *The Answer Man*

Once upon a time I was fat, broke, lonely, and miserable. Life was a fight. And I was losing. I was chained to my computer, but I was $50,000 in debt. I was always on a diet, yet I weighed 300 pounds.

The odd part about making a mess of my life is that, seemingly, I had done everything right. I wrote mission statements, ate my vegetables, and kept my promises. When I made up my mind to write a book, run a marathon, start a business, win a poker tournament, or learn guitar, I accomplished my goal.

The problem was that when I "got somewhere," I felt so empty that I started looking around for the next thing—the next deal, the next meal, the next *fix*. And that mindset led me right back to misery.

Asking seven empowering questions got me out of my rut.

Answering them led to a life of my own design.

I went back to school to become a holistic health coach, and when I got to the bottom of *why* I didn't feel full (or fulfilled), I lost 100 pounds.

I learned to reprogram my thoughts—a skill I will walk you through—and quickly earned enough money to erase my debt and travel for several years. Most importantly, instead of lugging around all that emptiness, I felt excited, fulfilled, and appreciated. I had earned the inner peace and outer confidence that is a byproduct of answering empowering questions.

I was finally living the life of a leading man.

Why Become a Leading Man?

The leading man has awareness, empathy, and intuition. He is coachable, open to criticism, and willing to work on his flaws. He trusts his gut instinct, which breeds the confidence to act decisively.

The leading man *gets it*. He commands respect and elevates others with his presence. His word is gold. When faced with adversity, he is the voice of reason. And for all his focus and success, he enjoys the ride.

But can we actually *learn* to be confident, grateful, and fulfilled? Can what seems intuitive be taught?

The Leading Man is not about how to talk to an investor or a woman you think is out of your league. It's about arriving at a place where you believe— where you *know*—that no one is out of your league. It's about figuring out who you are, how you want to live, and taking the steps to make it happen. It's about developing the mindset that makes you feel like you are constantly in the right place at the right time.

I can't teach you how to look like a bodybuilder or make a billion dollars. What I can show you is how to master the arts of listening and relating so you can truly connect with people. I can walk you through how to figure out what makes you tick, when you are at your best, and how to maximize your gifts. And when you struggle, as we all do, I can show you where to find the tools to get unstuck.

This book provides everything you need to discover your own answers. You'll create a map that leads to financial freedom, which is just another term for *life* freedom. You'll learn to think and act like a winner. Rather than be a pawn in someone else's agenda, you will gain the power to set the agenda and design your ideal day.

Imagine being the writer and director who has the power to create his own movie—and being the star who gets to experience it. A leading man is not just "living the dream." He is living the dream that he *created*. And while he makes it look easy, you will learn that leading men are not born. They are made. This book shows you how.

Skip the Bottom and Close the Gap

I ask my workshop attendees if they need to hit rock bottom in order to change. My favorite answer came from a guy named Chaz, who replied, "Not if you're paying attention." It's such a powerful answer that I wish I could plant Chaz in all my audiences. You don't need to wait for something bad to happen to build the life you want *if you're paying attention.*

The reality is that most of us need to get smacked upside the head to start paying attention. In fact, it's often the *absence* of extreme pain that lulls us into the doldrums of an unsatisfying life. I don't know many men who are down and out, but I know plenty who are fed-up—yet sadly remain stuck.

When a man asks me why he should bother asking all these questions, I reply by asking just one: Is there a gap between the life you want and the life you have? If not, he should carry on as is. If there is a gap—if he's not living up to his own standard—we continue asking questions.

Asking questions—like analyzing a blood test, reviewing video of a sporting match, or studying an annual report—is not the endgame. Questions are tools that lead to information. Like a mirror, they offer a unique vantage point to see our blind spots and gain perspective. If we take the time to answer them, they alert us to clues so we don't walk blindly through life.

If you are ignoring the signs of discontent in your life, what will it take for you to hear your own wake-up call? Maybe you picked up this book because you got fired or dumped. Perhaps you accomplished a life-long goal and felt an unexpected emptiness. Or maybe your buckle snapped on your fourth trip back to the Chinese buffet. Whatever your situation, you have made a choice that you are ready to ask questions in order to thrive.

Avoid the Guru Trap and Work Inside-Out

Has anyone ever told you that you must hear this speaker, read this book, or see this movie? You have to, because…wait for it...

It will change your life!

Newsflash: It won't.

Looking for answers outside of yourself only leads to the "guru trap"—the myth that another person, place, or concept holds the key to your success. The trap is thinking that being a spectator takes the place of making the sales call, saying you're sorry, or powering through that last rep.

Running from one guru to the next is like reading the menu at a restaurant over and over again. It won't nourish you unless you put in an order and eat the food. That's why the approach of leading men is inside-out. It's *not* the guru, the retreat, or the seminar that changes your life. It's the openness to the experience and the actions you take as a result.

My mom loves to say that the only guarantees in life come with appliances. I say that no program works unless it is your own. And *you* work *it*. Daily.

Let me warn you that I won't be telling you what to do. How could anyone design an *individualized* plan without knowing the individual? Our guru culture anoints experts to provide formulas that fail to account for our unique lifestyles, desires, and tastes. As a result, they end up failing us.

I emphasize that the answers are within. And while that sounds like a given, we still need to learn how to access them.

We access answers with questions.

Questions created specifically for men like us.

◎ ◎ ◎

My friend Richard, who is 62, has turned into an evangelist for *The Leading Man* because he has witnessed the depressing lives of men his age that stayed on autopilot and never asked questions. He has witnessed the consequences—

the heartbreak, the fear, the *regrets*—of guys who never paused to choose how they want to live. He echoes what Thoreau said about the mass of men leading lives of quiet desperation and said this book gives him hope that the next generation of men will not "buy our way to death."

What separates you from the masses is your willingness to ask questions. Questions create a pause, and that moment of reflection breeds the insight to make effective choices rather than fall back into destructive patterns.

What About the Leading Woman?

To the women who are looking for answers, this is not one of those books about figuring out how to get inside the head of a man. *The Leading Man* is about personal development, so only continue reading (this goes for everyone) if the person you want to gain more insight about is *you.* If, after reading this book, you (man or woman) feel there are others in your life who can benefit from it, please share your enthusiasm and let them know what you gained by asking questions.

The reason I wrote this book for men is because I have witnessed how much we want to evolve and thrive. I have also seen us get stuck when other books and tools didn't seem accessible. Experience has taught me that when we keep it real, when we add some humor and levity, we can reach new heights. Letting go of our masculine armor is often the most challenging part, which is why I'm offering you the best of what I know in an engaging way.

Whenever I'm at a yoga workshop or a relationship seminar (two places where men are scarce), women tell me that they wish their boyfriend or husband or brother or dad would attend something like this. Then they tell me that these men won't listen to them, but they might listen to *me.*

You kind of look like a meathead and you're here.

Thanks. I guess. Pass the kale chips.

Sadly, as my friend Becky and her kids experienced, an unevolved man can devastate everyone in his path. After years of abuse, Becky summoned the courage to leave her husband. In her support group, she kept hearing stories similar to her own, and in addition to the compassion she felt for the women, she also felt it for the men. Becky asked, "How miserable, confused, and worthless must these men feel if they're treating others this way?" Like all powerful questions, it made me reflect and work even harder to formulate questions for the men who want to find their way.

Our Dream Team Makes Us Laugh and Reach

Some say a coach's role is to support. Others say a great coach makes you reach. Usually it's a little bit of both. As your coach in this process, I ask that you stay in your comfort zone, read at your leisure, and look for a pearl of wisdom or two. Besides, you're only going to receive the message when you are ready for it. On the other hand, I encourage you to reach *outside* of your comfort zone. Browsing is for tourists. To get the most out of this book, you have to stop and sit with your answers long enough for them to sink in.

Crafting a map for your life takes time and effort, which is why I've extracted the most powerful nuggets from the ashes of my experience and provided examples of leading men. Like a DJ who curates the latest and greatest music, I will expose you to a dream team of talented voices.

If you like music, movies, sports, comedy, and insight from dynamic sources, you're in for a treat. The dream team includes: Dale Carnegie, Stephen Covey, Steve Jobs, Warren Buffett, Malcolm Gladwell, Joshua Rosenthal, Abraham Maslow, Joe Ehrmann, James Altucher, Tony Schwartz, Simon Sinek, David Deida, Byron Katie, Timothy Ferriss, Daniel Gilbert, Mark Hyman, and Deepak Chopra.

From the worlds of sports and poker, you'll see how Charles Barkley, Michael Jordan, LeBron James, Russell Wilson, Tim Tebow, Daniel Negreanu, and Phil Gordon use these techniques. You'll also hear stories of how coaches Pat Riley, Phil Jackson, and Mack Brown help others shine.

Since prophets often masquerade as musicians and comedians, you'll hear from some of the finest, including Tom Petty, Jerry Seinfeld, and Louis C.K. Keeping them in character, we'll gain insight from Tyler Durden, Tony Soprano, and, of course, "The Dude" from *The Big Lebowski*.

Before we begin your story, let's write the ending.

Picture the Leading Man's Movie

See yourself as the leading man in this story. You are the writer, the director, and the star. In the first act, you work through your challenges. In the final act, you break free.

Take a moment to look ahead and visualize the perfect ending for your movie. Ask what the leading man is after, what he truly seeks. Using the words from Joseph Campbell's "Hero's Journey," think about what it looks like to "return with the elixir." If you can write the ending, the rest of the story will start to write itself.

My friend Monte, who you will get to know in these pages, loved the idea of seeing his life as a movie. "When you asked what a fulfilling life looked like," he said, "I paused and imagined my house, garden, porch, friends in the living room on a comfy couch, guitar in the corner, eclectic art on the walls, and a loving wife who encourages me to be the best man I can."

When Monte took the time to see himself as the hero in his own movie, he realized the gap between the life he wanted and the life he was living. This image woke him up to the reality that remaining on autopilot put him on a collision course for disaster. But as soon as he envisioned what his triumphant life looked like, once he let it seep into all his senses, Monte started making choices to close the gap between the life he wanted and the life he was living.

Before we start asking more questions, consider what you are after. Use your imagination to think about where you want these questions to take you. Then see yourself victorious, basking in the glory of being a leading man.

MAN UP WITH 7 EMPOWERING QUESTIONS

"...I believe that having questions is better than having answers because it leads to more learning. After all, isn't the point of learning to help you get what you want? So don't you have to start with what you want and figure out what you have to learn in order to get it?"

—Ray Dalio, investor; on 2012 *Time 100* list
of the most influential people in the world

Not long ago, if you polled those closest to Monte for the one word that best described him, the most common response would have been "clueless." It wasn't from a lack of effort. In fact, Monte may be the hardest working guy I know.

His immigrant parents ran a restaurant in New Jersey, where he learned the hospitality business from the ground up. After working his way up the hotel ranks, logging 100-hour weeks with the tenacity of a pit bull, Monte founded a hospitality real estate firm that was about to go public.

During the Super Bowl a few years ago, Monte was on the phone with his bookie while I was talking about a relationship book called *The 5 Love Languages*. It wasn't exactly game-day material, which explained why Monte wasn't the only guy in the room looking to put a muzzle on me. The women, on the other hand, including Monte's fiancée Melinda, were enthralled and later bought the book.

Monte and I met as college freshmen when we were beefy linemen on the football team. Our conversations back then centered on sports, poker, and what we were going to eat next. In my 30s, when I started traveling to a health retreat in Thailand, Monte had a field day. I took the Kumbaya and colonic jokes in stride, though I felt frustrated that our friendship hadn't evolved. Even though I'm counted on among our friends as the heart-to-heart guy, Monte never showed any vulnerability with me. If his life was a deck of cards, he would only let you see the four aces.

Like me, Monte had a history of yo-yo dieting. Whenever he got too out of shape, he would jump on the fad diet of the moment and battle his way back into form. Now we could see he was losing the battle. What we couldn't see was that behind closed doors he and his fiancée were at each other's throats. When Melinda questioned his commitment to her because he traveled so much, Monte lashed out, trying to explain that he was doing so for *them*. Exasperated, he screamed, "How many frickin' times do I have to tell you I love you for you to get it!" Empathy wasn't his strong suit; nor was asking for help.

Monte had been socialized to steer clear of talking about his feelings, and embraced the "strong, silent man" as an ideal archetype. That's why I was surprised when Monte called me and showed the smallest tinge of vulnerability. As he shared his frustration and heartache, I learned that he picked up the book about relationships after his fiancée nearly took off his head throwing it at him—on her way out the door.

Your 7 Empowering Questions

Before we resume Monte's story, and focus on the heart of yours, it is important to note that all of our lives are unique. Monte makes a fortune doing what he loves but struggles with women and weight. Other men struggle with their finances and careers, while others seem to be in a perpetual existential crisis.

Like Monte, I crave a deep, romantic relationship with a woman but agonize about giving up my freedom. Then there's the lingering question of having kids. In some moments I feel a longing to be a father, and in others, I'm paralyzed with anxiety about the responsibility of raising children. Some of my friends who are already dads tell me the same thing. And how can you blame them, given the onslaught of news to induce panic about childhood health and development?

There's also the dread of the proverbial trap—that we'll have to give up our own dreams and work jobs we hate to pay the mortgage and placate the nagging wife. But for Monte and me, that concern pales in comparison to our struggle to fight our own demons and figure out if we'll ever find our place in the world.

This unease was the impetus for asking questions. I learned the hard way that hopelessness only gets worse when we hide from it. Breakdowns, bankruptcies, and ballooning bellies don't happen overnight. And when disaster *doesn't* strike, it may leave us worse off. As we touched on earlier, that place of quiet desperation makes us even more prone to accept the notion that fear and stress will forever get the best of us. Numbing ourselves with food, drink, and TV may help get us through the day, but ultimately, dulling the pain only makes our problems easier to ignore. Denial is the first step on the road to despair.

Watching the suffering of those who don't confront their issues, Monte and I included, has strengthened my resolve to confront fear head-on. We don't always find easy answers, but asking questions at least offers clues. With more self-awareness, we can identify the source of the fear. When we take action to alleviate it, stress dissipates and serenity seeps in. I can't say that I've kicked fear's ass once and for all, but on most days, I manage to keep it on the ropes.

Because only you know the intricacies of your life, I've constructed a path that will lead to your own unique answers. If you say, "Your way sucks, Dinkin," I'm coming right back with, "It's *your* winning way, jabroni. I only asked the questions."

Here they are:

1. Why ask?
2. What is my ideal day?
3. Who am I?

4. Where am I now?

5. How do thoughts propel me?

6. Which tools uniquely suit me?

7. What habits produce effective results?

You'll see in the diagram that follows that each of the seven questions can be reduced to one word:

DINKIN'S
7 EMPOWERING
QUESTIONS

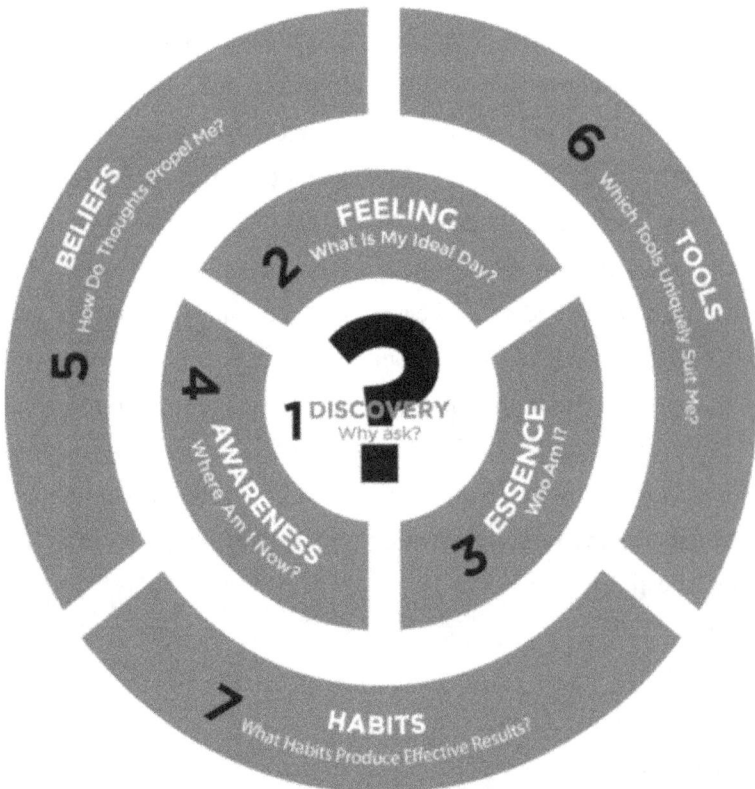

We'll dig into each question in its own chapter. At the end of each, you'll have the opportunity to create your own answers. This is where the real learning takes place, so have a pen or a keyboard handy. In the final chapter, "Commencement," we'll tie everything together.

The Real Danger Is Staying Inside Your Cave

As I do with all prospective clients, I sent Monte a list of questions and told him that our coaching process would begin when he answered them. This tactic weeds out those who are in the "guru trap"—who want *my* answers—as well as those who want to whine rather than win. If worrying, as the saying goes, is praying for more of what we don't want, then complaining is out-and-out begging for it. While others bitch and moan, leading men harness their power to take action.

Experience has taught me that embracing questions is the most reliable indicator of success. When Monte sent back his answers, I knew he would find his way. My concern is the men who aren't talking at all. One of our best friends, a renowned mathematician, recently told me he was getting divorced. My first thoughts were about what might have been. Where was the call when things started getting rough? With whom were you sharing your feelings when you felt confused and alone? Why didn't you reach out before it got to this point?

This wasn't the first time I watched a man put up a front that he was okay while suffering intense emotional pain. My friend later confessed that he never spoke of his marital anguish because he knew that the moment he did, he would be forced to take action. He was aware of his denial yet still chose to avoid a problem that put him in an even deeper hole. Part of the problem was that he had spent decades gaining scientific intelligence while overlooking emotional intelligence.

Vulnerability Is a Privilege Reserved for a King

Emotional intelligence, or EI, is street smarts, sensitivity, and interpersonal savvy. A *Forbes* article by Margie Warrell claims that 90 percent of leadership success can be attributed to high EI. You may also be familiar with the term EQ (emotional quotient), which measures EI. By any name, a leading man who "gets it," has it.

Low EI shows up in the form of arrogance and stubbornness. No matter how obvious it is that they are lost, rather than bite the bullet and own up to a mistake, lots of men refuse to ask for directions. Because we take such pride in figuring out things for ourselves, we often end up making life more difficult for ourselves and for others.

It's understandable that you want to figure out things yourself, but there's a fine line between pride and foolish pride. A fatal flaw of the old breed of men is their insistence on being right. Modern women, like my friend Maia, a tough-as-nails corporate recruiter, understand the value of not having all the answers. When she has a technology issue, admitting that she can't figure it out herself motivates others to move mountains to help her.

Conversely, many guys would put their fist through a wall in frustration and still have a broken computer. That's why today's leading man is brave enough to admit when he is lost and *does* ask for directions. Asking questions, and admitting you don't have all the answers, is the key to ultimately getting what you want.

I took a sales course from Sandler Training when I was 22 and ended up with a priceless education in human nature. One of those lessons is that our natural reaction can lead to undesired results. A speaker who perceives that he is losing his audience will raise his voice, which pushes the crowd even further away. Aggressiveness, man's normal response to adversity, often makes matters worse. If you want to get cozy on the dance floor, your first instinct is to step closer. This makes your partner step back. Get too aggressive and you'll end up with a drink in your face or a bouncer's arm at your throat.

That's why you learn to speak softer or back up to create attraction. To do so, you must be able to control your emotions in the heat of the moment.

If you're stuck at the airport and exhausted after missing a flight, barking at the customer service rep is a recipe for further disaster. This is the time to say something like, "I screwed up, and I am in a terrible bind. I could really use some help." Who could resist helping you with an approach like that?

In addition to keeping his cool, a leading man also must learn to unlock his heart. After keeping an emotional distance from a former girlfriend, I eventually felt safe enough to open up. As I started to share, I could feel the tears welling up. Taking my cue from generations of male conditioning, I shut down, afraid to show anything but strength.

I anticipated judgment, but when I looked at this beautiful woman, all I could see was profound love and respect. As I struggled to continue, she said, "Vulnerability is a privilege reserved for a king."

When the tears poured down, I realized that the ability to be vulnerable, to listen, to share, and to open our hearts, not only makes one more of a man—it defines the art of masculinity.

The Skin of the Leading Man

Over lunch one day, I asked Monte to think about what it would take for him to feel like a leading man. While you do the same, stay open to the idea that the traditional markers of male success—physical prowess, sexual conquests, and economic success—may be flawed. When I showed my friend Alex a list of my bona fides to establish my masculine credentials for writing this book—what I referred to as "dude cred"—Alex said I had "douche cred" for tooting my own horn. It forced me to probe even deeper about what it means to be a man.

When Monte asked for a flesh-and-blood example of a leading man, the first person I thought of was Mr. Skin. Mr. Skin (whose website was immortalized in the film *Knocked Up*) parlayed his savant-like knowledge of the "good parts" of films to create a multi-million-dollar business with 40 employees, including his mom. When I cofounded a literary agency, he was our first client, and I helped bring *Mr. Skin's Skincyclopedia* to Barnes & Noble and beyond. Boy, are my parents proud.

We became fast friends, and we had many fun nights out in Vegas and his hometown of Chicago. Mr. Skin's humor and wit made him the life of the party, but what impressed me most was that he thrived in all facets of life. No matter how late we were up, he always made it to the gym, took care of business, and brought more energy than anyone to the party that night.

When you're away at a bachelor party, a guy's weekend, or even on a business trip, your partner is going to be nervous. That's why Mr. Skin mastered the art of giving good *phone*. If you call from the casino or club, or send a lame text, you have made matters worse for both of you. You carry around the guilt or ruin the moment by spending half the night trying to appease her. *Oh, that's Destiny. She's just a friend. Promise. Love ya, Babes.* Meanwhile, Mr. Skin is footloose and guilt-free, because he had the EI to find a quiet place to give his then-girlfriend, now-wife, five minutes of his full attention.

It's human nature to judge a book by its cover. Part of the reason I've studied Mr. Skin's habits is that he's always in great shape yet never on a diet. Many guys live in fear of getting old and do everything they can to hide their age. On his 50th birthday, Mr. Skin wrote on Facebook: "Fifty is nifty." He celebrates life. He's the "old dad" to three kids under eleven, but whether he's coaching his kids' teams or creating a new line of business, he's running circles around guys half his age. He also supports his wife, emotionally and financially, in her role as president of a women's cancer charity.

Mr. Skin earned a college baseball scholarship and worked at the Chicago Mercantile Exchange before founding MrSkin.com. He's the consummate guy's guy, which allows us to expand our definition of masculinity beyond traditional stereotypes. Strength and confidence are not mutually exclusive traits from awareness and sensitivity. In fact, a big part of our focus is elevating all of these traits to redefine today's leading man.

The X Factor Is Execution

I wanted to make a powerful impression for my first meeting with Mr. Skin. Despite the fact that our agency didn't have two nickels to rub together, I took him to dinner at Gibsons, a high-end steakhouse in Chicago. Keep in mind that protocol in the publishing business dictates that agents pay for meals with authors. Even though I had a veteran poker face that knew how to conceal weakness, Mr. Skin saw through it and displayed the sixth sense that comes with being a leading man.

I still can't figure out how (did my eyes bug out of my head when I looked at the menu or did I leave the tag from TJ Maxx on my slacks?), but Mr. Skin had the awareness to see that I was in over my head. Perception is a critical skill, though it's not worth much unless you act on it.

Mr. Skin *didn't* say, "I know I'm your only client and I can tell you are broke as a joke." It happened to be true, but he allowed me to save face without calling attention to it by saying, "I was on Howard Stern today. Let's celebrate with surf and turf. I'm buying."

What seemed like a simple gesture—and if you asked him, Mr. Skin would have said it was no big deal—highlighted his emotional intelligence. He was able to pause, survey the situation, walk in my shoes, and execute. The ability to act on our perceptions is so important that we're adding an X after EI to show that a leading man not only can feel and think, but also execute.

The leading man's definition of EIX looks like this:

➤ **Empathy and Emotion:** He walks in the shoes of others and knows how to make others win. He also allows himself to feel and be vulnerable.

➤ **Intelligence and Awareness:** He can see things from multiple perspectives. He also has intelligence built on the awareness from knowing himself.

➤ **X Factor and Execution:** He's the man with a plan, and he is executing his plan. He makes the move. The X Factor comes from living the life he chooses to live.

If EI is getting it, then EIX is getting it and *living* it.

◉ ◉ ◉

Because of Monte's "no pain, no gain" mentality, I wanted him to see that he could have a better quality of life with less effort. Mr. Skin is the perfect example because everything he has accomplished is available to us. There was no trust fund or private school. Sure he put in the work, but plenty of chumps put in the hours. Leading men make the most of the hours. He's a smart guy, but intelligence is hardly rare (though emotional intelligence is). What set him apart was his *willingness to ask questions*—even when times were good.

Imagine a 33 year-old single guy pulling down a decent buck in Chicago during Michael Jordan's heyday in the mid-nineties. Then imagine the same guy having the foresight to ask: Is this work going to fulfill me five years from now? What is my ideal day? Who am I? Seven years before he was even married, Mr. Skin was aware enough to ask: What happens when I want to coach my kid's baseball game and my boss is in one of his moods? Now imagine him walking away from all that security to start an Internet company.

Socrates said, "The unexamined life is not worth living." Mr. Skin shows us how examining life allows us to maximize it. While he makes it look easy, Mr. Skin built the life of a leading man because of the way he embraced questions. It's all there for you as well.

Generous. Genuine. Grateful. Healthy. Wealthy. Aware. Involved father. Attentive husband. Dutiful son. Philanthropic. Purposeful. Hilarious. Happy.

Mr. Skin wasn't born with all of those qualities. No one handed him a phenomenal life. Because he asked questions, he earned that phenomenal life—and gave new meaning to the expression, "comfortable in his own skin."

Finding Your Own Answers

After peppering him with questions for weeks, one night Monte called me and asked, "Now can you tell me how to patch up things with Melinda?"

"Not a chance," I replied.

A quick-fix solution might stop the bleeding, but without finding his own way, Monte's wounds would return. If you're anything like Monte, you're looking for clues to solve the puzzle yourself. Whenever Monte brought up his fiancée, I hammered away at the seven questions to keep the focus on him. Once you make peace with yourself and master your internal world, your relationships with others will flourish. That's why I developed questions that turn off autopilot and force you to reflect.

Monte needed to know that success was in his own hands. I asked him questions and actively listened. By holding up a (metaphorical) mirror, Monte saw *why* Melinda was frustrated. When he stopped defending himself and started seeing things from her perspective, he was able to adapt. Just like improving his health required daily effort, that same commitment to his relationship brought him closer to Melinda.

When word got around to our buddies—the same guys who wanted to muzzle me during the Super Bowl—that these seven questions elevated Monte's life, they too were hungry for answers. Of course, I only fed them questions. By leading them to find clues inside of themselves, they found their own winning way.

You can do the same, provided you remember that the only guidebook for a leading man is the one he writes himself.

Now man up and write it.

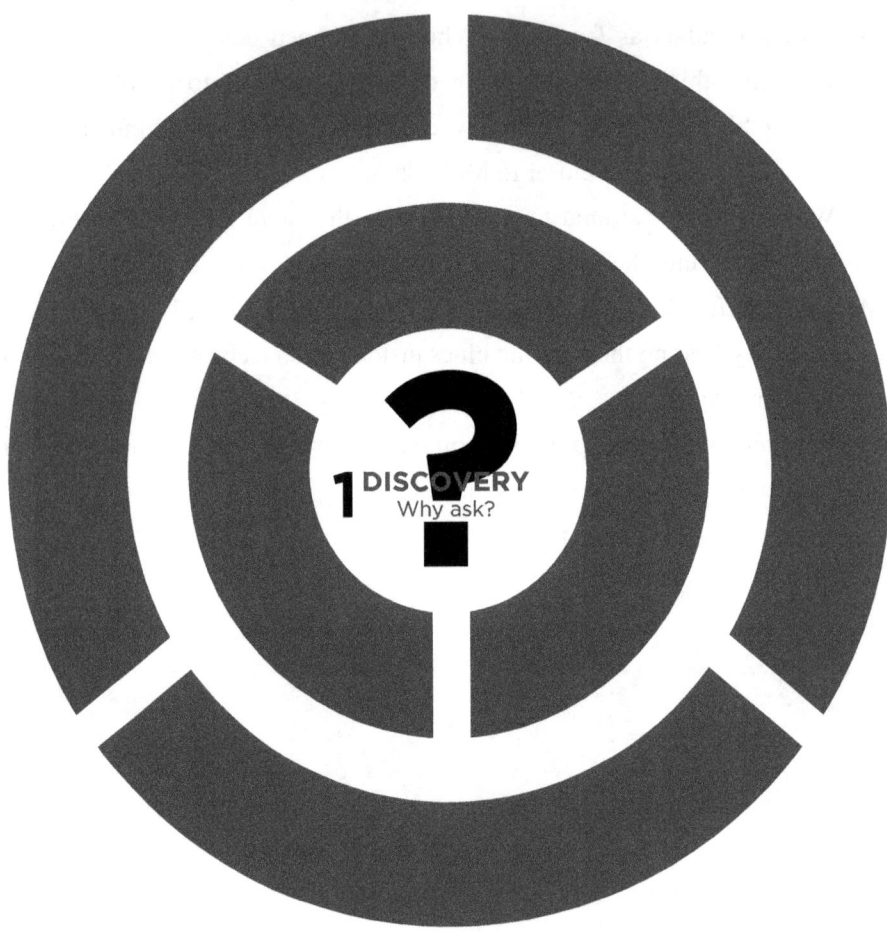

1 DISCOVERY
Why ask?

WHY ASK?

---

*"The two most important days in your life are the
day you are born and the day you find out why."*

—Mark Twain

Why ask?

Because the first step in achieving a dream is conceiving it. And the first step in eliminating angst is identifying it.

Is there a gap between the life you want and the life you have?

If so, how will you find the answers to close it?

By asking questions.

The first step in *finding* what you want is *asking* what you want. We can't change what we don't notice. Questions are like a mirror that forces you to stand up and notice. You check the mirror before you leave the house to make sure you don't look like an ass. You check in with yourself to make sure you don't *live* like an ass.

Questions open a portal for answers to come barreling down into our conscious thoughts—or be nudged out of hiding. We're often scared to ask questions because, deep down, we already know the answers. Acknowledging painful truths can hurt. The benefit of confronting the truth is that owning up to an issue is the first step in solving it. What's more, the downside of *not* recognizing our pain can be disastrous.

Minor problems that go unchecked end up as major catastrophes. Avoidance keeps us stuck. Denial, as already noted, is the first step on the road to despair.

Ignoring our issues leads to waking up one day feeling like life passed us by.

We take action to move away from pain or towards pleasure, or both. Picturing yourself as a leading man, triumphant in your own movie, may be all you need to dive into these questions. Or maybe you would benefit more by putting a microscope on your pain.

A detective asks questions to solve the case.

A leading man asks about pain in order to eliminate it.

As awful as it feels to get sick, there's a sense of relief upon hearing the diagnosis. Once you've identified the issue, you can devise a game plan to eradicate it and get well again. That's why I want you to think about the pain in your life. What does it look like? Where in your body do you feel it? What are its consequences?

As you identify the sources of your angst, do your best to tap into your emotions. Here are some examples:

- I feel like a total loser when I break my promises to myself.
- I'm exhausted from being disrespected by the idiots I work for.
- It depresses me to know I could be doing so much more with my life.

Questions are the GPS of life. They show you where you are now as well as how to reach your destination. Ask the right ones, and they'll even help you *determine* your destination.

Why do we get out of bed in the morning? Why are we obsessed with winning a championship, beating the earnings estimate, or perfecting that presentation? Why bother to do anything? We ask in order to understand what is driving us.

In this chapter, we'll ask questions to build a foundation for what it means to be a man. You'll learn to challenge the notion that happiness only resides in the future. Along the way, we'll explore the meanings of "provider" and "alpha male." The stories I share will allow you to consider the exact type of man you want to be and discover your own winning way.

Love Ourselves As We Are or When We Improve?

The starting point is to see ourselves as we are—perfect. Or at least perfectly flawed. The leading man is happy with his lot in life *now* and loves himself *as he is*. He asks questions to refine and enhance his life, not change who he is.

I'm as guilty as anyone of buying into the myth that one day we can figure everything out. I'm still searching for the empty inbox, the toxin-free body, and the perpetual bliss in every moment. Only now do I see that being a leading man means accepting the flaws both in myself and in life. The trick is to continue growing while loving ourselves as we are.

Hold it right there.

If I'm asking you to tap into your pain and think about what parts of your life you want to change, why am I telling you to love yourself as you are? It's an important paradox, which begs the question: Do we love ourselves as we are or do we work on evolving?

Both.

Can life be perfect today and more perfect tomorrow?

Yes.

Just as we tell a child that certain behaviors are unacceptable, we wouldn't tell him that *he* is unacceptable. We love him as he is *and* show him how to grow by improving his actions—not by changing his essence.

By answering questions, you will make behavioral changes. You will reprogram your thoughts. You will replace destructive habits with effective ones. You will change parts of your life while appreciating yourself as you are. You will take action *because* you love yourself now.

Get used to seeing things from multiple perspectives. Sometimes you might wonder what side I'm on and what conclusions I want you to draw. I want you to draw your *own* conclusions. If I say it enough times, maybe it will start to sink in: *Your answers are within.*

◉ ◉ ◉

Think of yourself as a perfect bell. Depending on how much gunk has built up, its sound may have changed but it still remains perfect. If you want to remove some of that gunk—whether it's grudges, extra pounds, or negative emotions—you'll learn how doing so will sweeten the sound of your own music.

The real juice in life (fulfillment, happiness, enlightenment—take your pick) comes from self-love and self-acceptance. If you believe that you need to change before you can love and accept yourself as you are—that you must complete your degree, cure your acne, or get a promotion before you can be lovable—then you are already at a deficit.

If you want unconditional love from others, you have to start by loving yourself unconditionally.

Now.

If you can only love yourself once you have done x, y, or z, you have put yourself on a treadmill to nowhere.

Feeling or Doing: What Comes First?

The late comic George Carlin wrote, "I do plenty. I get some. But I don't BE." Sometimes we forget that we are human *be*ings, not human *do*ings.

How many times were you asked what you want to *do* when you grow up? Or even now, what you want to do on vacation or do for work? Conversely, how many times were you asked, both growing up and now, how you want to *feel?* We tend to state goals as actions—we want to go public, make partner, get shredded—rather than focus on feelings.

The bulk of advertising focuses not on what the product offers, but on what is missing in us. Marketers highlight the "gap" between what we have and what we want. They call attention to what is missing in our lives—both the objects and the underlying emotions—to convince us that making a purchase will close the gap. But will driving a Ferrari or wearing a Rolex actually make you feel powerful and important?

I want a Ferrari because I want a frickin' Ferrari! Who doesn't want a Ferrari? Why all the questions, Dinkin?

When you ask questions, you take the power away from marketers and put it back in your own hands. You identify the gap to figure out if your best course of action is to stay on your current path or find a new one. You also gain insight about whether the things you are chasing will bring the feelings that you covet. Continue with questions and they will bring you even closer to your core desires. It's one thing to know what you want. Your life goes to another level when you know *why* you want it.

◉ ◉ ◉

The premise of "wrong knowing" is thinking that we know what we want but feeling unsatisfied once we attain it. Feeling loved or secure does not come automatically with a marriage certificate, just as career fulfillment does not arrive gift-wrapped when you start a charitable organization.

A friend of mine spent 12 years visualizing, designing, and working tirelessly to earn the money and know-how to build his dream home. The project was such a success that the home received acclaim in architectural journals. The day it was complete, guess what my friend did:

a) Jumped for joy.
b) Performed a gratitude ritual and oozed thanks.
c) Fist-pumped until his fingernails fell off.

Try none of the above. He cried his eyes out and claimed he never felt lonelier. Glass, concrete, granite, and a Sub-Zero refrigerator didn't elicit feelings. Where did he go wrong?

He created a vision that sprang from what he wanted to have, rather than how he wanted to feel. Because he never asked why he wanted the house, what could have been a celebration instead led to a breakdown.

Why ask?

The reward for asking is an efficient path that leads you to both the things and feelings you want. The penalty for not asking is working hard to achieve something with no payoff. Or even if it does bring material gain, it also brings confusion and anguish. That's why we ask what we want to attain as well as the feelings that go along with it—*before* we start a project.

◎ ◎ ◎

My former life coach, Vaughn Gray, introduced me to the premise of Have-Do-Be and its remedy Be-Do-Have.

Have-Do-Be looks like this:

- *Have* something (money, six-pack abs, a degree), in order to
- *Do* something (travel, find a partner, write that novel), so we can then, and only then
- *Be* something (happy, grateful, loved, complete, fulfilled).

Have-Do-Be is a recipe for endless seeking, a treadmill that you can't get off. The disease of the mind is believing that salvation is elsewhere. You chase and chase and chase until you realize that, wherever you go, there you are.

When you start by choosing how you want to be/feel, it takes you to the express lane, without having to buy a Ferrari, build your dream home, or sculpt your abs. Just choose to be and feel a certain way without chasing anything.

Sure, Dinkin, I'll be all happy in some cave while my family starves and my house gets repossessed. How about you break free from downward dog and pay my student loans and my family's medical bills?

I understand if you're skeptical. To many, "being" elicits visions of people philosophizing about utopia while sitting on their lazy asses. Yet I have found that *being breeds doing and having.* Getting in touch with how we want to feel leads us to the actions and activities that bring us those feelings.

When you invert Have-Do-Be, it becomes Be-Do-Have:

- *Be* (energized, happy, grateful, excited, loving) makes us want to
- *Do* (work, create, serve others, explore, play) and then we

• *Have* what makes us feel good (love, money, toys, peace of mind, freedom).

When you start by being, you naturally do loving, creative, productive things, which in turn leads to getting what you want. Most importantly, you arrive at being by recognizing you are already there.

Find the Juice

Juicy moments in life are the times you feel most alive. It's what you add after the phrase: *There's nothing better than...*

Here are some examples:
• Falling down exhausted after pushing myself to the edge.
• Sharing my deepest secrets and feeling loved.
• Morning sex, followed by coffee and a croissant.
• Figuring out a solution to a complex problem that serves humanity.
• Seeing the light go on when I teach someone.

List four juicy moments now:
• Being...
• Feeling...
• Doing...
• Watching...

We ask because we often forget what makes us feel most alive. Life gets busy. There are countless distractions. You ask what fulfills you in order to make sure it remains a prominent part of your life.

"F-You" Money and the American Illusion

When "Having" is viewed as the starting point, it's no surprise that the castle in the sky for many men is cashing out. The fantasy is to earn enough "F-you" money to never have to work again. We buy the yacht, the jet, the ski house, and the penthouse. We sleep with everything in sight. We eat and drink like kings and somehow think that will make us happy. Why is this such an alluring fantasy?

Think about your trips to Vegas, Atlantic City, Macau, or wherever you go for debauchery. Aside from gambling and escape, the drivers of these junkets for most men are food and sex. We go out for decadent dinners, eat steak and eggs late-night, and inhale the buffets. The rest of the time we are on the prowl, looking for a release. The first night or two is fun, but after a few days, we may be so miserable that we catch an earlier flight and get the hell out of Dodge.

It seems like a sick joke that what gives us so much pleasure also drains our life force. *Nothing saps a man's energy more than digestion and ejaculation.* As we succumb to one last sip, bite, or pump, a part of us knows that there can be, in fact, too much of a good thing. Yet somehow, even as our hangover and heartburn are making us say "never again," we still equate consumption with happiness.

Some may call it the American Dream. I call it the American Illusion. If this is your fantasy, consider if it would make you truly happy. Ask yourself what's driving those desires, and if what others call "the good life" would bring the feelings you seek.

A leading man has control over his appetites. If your energy is consumed seeking sex and substances, you're just a walking hard-on looking for a fix. Even worse, you dramatically lower your odds of finding a romantic partner. Does the guy wolfing down chili cheese fries and making cat-calls ever actually connect? Have the words, "You got some fries to go with that shake?" ever done anything but make a woman run away faster? Can you picture James Bond or the leading man in *your* movie using that line?

If you have too much leisure time, you will lose your appreciation for it. Isn't it a fascinating paradox that most of the wealthiest men also happen to be among the hardest workers? Think about Elon Musk, Bill Gates, Warren Buffett, and Mark Cuban. All of them have gobs of "F-you" money, but find doing what they love more satisfying than a life of consumption.

Curiosity and the Irony of Discomfort

We marvel at the rate at which toddlers learn. Their secret? Curiosity. The question "Why?" is omnipresent. Leading men maintain this curiosity through adolescence into adulthood. They remain in "wonder" at the world and have a "childlike" appreciation for life.

This is why we continue to ask questions…forever. Why do you do what you do? Why do you want what you want? What is the source of pain that led you to pick up this book?

Two days before I turned 35, in the summer of 2006, I made a score at the World Series of Poker. A year later, I sold my half of the literary agency and moved to the Thai island of Koh Samui, where a little "F-you" money goes a long way. A guy who had lived on the island for 10 years asked me what I was there to do. When I told him I was figuring it out, he said, "There's only two ways to go here. You find a purpose or become an alcoholic."

Luckily, I had found the perfect laboratory to look for my purpose—a community of healers at a health retreat. I avoided overindulgence (and did several fasts, ranging from seven to 15 days), and although I had productive days, something wasn't quite right about a life of leisure.

I needed to have my ass kicked. I still do.

The irony of working to find comfort is that *dis*comfort makes us feel most alive. When your favorite football team is up four touchdowns you start flipping stations. When they're down by six with two minutes left and you bet three months of rent on the game, your synapses are firing like an Uzi. It's an apt metaphor for life, which explains why leading men look for ways to push themselves. Just as you build muscle by pushing yourself to failure, you build character and grit through struggle.

Darius, a Wall Street executive, had the accelerator pinned for 15 years and crushed it professionally. He couldn't put his finger on it, but he felt like something was missing. In movies, the catalyst for change (what filmmakers call the inciting incident) is dramatic and obvious. The hero is betrayed by his wife, beaten by his teenage son in basketball, or wrapped around a tree while driving drunk. In real life, it's rare that we get smashed in the face with a wake-up call. We'll be spending a great deal of time focusing on awareness because it's usually a combination of noticing external factors along with deep introspection that gets us out of a rut.

What's nagging at you right now? What are those quiet voices in your head saying that you're ignoring? How is life creeping up on you?

It would have been great to get inside Darius' head and find out what he was thinking. What I do know is that he built the habit of asking questions. When he felt like he was getting caught up in the rat race, he slowed down long enough to ask questions in order to identify his rut. From there, he crafted a plan and made a conscious choice to ease off his career goals and focus on his family, which includes two young children.

You know how the story ends, right? He goes bonkers reading bedtime stories and reverts to his old ways. That's how it typically goes. But Darius, at age 39, channeled his need for challenges by competing in triathlons. To up the ante, he made bets with his friends and kept detailed records to track his progress. All the while, he reconnected with his family and still got his work done, only in fewer hours.

Why did Darius ask?

Because he treasures life and wants to make the most of it.

By asking questions, Darius found the balance that many of us are looking for and is now an athletic, centered, efficient guy who loves and values his family and friends. He is on to his next professional challenge, where I guarantee he'll feel even more alive in his discomfort.

Why is discipline important? When are you at your best? Why are you at your best?

Shining a Light on Your Discontent

1. What's nagging at me most right now is:

2. The quiet voices in my head that I've been ignoring are saying:

3. To prevent life from creeping up on me, I've pledged to confront:

Your Why Leads to Your How and What

In the absence of asking why, it's easy to fall into a routine. Then one day we wake up exhausted, wondering what it was all for. That's why we constantly ask questions.

Simon Sinek, author of *Start with Why*, explains the importance of starting with why—and communicating from the inside out. His Golden Circle shows "Why" at the center and "How" and "What" on the outside. As he explains in his TEDTalk (TED, which stands for technology, entertainment and design, is a nonprofit organization devoted to ideas worth spreading), Apple wasn't just making devices; they were changing the world. And as Sinek says, "People don't buy *what* you do; they buy *why* you do it."

If companies need to be clear about their "Why," it's easy to see that you must do the same. If you don't know why you do things, how will you inspire others? Martin Luther King, Jr. didn't detail what and how; he told us why. He gave the "I have a dream" speech; not the "I have a plan" speech.

◎ ◎ ◎

Let's pretend you have a job shoveling horse manure. If you have been held captive and been tortured for 37 years, and one day you are told that if you shovel manure for an hour, you will be freed, it will be the happiest hour of your life. You might also love this job if you only have to do it for a weekend to pay for Spring Break in Ibiza or front row seats to the Final Four. That's because, depending on the context, the action takes on an entirely new *meaning.*

Think about people who live as if they are possessed. If they are competing to honor their family, to avenge their ancestors, or represent their beloved alma mater, you can see it and feel it. Blake Mycoskie, founder of the company TOMS, runs a business because he's driven to provide shoes (and now water) to people in need. It creates a very different feeling among his customers, employees, and stakeholders than if his purpose was making shoes with the best arch support.

Some examples of "Why":

• I take risks and live on the edge because I never want to wonder "what if?"
• I'm here to give back to others because I received so much.
• My "Why" is the desire to fulfill my destiny.

I've known Daniel Negreanu, the world-class poker player and passionate author, for 12 years. The key ingredient in his success—in poker and life—is inquiry. With regard to his "Why," he wrote:

> To be a billboard for what's possible for others who don't see hope. To inspire people to dream bigger and be kind to each other. To be a loving, attentive, present father and husband. To raise kids that will make a difference in the world. To use the position I have been given in life and leave a legacy that inspires people to just keep giving of themselves.

What is your "Why"?

A Poor Why Makes You Poor

Despite being a smart guy who has played poker for 30 years, John is a consistent loser. One day at Hollywood Park Casino he was going on and on about how much he hated poker.

"Go ahead; ask me," he said.

I couldn't resist. "Ask you what, John?"

"Ask me why I'm here every day if I hate poker and lose all the time."

I had been dying to know for years. In fact, I've always been fascinated with what goes on inside the head of a person who punishes himself.

"Why are you here, John?" I asked.

"Because I've got nothing better to do," he said.

Credit John for having a little awareness. If you go deeper, you can see he plays poker to meet some of his needs—companionship, uncertainty, and feeling a rush. He has some purpose, but because it is so poorly defined, he feels uninspired and leaves unfulfilled.

Your purpose may be to get through the day. It may be to make your parents or children proud. It may be to leave the planet in better condition than the way you found it. Maybe your purpose is to serve your creator. Look no further than Heisman Trophy-winning quarterback Tim Tebow for an example of a man with a definitive "Why" behind all of his actions.

If you are not quite clear on your "Why," you have plenty of company. Unfortunately, that crowd is full of confusion, fear, and discontent. Once you understand the "Why" of your business, your life, and your relationships, you'll reap the benefits of that clarity.

Man As Provider

Why ask what it means to be a provider?

Because without awareness, patterns get repeated. Unfortunately, that often means destructive patterns.

According to the nonprofit organization Childhelp, "about 30 percent of abused and neglected children will later abuse their own children." We often hear how it's inevitable that we will turn into our dads. That may be true for those who are stuck in old habits, but an inquisitive man gets to *choose* what type of man he becomes.

Generations of men have resisted asking questions, and it has caught up with us in school and in the workplace. The statistics force us to face the blunt truth: Women are kicking our asses. The fairer sex outnumbers men seven to five in graduate school and earns more doctoral degrees. A Pew Center study revealed that women in the workplace rate higher on leadership qualities—including intelligence, compassion, honesty, and creativity.

We're falling to such depths that books are being written about our collapse. In 2012 alone, both *The Demise of Guys* and *The End of Men* dissected our downfall. In the latter, Hanna Rosin wrote that women have pulled ahead of men by almost every measure, and that "the post-industrial economy is indifferent to men's size and strength." Goldman Sachs and Google aren't handing out promotions for prodigious pecs.

The fact that one in three kids in America grows up without a father is a stark reminder that we have work to do. We ask why men are struggling because identifying the problem will help us to solve it. The goal, however, is not to compete with women. It is to find our own winning way, which, in turn, will help us to connect with them. Everyone wins when we show up as leading men.

◎ ◎ ◎

My friend Hal, a wealthy 64 year-old real estate developer, reads mostly historical non-fiction, but that didn't stop him from devouring all three books in the *Fifty Shades of Grey* trilogy in one week. In the summer of 2012, those erotic romance novels by E. L. James, which have sold more than 90 million copies worldwide, were all the rage.

I asked why.

I read the first two books and polled dozens of women for their opinions. Almost all of them told me that they want a *man to be a man*. Christian Grey, for all his deviance, is a provider. He's decisive. He's strong, nurturing, and powerful. He plays the piano and appreciates art. And most important, he's clear about his purpose. Many women long for some version of Christian Grey because he knows how to *take a woman*.

Hal insisted that all men, including me, have a lot to learn from Christian

Grey. I've never seen Hal as irate as the day he carried on about a wealthy friend who "bragged" about only paying $400 a month in alimony. I've been with Hal while he drove his *ex-wife* all over town, picking up special water and health food. When I asked him why, he said, "That's the mother of my children! What type of example would I be setting about how to treat a woman, both during and after a relationship, if I did any less?"

Beginning at age eight, I lived through five years of my parents' contentious divorce. My mom hung out with other divorced women who also felt let down by men. Listening to their struggles helped me develop empathy, but I had few opportunities to study men who were providers. Since my other male role models were primarily coaches, whom I seldom saw with their wives and kids, I rarely witnessed the art of male providing.

Trying to understand what it meant to be a provider had my head spinning. I began dating in the late 80's and attended a liberal university where it was blasphemous to use the word "chick" and disrespectful to open a door. Protocol for a first date was to go Dutch. Yet, the more questions I asked women, it was clear that their expectations were still not being met.

The consensus was that women were tired of weak, indecisive men. All that sensitive stuff I had learned seemed to be part of the problem. Almost every woman I spoke to told me the same thing: *Men need to get their balls back.*

One word of caution about what I gleaned from *Fifty Shades of Grey:* It only provided another perspective. Before we swing the pendulum too far in the other direction, let's avoid stereotypes that pigeonhole men. Decisiveness and clarity are important traits of masculinity, as are sensitivity and compassion. In other words, defining masculinity goes beyond labels, and it's up to you to come up with your own definition that *transcends labels.*

Why ask all these questions?

You ask in order to determine what type of man you want to become. You ask because we are prone to repeat the patterns of our role models—often ones we do not want to emulate. You ask in order to grow into the man you have chosen to be, rather than duplicate family patterns or societal stereotypes.

What childhood influences have led to your definition of what it means to be a man? What is your ideal of a man? Are you embodying it?

You, Not Charles Barkley, Are a Role Model

When we consider what traits we want young men to develop, it reminds us of the traits we want to exemplify. We ask because it's natural for a man to think about how he affects others. Therefore, there is value in asking what type of role model you want to be for kids, either your own or others'.

In college, I was in a jock fraternity and know all about the perils of testosterone-fueled displays of bravado. I also know the value of being put to the test to mature, bond, and grow into a man with grit. When rituals are led by responsible older men, they can be valuable experiences that develop a young man's emotional, physical, mental, and spiritual well-being.

Robert Bly's book *Iron John* shines a light on the need for boys to be challenged. Mothers the world over are overprotective, which is why it's incumbent on the older men in the village to initiate boys into manhood. After reading Bly's book, I noticed that my godson Reed, a 16 year-old junior in high school at the time, was displaying the traits of a kid who had not been tested. I love him to pieces, so it was easy to rationalize his disrespect and white lies as typical teenage behavior. I could also tell myself that there were minimal expectations of me in my role as a godfather.

Then it dawned on me that I am one of the old men in the village—and so are you. When he was an NBA all-star, Charles Barkley was vilified for saying "I'm not a role model." Folks in the media pointed out that many kids do, in fact, look up to NBA stars and that he should accept his role and set an example. Barkley fired back in a Nike commercial with: "Parents should be role models. Just because I dunk a basketball doesn't mean I should raise your kids." Sir Charles was calling attention to the need for children to find role models, not from sports or pop culture, but from people who are actually a part of children's lives.

All leading men are role models. The more proximity we have to kids, the greater our opportunity to show them the way. Whether you are an uncle, brother, father, grandfather, coach, coworker, or friend, you have an opportunity to step up. Being a provider starts long before getting married or having kids of your own. In fact, copping out of that responsibility will make you less attractive not just to women, but to peers, colleagues, and family.

Leading Men Elevate Others

Aaron is a 26 year-old music teacher who, after working all day, met me at Hal's for a guitar lesson. Hal invited friends to sing along with us after dinner, and one of his friends brought her 12 year-old son. Seeing that he looked out of place as the only kid at an adult party, Aaron handed him a djembe drum and gave him a quick lesson, transforming an awkward moment into an affirming one. With a simple gesture, he inspired everyone at the party.

Like Aaron, my brother has elevated me by his example. When a boy from the neighborhood knocked on his door, selling magazines for his youth group, Andy asked him how he differentiated his product line from the competition. Sure, the boy might think of him as the crazy neighbor, but he'll benefit from that crash course in salesmanship. Andy also had a talk with his niece before she went to college about how to protect her boundaries around those sweet college boys who can get a little frisky at their first keg party.

Andy's example reminds us to contribute to the next generation of leading men and women. Play catch, lend a hand with a science project, or offer a kind word. More importantly, *be* a leading man. Young people will respond more to who you are than what you say. And in the absence of leading men in their communities, kids will take their cues from those they see on television, including those who, as Barkley said, are only "paid to wreak havoc on the basketball court."

You may be afraid of overstepping your bounds, but every parent I know wants more positive influences for their children. You are correct that the guy who criticizes parents for how they feed their kids will be told to mind his own business. But the one who leads by example and prepares a healthy meal with them will be met with genuine gratitude.

◎ ◎ ◎

When Reed was rude to his mom, I called him on it. I calmly listened to his side of the story, but when he started in with excuses and manipulation, I lost my temper. I screamed so loudly that I was afraid I had gone too far. To my surprise, his mom *thanked* me, as did Reed's step-dad. The message from his family was loud and clear. *It's about frickin' time an older man from the village showed up.* And to my surprise and delight, Reed's behavior shifted immediately.

Though I've heard a million times that kids crave discipline, it didn't sink in until I experienced it for myself. To this day, Reed continues to thrive from my challenges. He also flourished when he worked as a kitchen assistant at Fenway Park. Despite his history of tardiness at school, a paycheck and accountability put that concern to rest and he was a model employee. The simple initiation ritual of a first job served as a valuable catalyst for his maturity.

Before his senior year of high school, I sat down with Reed for a man-to-man conversation. I outlined how few college and career choices he would have if he didn't step up and how many choices he would have if he did. As long as he committed to drive the process, I promised to take him to visit colleges and assist with applications.

This gave me more opportunities to show him that a leading man's word is gold. As his performance in school improved, I took him to visit colleges, and on one of our trips, we spent the night with friends of mine. I modeled leading man etiquette by showing up with a gift, having us make our beds when we left, and mailing a handwritten thank-you note the next day. I explained to Reed that this not only shows appreciation for our hosts, but also ensures that we would be welcome to return. I made it a point to let him know that when done genuinely, these are the types of gestures that foster deep friendships.

As much as I learned from studying other leading men, my own initiation into manhood came from accepting my responsibility as a role model. As a result, both Reed and I started to come into our own. As we'll explore shortly when defining the alpha male, I also learned that my words were more effective when delivered with calm and compassion. I apologized to Reed for screaming at him, and in doing so, modeled two critical elements of masculinity—owning up to a mistake and genuine humility. I also found that he responded best to boundaries, clarity, and high expectations—without raising my voice.

What kids could you be leading? Do they look up to you? Why?

Seven Words That Best Describe You

I want to be (and be seen as) a man with these qualities:

1.

2.

3.

4.

5.

6.

7.

Feel free to choose from this list, though do your best to find your own words:

Inspiring, Generous, Loving, Loyal, Grateful, Genuine, Aware, Happy, Wealthy, Ethical, Intelligent, Purposeful, Philanthropic, Strong, Dependable, Badass, Hilarious, Honest, Nurturing, Thoughtful, Controversial, Healthy, Attractive, Athletic, Adventurous, Curious, Expressive, Articulate, Flexible, Trustworthy, Worldly, Brave, Faithful, Creative, Spontaneous

Time to Break the First Rule of Fight Club…

...and talk about *Fight Club*.

Fight Club highlighted the disempowerment of men who grow up without proper challenges. In the 1999 David Fincher film starring Edward Norton and Brad Pitt, men responded to the protagonists' complaints about Ikea-built, white-washed comfort. In response to the doldrums of a safe, comfortable life with all the trimmings, men reveled in the idea of getting their faces beaten in. With words like these, Tyler Durden became a prophet:

> You have a class of young strong men and women, and they want to give their lives to something. Advertising has these people chasing cars and clothes they don't need. Generations have been working in jobs they hate, just so they can buy what they really don't need.

Fight Club offered clues about how men develop, as did *Season of Life* by Jeffrey Marx. The book is a true story about Joe Ehrmann, a former NFL star who became a high school football coach at the Gilman school in Baltimore. Ehrmann explains that the traditional measures of masculinity (what he calls "the three lies of masculinity," and what my friend Alex calls "douche cred") are based on athletic ability, sexual conquests, and economic success.

For teenage boys, these yardsticks consist of how much they can lift, how often they've hooked up, and what type of car or electronic device they've managed to acquire. As we get older, fantasy football or weekend golf may replace athletic prowess. Sexual conquests may take the form of flirtations outside of marriages. Economic success ranges from bragging about the square footage of our homes to sporting a watch that costs more than the GDP of East Timor.

Ehrmann dedicates his life to showing that we need to teach empathy, love, and vulnerability rather than greed, ruthlessness, and machismo. In his own book, *InSideOut Coaching*, Ehrmann writes, "Having emotions and the ability to express feelings doesn't feminize boys, it humanizes them. It enables them to have healthy relationships."

Because we're socialized to believe that success in sports comes from pushing kids to the limit, people wonder if Ehrmann's "soft" message works. His team's championships silence that argument. What's more, does winning games—while raising shamed boys who can't express or feel love—qualify as success?

Men want to be loved *and* tested. We want an outlet for the testosterone that courses through us. Maybe your nephew, son, or student will never feel the need to fight bare-fisted in a decrepit basement. But whether their challenges come from music, martial arts, or permaculture, if they never reach into the core of their manhood, they will be living a slow death. As Bob Dylan sings in *It's Alright, Ma, I'm Only Bleeding,* "He not busy being born is busy dying."

This gets us back to asking the right questions, ones that point us towards becoming leading men. How are you testing yourself now? Are you chasing the right things? With yourself and others, have you found the right combination of challenge and compassion?

The Four C's of Today's Alpha Male

We ask what it means to be an alpha male so we can formulate our own definition of masculinity. It is all too common to fall into the trap of trying to fit into the expectations of others. The term "alpha male" is especially confusing since it's often accompanied with aggression. "Shut the f$%k up," he says, while pushing his girlfriend or kid. "I know what's best for you. Now get in the car and don't say another word or I'll beat the living crap out of you."

The yelling, cursing, and pushing are the macho BS that lead us to characterize the alpha male as a domineering jerk. As we say in poker, courtesy of (Mike) *Caro's Book of Poker Tells,* "Strong is weak and weak is strong." When you have a strong hand (in poker, business, or life), there is no need for aggression. It is when you are weak (bad cards, no leverage, no respect) that you overcompensate. The loudmouth in the bar talking smack never throws a punch. The more I hear someone brag, the more I realize that they believe, deep down, that they feel they are *not enough.* Because a true alpha male has clarity and certainty in his words and actions, he doesn't need to put on a false front of bravado.

An even bigger lesson from poker is to walk in other people's shoes. I started playing poker when I was 15, and I made a living from the game because I took the time to figure out what others wanted. It built the muscle of compassion and taught me that the best way to get what you want is to help others get what they want.

Like everything, there is a delicate balance. There have been times when I have taken this concept too far and been so accommodating that I created "I lose/you win" situations. Too much compassion and not enough courage is the polar opposite of macho BS and both are weak. Being a wimpy doormat stems from lacking the courage to speak your truth because you want to please others. It's swinging the pendulum too far in the opposite direction—so far that I don't know one child, employer, or woman who would count on that man.

Put it all together and today's alpha male possesses all four C's: certainty, clarity, compassion, and courage. As you continue moving through this chapter, think about which parts of my definition of alpha male you agree with and which parts you don't. What I really want to know is: What does the leading man look like in your movie?

Getting Our Balls Back and Using Alpha As a Verb

The word "alpha" has not relinquished its hold on America. *Man 2.0: Engineering the Alpha* was published in April 2013 and went straight to *The New York Times* Bestseller List, suggesting that "alpha" remains a trait we covet but don't quite understand.

Authors John Romaniello and Adam Bornstein explain that the average man's testosterone level has dropped 20 to 30 percent in the last 20 years alone. The decrease has affected our fitness, personality, and sex drive. The book examines how food and exercise impact our hormones, including testosterone, cortisol, and insulin. The authors illustrate that all the crunches and curls in the world will have little impact unless our hormones are optimal.

Mind and body work together. As men navigate ever-shifting societal expectations, we're also dealing with a host of biochemical changes (stemming from poor nutrition and gut health, not enough sleep and sunlight, EMF, BPA, GMO, and a bunch of other acronyms) that are keeping us from living the fullest expression of our manhood. In other words, needing to *get our balls back* is quite literal.

As we'll discuss in chapter six, looking good is also an inside-out approach. For now, let's continue to ask what it means to be an alpha male. Also remember that the central question of this chapter is: Why ask?

The question requires you to identify the gap between the life you've envisioned and the one you are living. When you read about what it means to be a provider and a role model, think about your own life. Where are you thriving? Where are you not living up to your ideals? As we forge ahead with more examples of leading men, we'll see what it takes to earn the reverence of both men and women.

◈ ◈ ◈

Just as women won't trust a man without a plan, neither will men. And becoming a leading man means earning the respect of other men. In *The Game,* a book that has become a dating bible for countless men, author Neil Strauss writes that if you get the guys, you'll get the girls.

After winning $18 million at the World Series of Poker in 2012, Antonio Esfandiari appeared on the *Howard Stern Show* and Howard asked if his fame helped him meet women. Antonio explained that women rarely recognize him, but men frequently do. And once men see he is worthy of admiration, his company is coveted by all. If you get the guys, you get the girls.

Antonio is more than an exceptional poker player. He is a man who is dedicated to improving his life and his craft. When I spend time with Antonio, I can sense that certainty. He's a man with a plan, and he elevates others with his presence.

Because I'm always curious to learn more about what attracts women to men, I've had many conversations with my friend Hemalayaa about the art of masculinity. She told me that she'll often say to a man, "Alpha me, baby." Now that I see that she is looking for certainty, clarity, compassion, and courage—rather than disrespect and aggression—I will *alpha* when the situation calls for it. The women I talk to are demanding that blend of strength and sensitivity.

The Four C's are certainty, clarity, compassion, and courage. Are you man enough to bring the complete alpha package?

The Alpha is the Man With a Plan

Women tell me that one of their biggest turnoffs is indecisiveness. If you ask one of your guy friends to choose whatever he wants to do on his birthday, he'll be thrilled with the freedom of possibilities. Ask the same thing of a woman and she'll ask if your mangina hurts. At least that's what she'll be thinking as she wonders if you are worthy of being her mate.

Yonnus Becker illustrates the point in the online magazine *Elephant Journal*: "This morning, when my guy announced that he was taking me on a surprise trip and that all I needed to do was pack my bag and that I would learn the destination once we arrived at the airport, my first thought was, *'I have the world's greatest boyfriend.'*"

Her man made her feel loved by taking charge and having a plan. Stepping up with a trip for which she didn't have to make any decisions put her at ease. As Yonnus explains, the decisiveness that made her feel cherished, safe, and loved also extends to every-day actions. Her man keeps his word. He knows when to be quiet and how to nurture. And in a crisis, he goes into "get shit done mode," which also makes her feel safe.

There are different theories about why women like the "bad boy." I believe women are not attracted to a people pleaser because if he can't stand up for himself, he is not capable of standing up for her and her family. It is not the motorcycles, cigarettes, or tattoos that make the bad boy attractive. It is the courage he shows by living according to his own rules. When you move beyond the stereotype, it is the essence of the man, not what he wears or does, that earns the respect of others.

◎ ◎ ◎

Among a group of my friends, many are powerful, driven guys. Yet the alpha of the group, Jim, is the least aggressive and the furthest from a stereotypical ladies' man. When we're planning a dinner or an event, Jim sets the agenda and we all fall in line. We don't follow him because he can bash in our skulls or because he's got a harem of models on his arm. We trust him because his track record shows that he considers all of our needs. With full knowledge that he can't please everyone and will be subject to criticism, Jim's courage allows him to execute the plan.

Another buddy, Kaiser, sold his dot-com and made enough "F-you" money to retire at 28. For a few years, he traveled the world and had the time of his life. Ten years later, Kaiser still has millions in the bank, but he can't get a date to save his life. Women are repelled by his lack of purpose. That's why a plumber—who knows his purpose and carries himself with confidence— earning $40,000 a year can make a woman feel safer than a man with buckets of money and no clue as to what to do with himself.

A sure way to lose the respect of everyone is to be unhappy with your lot in life and do nothing about it. Kaiser frustrates me because he talks in circles when making dinner plans. At first I thought his affliction was diarrhea of the mouth. Now I see his lack of clarity is a symptom of not knowing his why.

Pat Riley, the Basketball Hall of Famer who is the only North American sports figure to win a championship as a player, coach, and executive, embodies how certainty earns the respect of other men. In 2010, he had to convince LeBron James, Dwyane Wade, and Chris Bosh to accept less money than their market value in order to form a "Big Three" for the Miami Heat. Riley could not have done so without personifying all the qualities of today's alpha male.

"You listen to what he says, and he knows it," Bosh said, according to espn.com. "He just has that 'been there, seen it all and this is what you have to do [element]' about him. He comes around you, and you stand up straight."

We stand up straight in the presence of a man who keeps his promises—

both to himself and to others. A leading man has a plan and can *alpha* when the situation calls for it. My definition of alpha is certainty, clarity, compassion, and courage. Does that jibe with your view?

Another Hero's Journey Brings Us Back To: Why Ask?

In the HBO series *Entourage,* Jeremy Piven's character, workaholic super-agent Ari Gold, neglected his home life and lost his wife and kids. After playing every card in the deck, retirement was the only move that would reunite him with his family. The final scene of the last episode showed him and his wife poolside, overlooking a cliff on the Amalfi Coast in Italy, drinking wine in the afternoon. Ari had made it to the top of his profession, collected his "F-you" money, and rode off into the sunset.

Then he got *the call.* They wanted him to be chairman and CEO of a film studio and knew just how to tap dance on his ego. "You want to know what heaven really is, Ari? Try being God."

Ari Gold, like others who have cashed out and don't "need" to work, has a choice. When you remove money from the equation, when paying the bills becomes a non-issue, it brings us back to the question: Why ask? If not to pay the bills, what is it that gets us out of bed in the morning?

We talked about the American Illusion. Will having fistfuls of money so he can consume to his heart's content make Ari happy? Would it make *you* happy? Is it true that we either find a purpose or become an alcoholic? Might Ari be able to live on the Amalfi Coast, never return to the cut-throat world of Hollywood, and find a way to be fulfilled?

Tom Petty, for one, would bet against it. As the profound Petty said, regarding the choice to stop doing what's in your blood, "You could quit, but it's kind of like the sailor and the sea. If he never goes back, he's going to think about it forever."

It's the same scenario for entrepreneurs or coaches who retire young with millions. Some can get the "juice" they need from broadcasting or philanthropy. Others have to go back to the grime of building a company or coaching because it's what fills their soul.

We ask questions to gain perspective. What would you do if you were in Ari's situation? Are you working to find happiness in the future or to enjoy each day?

We know Ari Gold's character well enough to know that he will go back. Trading comfort for discomfort, he'll feel more alive than ever. His biggest challenge will be to perform on the job while ensuring his wife and family feel loved. Since past behavior is the greatest predictor of future behavior, anyone with an affinity for odds would bet against him. But gosh darn it, we want to see him do it. For all his flaws, we recognize Ari's humanity and hope he can man up and put it all together.

I'm rooting for Ari Gold because I want to see all of us become leading men. Reward my faith by answering our first set of questions.

Note: We've asked a lot of questions throughout this chapter, as we will in those that follow. Whether you have answered some or all of them, be sure to answer all the questions at the end of each chapter. Write down (or type) your answers as they comprise the most important parts of the map you are creating.

QUESTION ONE: WHY ASK?
More Empowering Questions

1. Is there a gap between the life you want and the life you have? If so, describe the emotions it creates in you.

2. What pain are you running away from? What pleasure are you running towards?

3. How will you know if you have been successful on your hero's journey? What is your leading man's ending?

4.   What is your "Why"?

◎ ◎ ◎

Once you have answered these questions, you will have clarity about why you are going down this road. You have also started to build the muscle of asking questions. That muscle will continue to develop in the next chapter when you ask: What is My Ideal Day?

FEELING
2 What Is My Ideal Day?

?

QUESTION TWO

WHAT IS MY
IDEAL DAY?

"The great lesson from the true mystics ...[is] that the sacred is in the ordinary, that it is to be found in one's daily life, in one's neighbors, friends, and family, in one's backyard."

—Abraham Maslow, humanistic psychologist
and creator of the *hierarchy of needs*

My brother Andy may be even more relentless than I am when it comes to asking questions. After college, he channeled that inquisitiveness into sales and had great success. As he approached 30, his quest for life's answers led him to ask new questions. In fact, one simple question he asked is the focus of this entire chapter, as well as a pivotal tool for clarity and direction.

One day Andy casually asked several of his friends to describe their ideal day. "I'd want my business to be doing 80 million a year in revenue," one said. Another said that he'd want to own a villa in Tuscany, a ski chalet in Aspen, and a penthouse in Tribeca. One told him, "I want to have all three of my kids' tuitions paid, through graduate school, before they turn 10."

Andy's reply to all three of his friends was the same, "All I asked was to describe your ideal day. Just answer that one question."

He got nothing but blank stares.

During the housing boom in 2004, Andy ran a regional branch for a mortgage company. At the firm's annual meeting, a fellow branch manager who was one of the company's biggest earners kept emphasizing the need for growth.

Love for the word *why* must be in our genes.

Andy asked, "Why do you want to grow?"

His colleague hesitated. What a ridiculous question to ask at a *business* meeting. In the midst of searching for an answer, veins were popping out of his forehead. With more spit than words, he managed to summon the stuttering response, "Gr-gr-gr-gr-grrowth. Just gr-gr-gr-gr-grrrowth!"

I asked Andy why he had posed the question. I wondered if there was some philosophical answer he was searching for. Maybe he was getting at the deeper question of whether we can find fulfillment in the moment, or if the need to strive for more is essential. It turned out that Andy's motives were much simpler. He told me that all he wanted to know was how growth affected an ideal day.

The Fisherman and the Businessman

The parable about the Mexican fisherman and the Harvard MBA, even if you already know it, is worth repeating. The gist is that the businessman can't understand why the fisherman only works a few hours when he could make a lot more money by putting in a longer day. The fisherman says, "I sleep late, fish a little, play with my children, take a siesta with my wife, Maria, stroll into the village each evening where I sip wine and play guitar with my amigos; I have a full and busy life, señor."

The MBA explains what he's missing by not growing. He maps out a plan and explains that if he works harder and sacrifices for 15 or 20 years he can build a huge enterprise, live in a big city, and cash out for millions.

"Millions, señor?" the fisherman asks. "Then what?"

"Then you would retire. Move to a small coastal fishing village where you would sleep late, fish a little, play with your kids, take a siesta with your wife, stroll to the village in the evenings where you could sip wine and play your guitar with your amigos."

The fisherman, still smiling, looks up and says, "Isn't that what I'm doing right now?"

◉ ◉ ◉

In *Save the Cat,* the late Blake Snyder's book on screenwriting, he wrote, "Stasis is death." We either grow or we die. Tony Robbins believes that "growth" is one of the six human needs. He also lists "uncertainty/variety" as another, so Robbins may argue that if the fisherman maintains his routine forever he'll be missing two of his six needs.

What I love about the fisherman is his clarity about what an ideal day looks like, which brings us back to the starting point for this chapter. There are other words like intention, mission, and vision, but let's keep things simple by describing one day. You can type it on your phone, tablet, or computer, or write it in pencil, pen, or blood on the surface of your choice. Just free-flow and write what comes naturally. You'll get more guidance as the chapter progresses.

_____

_____

_____

_____

_____

_____

Did you want to know how specific you should be? Before I address that question, here's a partial description of the day my friend Ken described:

> I wake up in the morning in a comfortable bed as the sun is rising at our beautiful beach home in Maui. I make love to the most beautiful woman in the world, take a shower, and meditate for 20 minutes. After a healthy breakfast with my wife, we take a walk on the beach together and remind ourselves how lucky we are.
>
> We make plans to fly to L.A. so I can play in the L.A. Poker Classic. My wife and I head out to the animal shelter where we volunteer. After a healthy lunch and the satisfaction of a productive morning, my friend and I decide to play 18 holes of

golf before dinner. I shoot a 70 for two under and beat my friend
by one stroke.

The details are important. Ken wrote "comfortable" bed because he doesn't
care if it's a four-post bed with 1,000 thread-count sheets. His golf score is
specific because he very much cares what he shoots. If you have visualized
sitting behind an antique, wood-carved desk on the 125th floor of a skyscraper
with floor-to-ceiling windows, then write exactly that.

Create Believability Factor

The choice of writing goals (and your ideal day) in the future or past tense is a
function of Believability Factor (BF). Some people feel more of the BF if they
talk about it in the future tense, as in what they are *going to do*. Some get a
higher BF if they talk about it in the past tense, as if they *have already done it.*

If you lack a clear vision (come on, leading man, think about that movie
ending again), or aren't sure how you want to feel, here are five more questions
to spur your creativity.

1. What did you love to do as a kid?
2. What gives you the most energy and makes you feel most alive?
3. If you cut class or call in sick, what do you want to do?
4. What are your happiest memories?
5. What is your biggest dream?

Money's Role in Your Ideal Day

Many people get stuck because they don't want to describe an ideal day they
can't afford. What I've found is that when you perform this exercise, you
realize one of three things: that you need more money than you think, less
money than you think, or you can make smart choices and still do everything
you want. You also may see that you are using money as a crutch, when the
real issue is a lack of clarity.

Suppose your ideal day starts by waking up overlooking the Pacific Ocean,
less than an hour's drive from your courtside seats to the Los Angeles Clippers.

Your first thought might be, "I need a boatload of cash to pull this off." And you may be right. Without even getting into why you desire those things, the simple answer might be that you need to find a way to make tens of millions of dollars a year.

However, if that is your ideal day, and you want to experience it now, it's time to be creative and stay true to your vision. Find a campground for your tent or trailer that overlooks the ocean or take a job as a resident manager of a hotel or condo on the beach. If you are a chef, gardener, or pet-sitter, find a job working for someone who wants you to live in their home and build such a remarkable reputation that you're always getting paid to live on the beach.

Remember that *owning* a house on the beach wasn't part of your description. If that's important to you, go back to your ideal day and make that change. Like Ken's golf score, the level of specificity is critical.

If you're not a billionaire or an A-list actor, courtside Clippers tickets might be tricky, but perhaps you're a doctor, a physical therapist, or a statistician and can work for the team. Maybe this ideal day makes you realize that you want to be a sportswriter. Maybe you're an attorney, an agent, or a banker thinking about changing jobs, and one of the firms you're looking into has courtside seats and part of your job will be to sit in them and entertain clients.

When you start by defining your ideal day, you move away from results and outcomes and shift to actions and feelings. Instead of saying, "I want to be a famous actor," you say, "I act daily. I spend a half hour every morning being creative. I feel alive when I'm creating with other actors." These are things that you have control over and can start doing today.

More Questions to Arrive at Your Ideal Day

1. How would my obituary read?
2. If I won the lottery for $50 million, what would I want my life to look like?
3. When am I at my happiest? What does it feel like? What does it look like?

Honest Abe or *Not* Nixon the Crook?

While you continue to think about your ideal day, let's talk about a powerful tool that I learned from emotional detox expert Mark England. Mark studied dozens of healing modalities until his work revealed that language plays the most pivotal role in our success. When you talk about what you don't want (stress or debt) or what you want to quit (smoking or complaining), you embed these words in your subconscious and create images of the very things you are trying to avoid.

When I was a literary agent, I met Hajjar Gibran, a descendant of Khalil Gibran, and sold his sequel to *The Prophet,* an inspirational book that is revered by millions. When I asked Hajjar to review a sensitive email for his publisher about the launch of *The Return of the Prophet,* his response was, "I deleted the part about not wanting to sour our relationship, because the subconscious doesn't register negatives. Like if I say, 'Don't think about Lao-tzu [his dog].'" Of course, all I could think about was Lao-tzu.

The subconscious does not process negatives. The subconscious *does process* what you say and hear. Adding a negative modifier before a word doesn't erase that word.

In sports, the oldest trick in the book is to plant a negative word in your opponent's mind. Right before a pressure-packed moment like a free throw, field goal, or a clutch putt (think "Noonan, miss it" in *Caddyshack*), you say to your opponent, "Don't choke." What else could they think about? You certainly wouldn't say, "Don't visualize the ball going in." We hear coaches, parents, and managers say things—precisely at the times they demand focus—such as, "We can't look ahead" or "It's not going to do us any good to complain about the things we can't control." By giving attention to those ideas, isn't that *exactly* what they are doing?

Richard Nixon uttered these four infamous words, "I'm not a crook." To this day, what does everyone think about Nixon? That he's a crook, of course. Abraham Lincoln, on the other hand, was known as "Honest Abe." In our minds, more than 100 years later, we still think of honesty and Abe Lincoln as one and the same. The key point to remember is that the "not" doesn't register. That's why the words "honest" and "Abe" and "crook" and "Nixon" will forever be embedded in our minds.

The words that will be associated with the hero in your movie are the ones you say, see, and hear the most. If you were to read a transcript of your typical day, would you sound like a leading man?

Winning Words Make You Money

Is there any utility in writing about a day you *don't* want to have? Would you devise a strategic plan and create 777 PowerPoint slides for how you *don't* want your business to succeed?

When negotiating the fee for a speech, I started to write, "I don't want to quibble with you over a few dollars but..." Then I realized that by writing quibble, I was, indeed, quibbling. Instead, I wrote what I wanted, which was to deliver a dynamic event and agree on a fair price. When I wrote exactly that, I got exactly that.

When my friend Kevin sent out a business plan to potential investors, I asked him what he wanted. "I don't want to push anyone," he said. I asked Kevin what he did want. "I don't want anyone to feel like I'm pressuring them or that I'm desperate." I told him that he was crystal clear on what he *didn't* want and could benefit by clarifying what he did want. Just like it can be frustrating to learn a new language, Kevin was ready to beat me to a pulp.

His frustration boiled over when he kept getting rejections from those he didn't want to push. It should be clear by now that people responded to Kevin as if he were pushing them, pressuring them, and as if he were desperate because of the words that were most prominent in his mind. Subconsciously, he sent the signals for exactly what he did *not* want.

The pain from a lack of results opened him up to changing his language. Through inquiry, he became clearer. Switching from the negative to the affirmative, he said, "I want people to be so wowed by the business plan that they're beating down my door to invest." With that very statement, he went back and retooled his business plan and pitch.

Thoughts turn into words and words turn into thoughts. Both lead to feelings and ideas. Feelings and ideas lead to success or failure, suffering or bliss. The results you achieve are rooted in the words you choose. There's a massive difference between, "I'm not going to be miserable any longer," and "I'm going to be happy." There's an even bigger difference when you say, "I *am* happy."

How do you want to feel right now? What words are you using to create that feeling?

The Power of Negative Words

It's far from an iron-clad rule to use only positive words. In fact, a strong case can be made that negative words may be useful to steer you away from what you don't want.

Words such as quitter or loser might be so repulsive that hearing them sparks an intense desire to do the opposite. Some people will move heaven and earth to do what someone tells them they cannot do. If a trainer or a boss is aware of this emotion, he may say, "I'll bet you're going to quit, you loser," every time he wanted to motivate you. My best friend Bryan's high school basketball coach told him he was the team's thirteenth man. There were twelve players on the roster. His coach's insults motivated him, and he became a starter and a team leader.

Speaking of degrading basketball players, in March 2013, Hall of Fame basketball coach Bob Knight came out with a book titled *The Power of Negative Thinking*. He explained that he prepared for a game by asking his team what their opponent could do to beat them and what they needed to eliminate. Knight's choice of words led him to win three national championships and author the rebuttal to Norman Vincent Peale's *The Power of Positive Thinking*.

Would you rather bet on a team that is playing to win or playing not to lose? Do you want to run towards pleasure or away from pain? Either may work for you. Much of the work you're doing in this book comes in the form of words—writing about who you are and your ideal day, as well as creating visuals to reprogram belief systems. Whether you focus on your desires or fears, choose your words wisely. Find out what motivates you best, then determine the words that trigger you, and you'll be on your way to creating the images that make your ideal day a reality.

Creating a Fulfilling Career

In his blog *Milk the Pigeon*, Alexander Heyne explains how it can be a trap to believe that a life of exotic travel will make you happy. To explain why, he cites Timothy Ferriss' *The 4-Hour Workweek*, the popular manifesto on how to create a mobile lifestyle. Heyne says, "The irony is that when Tim was interviewed regarding his 'day in the life,' he said the following: Morning meditation, meet with people he advises, exercise, a bunch of hours of work in the afternoon, long, multiple-hour dinner with a couple glasses of wine and tons of friends. He didn't say fly to Thailand, bungee jump, swim with sharks, and then bang a tranny."

Heyne's perspective reminds us that happiness isn't "out there" somewhere. Life is a bunch of days. Create the vision of a day that satisfies you. Then live it. Who said this had to be hard?

Seeing his life as a movie allowed Monte to see the big picture that he had been missing. Describing his ideal day brought even greater focus. Here is part of what he wrote:

> After watching the sunset with my lady, I turn off the 'thinking' part of my brain and focus on relaxation and pleasure. If I stay home, I play guitar, watch a movie, read a novel, or play a game. If I go out, I'll spend time with people I love—watching a sporting event, listening to live music, singing karaoke, going to a show or movie, or just hanging out.

This specificity led Monte to turn off his computer once the sun went down, which helped him to overcome his insomnia. As his days came into focus, his life did as well.

☻ ☻ ☻

When it comes to building a lifestyle around your skill set and passion, there may be no stronger tool than describing your ideal day. Dig deeper in order to create the type of career/calling that suits your unique skills and quirks.

My friend Trey is a wise-ass who never met an argument he didn't like. From the moment he could speak, people told him he was born to be a lawyer. He loves structure, family, and competition, and values financial security more than flexible work hours. Does this sound like a guy who would be happy working as a freelance scuba diving instructor in the Maldives?

Trey laughs at the jokes about lawyers and tolerates the long hours because being a partner in a law firm fits him like a glove (insert bad O.J. Simpson joke here). It's such a cliché to put down the attorney or banker living in the suburbs, or the nine-to-five middle manager driving a minivan. It's also an indication that we're feeling "less than" about our own day and who we are. Putting down others is an indication we haven't found our own sweet spot in life.

I used to be one of those entrepreneurs who boasted about being my own man. Sure, I could have kept my own schedule and worked from *anywhere,* but what it actually meant was that I worked from *everywhere.* While I was building my business, I was fat, lonely, and on the run from bill collectors. Trey, meanwhile, was building a family and a fortune. And here's the thing: I wouldn't have had it any other way, and neither would Trey. We live such different lives, yet we are equally fulfilled because we've each made the conscious choice to create ideal days that uniquely suit us.

Most of us tend to overvalue leisure. Our first reaction may be to describe a day in which we lounge around and do nothing. Ask yourself how that would feel after a month. Also ask what brings you the most satisfaction, where the real juice is. Think about the times you felt most satisfied professionally. Then continue to think about all your needs—social, financial, intellectual, and spiritual. In doing so, keep asking: What type of day gives me the best chance to thrive?

Your Ideal Day Is a Moving Target

When I was 22, my mission statement began, "I wake up when I want and am only accountable to myself." After Andy showed me the power of describing my ideal day, here's a snippet of what I wrote in 2007:

> The order of my day isn't too important, since I'm keeping my own schedule and 'report' only to myself. Over the course of the day, I will be creative, intellectually challenged, and of service. I can do those three things in a number of ways: by writing, working on a speech or giving a speech, developing a proposal for an author's book, creating a plan for a client, coaching a team, reading a journal entry of one of my godkids, or having lunch with a friend or colleague.

The insistence on freedom has dominated my life's decisions. I'm a night owl and have done my best work as a poker player, salesman, and author between sun down and sun up. If you're a music critic, a late-night TV producer, or a club owner, going to bed at 6:00 A.M. and waking up at 2:00 P.M. may work perfectly for you.

Those hours served me until I realized that contribution and service come with accountability. Clinging to a story that left me feeling isolated and unfulfilled would have only kept me stuck. There was nothing wrong with what I wrote in 2007. But after seven years of internal and external discovery, it no longer fit who I was and what I wanted to create in 2014.

Who you are and what makes you tick are moving targets. The man you want to be at 61 will likely be different from who you were at 21. If Trey continues to enjoy law but finds himself craving flexible hours or more financial upside, he may rewrite his ideal day and open his own practice or join one that fits his new script. If his wife wants to start a business, and he wants to spend more time with his kids, he'll go back to the drawing board and come up with a new version of his ideal day.

Your ideal day will always be evolving. Is it working for you now? Are your ideas about your day still in concert with the way you view your role in the world today?

Describe your ideal day without any hedges or concessions. I could choose from a million metaphors, but if you don't have a map, you're going to end up lost.

Fill in the Blanks to Create Your Ideal Day

If you like to freestyle or have already written your ideal day, you can skip these questions. If you like structure, filling in the blanks will give you a solid start.

Your Ideal Day

- I wake up... (where)
- At... (what time, with or without an alarm)
- Next to… (person, pet, neither or both)
- Looking at… (nature, art)
- I feel…
- I'm excited about...
- The first thing I do is…
- The first thing I eat or drink is…
- I earn my income from…
- I feel most alive when I…
- I spend time with…
- I stay fit and healthy by…
- I stop to smell the roses when I…
- I connect to my heart by…
- I wind down by…
- I get in bed…(time, setting, company, sheets, temperature)
- I close my eyes feeling…

You'll have another chance to refine your responses. At a minimum, make sure you have filled in these blanks to give yourself a starting point from which to work.

Power of the Word Because

In his book *Influence: The Psychology of Persuasion,* Robert Cialdini cites a 1989 study by Harvard social psychologist Ellen Langer about the power of the word "because." People waiting in line at the library to use the copier were asked a favor.

Excuse me, I have five pages. May I use the Xerox machine?

Sixty percent said yes.

In the next test, under the same circumstances, the explanation "because I'm in a rush" was added.

Excuse me, I have five pages. May I use the Xerox machine because I'm in a rush?

Ninety-four percent said yes.

When you tell people you're in a rush, they empathize and are more likely to help you. But here's where things get interesting.

Excuse me, I have five pages. May I use the Xerox machine because I have to make some copies?

Ninety-three percent said yes.

The word "because" is so powerful that it created nearly the same response whether followed by meaningless verbiage or a legitimate reason!

Don Miguel Ruiz, author of *The Four Agreements,* wrote, "I am worthy of my own love, simply because I am alive." While that's a lot deeper than saying, "I am worthy of my own love, because I added more cowbell," remember that the word because is more important than the words that follow it. When you say because, you are forced to think of a reason, and in that pause, you take yourself out of habit and into conscious choice. In addition, as evidenced by the study, it has a profound impact on the listener. When you hear the word because, you assume that what follows is a legitimate explanation and are more likely to acquiesce out of habit.

◎ ◎ ◎

Another clever use of because is to give a reason that creates urgency. A year after college, I sold windows and siding to homeowners (think Danny DeVito and Richard Dreyfuss in Barry Levinson's film *Tin Men*). I would lower my price if the homeowners allowed me to take before and after pictures and put a sign on their lawn for marketing purposes. *Because you're helping me out, I can give you a great deal* (the proverbial model home pitch).

Our minds tend to think there's a catch or that it's too good to be true without a reason. That's why a great salesman uses the power of because to create a reason by telling a story that makes you feel like you're getting a deal. Closeout, inventory reduction, overstock. These words signal a purpose. We're giving you a great deal because...and you better get in here soon.

What words can you use after because to trigger yourself?

One of my clients used my template to write out his ideal day, and then took it a step further by adding the word because in each sentence. It looked like this:

- I wake up with no alarm, at my own pace, *because* I like my mornings to be chill.
- I wake up—some days next to a woman, some days alone—*because* I enjoy both.
- I feel most alive performing and writing music *because* the work has meaning.
- I spend time with my son *because* we thrive on each other's love.

Act "As If"

A vital tenet of visualization work is to act and talk as if what you want is already happening. When you talk about how you *want* to feel, it creates longing. When you say what you *can* feel, it's an improvement. An even more powerful method is to state it, see it, and feel it as if it's already happening. Adding the word because adds to the power.

Fill in the blanks for:

I feel _____ because _____.

During a moment of clarity a couple years ago, I knew if I sent my thoughts to someone, it would make me more accountable. I fired off this email to my coach.

1. I want to be in the game.
2. I want to be on a bigger stage.
3. I want to serve more.
4. I want to fall in love with a woman.

James Altucher, author of the blog *Altucher Confidential* wrote, "Whenever you say 'I want to be' means first (by definition), 'I am not.' I don't want to be a NOT." My coach was equally wise and wrote back:

1. I AM in the game.
2. I AM on the world stage.
3. I AM serving.
4. I AM in Love.

It took me a second to notice that she changed "bigger" stage to "world" stage. I liked it. Since I understood the value of the word because, I took it a step further.

1. I AM in the game *because* I am working on my craft.
2. I AM on the world stage *because* I share my work with others.
3. I AM serving *because* it's what I'm here to do, and I love it.
4. I AM in love *because* I am love.

The reason helps, though the key factor is to use because.

You Decide Whether You Are Your Own Man

While traveling, I met a guy named Oliver, a free spirit who wanted the same things from his career as from backpacking around the world. Thinking that he knew who he was, a lover of risk and freedom, he started a small business. He turned a profit, but the unpredictability and chaos drove him mad. With his mental health waning, he took a job in the Corporate America he had once railed against. He was surprised to see that his coworkers were some of the happiest people he'd ever met. Much of that contentment, he said, was because of their jobs.

How you frame your job adds or detracts from your power. I sat on an airplane next to a fidgety manager of a Fortune 500 company that had just announced layoffs. He survived the cut and said that he just had to stick it out for 12 more years and hope to be spared from further layoffs. He also told me that it kept him up at night knowing that his entire fate was at the mercy of the whims of a consultant or stock analyst. He's a slave to the system because he *chooses* to be.

You can work for a company without being a "company guy" by building your savings, keeping your skills current, and knowing your value. When you describe your work (to yourself at the very least) as "leasing" your services to your employer, it puts the power back in your hands. You can let the business do what it does best, live your ideal day, make plenty of money, and be your own man. If you get laid off, you know their loss is greater than yours and you are prepared for your next move. You always have a plan to be your own man.

In *Linchpin,* Seth Godin writes, "It's okay to have someone you work for…But the moment you treat that person like a boss, like someone in charge of your movements and your output, you are a cog, not an artist." Godin then adds, "If your agenda is set by someone else and it doesn't lead you where you want to go, why is it your agenda?"

Are you setting your own agenda? Does your career work for who you are? Are you living your version of the ideal day?

QUESTION TWO: WHAT IS MY IDEAL DAY?
More Empowering Questions

1. What is my ideal day? Be as specific as possible.

2. Describe how you want to feel as if it's already happening. Say it out loud and write it down. Be as specific as possible. Words like intellectually stimulated, fulfilled, loved, challenged, excited, and grateful might be applicable. Write in the affirmative.

I feel_____because_____.

◎ ◎ ◎

In the first two chapters, you gained clarity about what's driving you and described your ideal day. Now you're going to ask questions to find out who you are.

3 ESSENCE
Who Am I?

WHO AM I?

---

*"It would be easier to roll up the entire sky into a small cloth
than it would be to obtain true happiness without knowing the Self."*

—Upanishads (Vedic texts), from
Catching the Big Fish by David Lynch

As we ate dinner in January 2013 near his New York City apartment, my friend Noah said, "Know who you are," at least a dozen times. Noah was the wide receiver on our high school football team that went to the 1988 Maryland state championship. Our star running back, Mark Mason, was destined for the NFL (he played briefly for the Dallas Cowboys) so we had run the ball almost every down throughout the season.

In the championship game, Mason injured his knee and we fell behind. We were forced to air it out, and Noah turned in a dazzling performance with 14 catches for 300 yards and two touchdowns. We all figured that the top schools would recruit him, so it was a shock when he received no scholarship offers. After walking on for a few practices his freshman year at Tulane, he quit.

Now 42 and with a baby, Noah still watches that championship game. His wife can't resist doing her best Bruce Springsteen impersonation. *Glory Days, well they'll pass you by, Glory Days.*

Eventually they turn off the Betamax and turn on the NFL games. When they see The Denver Broncos' wide receiver Wes Welker on TV, Noah's wife asks him if he wishes that were him. Noah may drift into fantasy for a second, but because he knows who he is, he's at peace with his job as a financial advisor. Keep in mind that Noah is two inches taller than the 5'9" Welker and, back in the day, ran the 40-yard-dash in 4.50 seconds, which is significantly faster than Welker's 4.65. On natural ability alone, I would argue Noah was more blessed than the guy who was the first player in NFL history with five 110-catch seasons. So why didn't Noah do it?

Know who you are.

Wes Welker's work ethic at Heritage Hill High School in Oklahoma City was legendary. Welker was the guy who stayed after practice to do extra drills and hone his craft. Noah was the guy who bolted the minute practice ended to look for mischief. The truth is that Noah never loved football. It wasn't in his blood. He wasn't going to sacrifice a fun college lifestyle or a business education to be bothered with football practice, much less stay late to watch extra film and refine his routes. Wes Welker was that guy. Noah recognized that he wasn't.

Know who you are.

These four words from Noah resonate because he radiates fulfillment and is happy with his lot in life. Now. We've been so programmed to aim higher and strive to be more than we are, that we lose sight of accepting and loving ourselves as we are.

◎ ◎ ◎

Noah started to tell me something and then held his tongue. I believe that a hallmark of masculinity is the ability to take criticism from other men. If your friends are *not* making fun of you or calling you out on your BS, it means you either take yourself too seriously or are overly defensive about your flaws. It ends up being your loss because without the gift of their awareness, you lose the opportunity to see your blind spot.

Byron Katie, author of *Loving What Is,* goes so far as to say that, "the most spiritual practice is to hang out with people who criticize you." As we delve further into this concept, you'll understand why it benefits us to seek criticism from our friends and why I wanted to hear what Noah was about to say. Especially if it was negative or unflattering.

"We've known each other since sixth grade," I said. "Out with it."

"I feel like you've been coasting," Noah said with trepidation.

I did what I always do when someone offers criticism: I thanked him. Then I started asking myself the question that we will explore in this chapter: Who am I?

The Directionless "Anti-Dude"

Upon reflection, Noah's words started to sink in. Deep down, I knew who I was but parts of me were denying it, and I was paying the price. A week later, I was in Key West for a wedding and his words about coasting resurfaced.

I felt lonely as hell.

Completely ungrounded.

Totally directionless.

Even worse, for all my work on acceptance, I was angry at my dad for no other reason than because he was the exact same person he has always been. Hundreds, maybe thousands of times, I have repeated the premise that suffering lives in the gap between reality and expectations. I was aware enough to know that my issues with my dad were a result of my expectations. Yet rather than accept reality, I clung to them and suffered. Here I was, at 41, this seemingly evolved, holistic man of the world, and I felt lost. Even worse, for all my work on acceptance, I was having daddy issues.

How pathetic.

My friends asked me my plans and projected their own fantasies. "Why not just stay in Key West and get a guitar gig? You would have the life." Never mind that I've been accused of being tone deaf and my greatest fear is singing in front of others; it still crossed my mind. I had steady, mobile employment as a Health Coach so I could find a way to live the "4-Hour Workweek." I was in a position to live the dream existence that many would envy, but every time I considered it, Noah's words came cascading down.

Know who you are.

When I lived in Thailand, I focused on *being* rather than *doing* and felt a sense of peace from not having to do anything to feel whole or loved. But after a few months, fewer challenges led to more comfort and less fulfillment. While the idea of a life of leisure sounded appealing, it taught me that I'm most energized by contribution.

You can see that I'm a far cry from "The Dude," played by Jeff Bridges in the Coen Brothers' film *The Big Lebowski*. For all my talk about purpose, it makes me wonder if it might do me some good to lighten the heck up and take a page out of "Dudeism," an actual religion with nearly 200,000 Dudeist priests ordained. The founder is a California transplant who, aptly enough, lives in Thailand. What the "Dudely Lama" Oliver Benjamin said in *Backpacker* magazine hit home with my often uptight self:

> Life is short and complicated and nobody knows what to do about it. So don't do anything about it. Just take it easy. Stop worrying so much about your life purpose. Kick back with friends, go with the flow and whether you roll strikes or gutters, do your best to be true to yourself or others.

Great advice for *some* people. The Dudely Lama knows exactly who he is, so that philosophy works for him. You need to figure out what works for you. Would you be happy living on an island with cash in the bank and nothing to do? Why or why not? Are you more like The Dude whose motto is "Take it easy" or Gordon Gekko (Michael Douglas in the film *Wall Street*) whose motto is "Greed is good"?

Better question: What is the motto of the leading man in your movie?

You? Or Your Representative?

Social media displays only the parts of people they want you to see. Few are brave enough to show their entire selves, which is unfortunate, because our best and worst moments are *all* part of who we are. When we reveal our shame, it not only makes us more real, it also helps us to connect with others. Sharing our vulnerability gives others permission to share theirs.

Comedian Chris Rock contends that for the first six months of a relationship, you are dating a person's "representative." The same could be said for new friends and business associates. We only show the parts we want people to see until we feel safe enough to let down our guards and reveal our true selves. If the ultimate goal is unconditional love, wouldn't it be more efficient to be yourself from the moment you meet? We don't because we fear rejection or we think we know what the other person wants.

What people want is the real *you*. And if others don't love you as you are, why waste six months creating a façade? The willingness to show someone your true self, flaws and all, starts with accepting and loving yourself as you are.

Our greatest fear and our greatest desire are one and the same: to be seen for who we are. The fear prevents us from showing our true selves. If we succumb to the fear, it also ensures that we'll never be seen—or loved—for *all* of who we really are.

◎ ◎ ◎

The formula for meeting the right partner is finding the right person and being the right person. Most people focus on the search, the finding, and don't understand that how we feel about others is directly proportional to how we feel about ourselves. That's why your inside-out approach starts with knowing who you are.

In order to break out of your shell, you must first eliminate the things that prevent you from being your true self. Figuring out who you are shatters the shell. There's no need to go looking for yourself when you already know who you are.

Being content as we are is challenging because we have been conditioned to see ourselves as flawed (by those selling us things or those not content with their own lives). As a result, we believe that we only attain happiness once we have or do something specific. I give you permission to let go of that notion with your next exhale.

Before we continue, here's a concise answer from Love Coach Shelley Bullard to the question: Who Am I?

> I'm a humanitarian. I'm an adventurer. I'm a seeker and experiencer of bliss. I'm a believer. I'm extremely compassionate. I laugh loudly. I feel deeply. I've got a lot of heart. I'm fiercely dedicated and clear about my beliefs about Love. I want to share those beliefs with you.

Projecting: I Know You Are, But What Am I?

Paying attention to what you say to others is an excellent tool to find out what you are saying to yourself. *You need to get your act together* can be translated to *I need to get my act together.* With a little reflection, you might learn that what you see as faults in others might actually be your own faults. Psychologists term these "ego-defense mechanisms."

For most of my life I've been the perfect cheerleader. I let people know how awesome they can be by telling them I see their potential. If only they could buckle down and lose those last 20 pounds or make a leap to that dream career, they would be perfect *then*. If only they would join Toastmasters to become a better speaker, they would be able to unlock their talent. They're okay now, but man, they could be so much better if they *improved*.

I could blame sports for indoctrinating me with the belief system that complacency leads to someone taking your position. I could blame business for teaching me that you can't rest on your laurels or someone will take your customers. I can point to a million ways I was socialized to believe that I always need to be improving. The core of marketing is showing people what they lack and how they can get it by buying XYZ. If we see ourselves as whole, why would we need to buy anything?

Does telling people how powerful they could be if they improved sound unconditional to you? Now do you get a sense of how I was talking to myself? Make it a point to study both your inner and outer dialogue. I'll bet they are one and the same.

Also pay attention to what others say to you and you'll see it's what they are saying to themselves. If someone puts you down, as much as it may hurt, consider that their inner dialogue is even nastier. They need to make you, or anyone in their wake, *less than* in order to make themselves *more than*. If they lack esteem or find your success threatening, they'll tear you down a few notches in order to feel better about themselves.

◎ ◎ ◎

If someone calls you stupid or gross or weird, any kindergartener will tell you that the perfect response is, "I know you are, but what am I?"

When did we forget such simple wisdom?

As disparaging as it is to put down others, fixing them can also be destructive. Whether you say it or show it, "I can help you" casts you in a savior role. If you consider that it is also a projection—a statement that you need to be fixed—it also casts you in a victim role.

The number one commonality I see in the people I coach for weight-loss is that they take care of others better than they take care of themselves. These people are the fixers and the helpers. It takes one to know one. I had a client say that his coworker was selfish for going to the gym while he had to hold down the fort and be miserable. That martyr mentality masked the fact that he was creating an excuse not to exercise and never developed the habit of self-care. As trite as it sounds, if you really want to help someone, you must put your own oxygen mask on first.

The more you accept yourself as you are—and know who you are—the less you try to fix and change others. You also stop making excuses for not taking care of yourself.

No one, besides you, has the power to make you feel good or bad about yourself. Even so, it's human nature for us to allow others to have an impact on us. Since everyone is projecting, spend your time with those whose projections suit you. *You are brilliant and generous.* I know you are, but what am I? *You are a rockstar.* I know you are, but what am I? *You can achieve anything you set your mind to.* I know you can, but what can I?

Here are questions to ask when deciding with whom to spend your time:

1. How do they talk to others?
2. What do they project on to you?
3. What do they really think of themselves?

Schadenfreude Means Broke and Miserable

There is a time-honored tradition of spending an evening with your favorite people in the world only to reconvene with your inner circle the next day at the diner or the gym to gossip about the rest of those favorite people. *Bill is folding like a cheap suit under all that pressure. Stan's girlfriend is using him like a receptacle. Ever since Bob got that bonus he grew three chins and turned into an uppity prick.* Rich people are frequent objects of this ridicule because we try to hide our jealousy—and make ourselves feel okay—by pointing out their flaws.

How can I be so sure that others do this? Because I've done it. When you examine your own projections, you see where you have work to do and learn more about who you are. That's the value that comes from thinking about what frustrates you most about others. Whatever you are pounding your fist hardest about when you're being critical will lead you to what you can't stand about yourself. *We teach what we need to learn.*

I figured out that a sure-fire way not to get what I want is to belittle those who have it. Nothing creates a feeling of scarcity more than rooting against others. Envy is your mind's way of saying there's not enough left for you. *Schadenfreude,* the German word for malicious joy in the misfortunes of others, is a common affliction. It's a loser's mentality, since begrudging the success of others is the surest way not to attain it yourself. If you don't want Richard Branson's boats or billions, rip him to shreds. If you do, celebrate his success. If you're happy with your lot in life, like Noah, you'll root for Wes

Welker. If you're not, you'll tear him down.

When you characterize those with abundance as rich jerks, your subconscious will do everything in its power to prevent you from having money. Better to be broke and righteous than a rich jerk. Or is it? What question could you ask that will lead you to believe you can have both riches *and* integrity?

Schadenfreude, Tony Soprano, and You

When asked about all the haters in the poker world, Daniel Negreanu, whose career tournament winnings exceed $19 million, referenced "The Happy Wanderer" episode of *The Sopranos*. Tony rants to his shrink:

> I see some guy walking down the street, you know, with a clear head. You know the type. He's always f$%king whistling like the happy f$%king wanderer. I just want to go up to him and I just want to rip his throat open. I want to f$%king grab him and pummel him right there for no reason.

His very next sentence is, "Why should I give a shit if a guy's got a clear head?" You got to love Tony's awareness.

Why would you ever care about—much less want to annihilate— someone who is happy or successful? Negreanu said, "…people who are depressed or down and not happy with their lives…Instead of [taking responsibility] they would rather hate on others and call you lucky…It's also a fear."

Recognizing judgment and envy helps show us who we are. Those who get angry at celebrities who put up a false front of perfection may have issues with their own authenticity. Those who are ticked off about greedy athletes or corporations may not have come to terms with their own greed. That doesn't make them piglets. It simply means there is value in examining their shadow side.

Whether it is people or events, the things you hate give you clues about yourself. When I discussed this with Monte, his nostrils started flaring and I braced myself for a beating. "My hate of greed is far from a manifestation of a shadow greed in myself," he said. "The inhumanity of greed maddens me because it's antithetical to my own inner nature and the way I believe others can live."

I know Monte well enough to recognize that this rings true, and I also know he became irate for a reason. People are most offended if they know deep down that what you're saying is true, but they haven't accepted this truth yet. When you pay close attention to the people and situations that trigger you, you'll find a mother lode of self-knowledge.

Also remember that fulfillment comes from within, so it's pointless to compete with others for it. Envy directed outward is only a distraction from asking the questions to discover who you are.

Four Ways to Uncover Who You Are

1. Ask yourself questions.
2. Ask others questions and listen when feedback is offered.
3. Spend time alone, without distractions.
4. Explore tools that lead to self-discovery (more on this in a few pages).

There is No Objective Reality

A person wearing blue-tinted glasses sees everything as blue. If you are wearing a red shirt, and he insists it is blue, would you engage in a spirited debate? Would you write him a lengthy letter, complete with expert testimony, explaining that your shirt is red? Would you shake him and get so worked up that you *turned blue* trying to make him understand?

This issue hits home for me because I have a pattern of setting the record straight to make sure people see things as they are. At least, as *I think* they are. I identify as a clear-the-air kind of guy because I believe that what we resist persists. Like everything, this is double-edged and I've acknowledged this flaw in my personality.

Think about why, at times, you feel the need to set the record straight. Katie Rubin, a brilliant comedian, diffuses every argument by saying, "You may be right." Some of us are colorblind. Have I considered the possibility that it's me? But I know it's red, and I need you to see it's red too. Why?

As my friend Hajjar often has to remind me, "Let people have their stories."

He also reminds me that there is no such thing as an objective reality. We can only see things through our own eyes. The person wearing blue glasses, just like that "objective" TV journalist or film critic, doesn't recognize that he's wearing them.

The author and diarist Anaïs Nin said, "We don't see things as they are; we see things as we are."

On most political shows, issues are argued from the point of view that one party is wrong and the other party's objective opinion is right. If you heard someone frame *every* issue this way, would you keep fighting to correct them or would you accept their point of view? Note the word accept. It doesn't mean you need to agree with them, and you certainly don't need to break Brussels sprouts with them. If they entertain or challenge you by playing the role of devil's advocate, then you may want to keep them in your life. If they bring you down, you can move away from the relationship. But...and here's the rub: Do you first need to set the record straight? The more certainty, clarity, compassion, and courage (our four alpha traits) you have about who you are, the less you care what others think.

We get frustrated with others when they are not who we want them to be when we want them to be that way. This understanding leads us to two questions:

1. Can you accept other people as they are?
2. If not, why are you spending time with those people?

◎ ◎ ◎

Twelve-step programs require a "fearless moral inventory of ourselves," which includes the courage to make amends. Note that I haven't been in one (though I have attended three AA meetings), but just as I encourage you to pluck the best tools from this book, I gather resources from wherever I can. *Suuuure, you're not an alcoholic.* I can hear you snickering. Have I failed to mention that food, especially of the deep-fried variety, is my substance of choice?

Forgiveness is independent of someone else's reaction. The person who needs to forgive is *you*. It's tough to live a good life, much less a spectacular one, if you are holding on to resentment. How can you focus on being a leading man if you're letting toxic thoughts rent space in your head and heart? And after all, who does the resentment really affect?

If you are intent on setting the record straight or getting someone to see things your way, examine how certain and clear you are about who you are. If someone said to legendary investor Warren Buffett, "You are the dumbest, red-haired, Asian woman on the planet," do you think he would take the time to refute this claim?

When words annoy you, consider why. If you feel the need to offer a parting shot before you walk away, ask yourself if there is a kernel of truth in what that person said. People who trigger us can be our teachers and help us learn who we are.

Who are you?

To gain more direction about who you are, fill in the blanks.

• I am most proud of _____

_____

• I am most afraid of _____

_____

• I believe in _____

_____

• I'm at my best when _____

_____

• I'm at my worst when _____

_____

• I am driven by _____

_____

The Wisdom of the Enneagram

The most valuable self-assessment tool I've come across defines nine personality types represented by the points of a geometric figure called an enneagram. Tony Schwartz, founder and CEO of The Energy Project and author of *Be Excellent at Anything*, recommended *The Wisdom of the Enneagram* and, within five minutes of meeting me, was able to predict my number. When I read the book (hereinafter noted as *TWE*), written by Don Richard Riso and Russ Hudson, there was no doubt Tony was correct that I am a Seven—The Enthusiast.

The "deadly sin" of the Seven is gluttony and three of our fatal flaws are looking ahead to the future, fear of boredom, and feeling like life/ourselves are not enough. Check, check, check. *"On a very deep level, Sevens do not feel that they can find what they really want in life."* Bingo.

We're touching on enneagrams to show you the value of tools to learn more about who you are. If you're intrigued, go to www.enneagraminstitute.com. *TWE* came along at a time in my life when I was ready to receive it and it helped show me who I am. I may break my arm patting myself on the back for my openness to criticism that can deepen my understanding of myself (See, I'm an enthusiast!). I do feel lonely and bored, but not depressed, and I lack a self-destructive side. Or do I? According to the book, The Seven analyzes himself but often does so *incompletely*. I was once 300 pounds and $50,000 in debt. Is that not self-destruction due to gluttony? Or was I uncertain about what I was hungry for?

What Are You Hungry For?

Geneen Roth, author of eight books, including the bestseller *When Food is Love*, spoke to my class at the Institute for Integrative Nutrition (IIN). She asked us to turn to the person next to us and answer one question: What are you hungry for?

I was floored. Speechless. Embarrassed.

When I snapped out of it, that question became the catalyst for me to look at food and addiction in a whole new light. When we look at anything done to excess, it's an indication that no amount is enough. There's a void so deep within us that it can never be filled. My friend who has attended AA meetings daily for 17 years, said, "I never had a *drinking* problem. I had a *living* problem." Then there's rocker Keith Richards, who said, "I've never had a problem with drugs; I've had problems with the police."

Humor aside (though I don't think Richards intended to be humorous), those of us with food issues can learn from those with other addictions. The focus of weight-loss too often centers on food—when to eat, what to eat, counting calories, etc.—which may miss the underlying issues. I ask my clients what they're really hungry for because overeating is often a symptom of not feeling full from life. Joshua Rosenthal, the founder of IIN, goes so far as to call the food we eat "secondary food." "Primary food" comes from relationships, physical activity, a fulfilling career, and spirituality.

Roth's question forced me to look at my patterns around food. I learned that when I traveled, I craved salt. This suggested that I was looking for food to ground me. I uncovered that when I couldn't sleep at night, I used food as a way to slow down my mind and help me sleep (the proverbial food coma). When I looked deeper, to places that weren't as comfortable, I discovered that I looked to food as a way to fill up the loneliness and emptiness in my life. I also realized that I developed a pattern from my family, who for many generations turned to food as comfort, or even worse, to dull their feelings completely.

Did I have a food problem or a life problem?

Ask yourself what you are hungry for. Now answer the question: What *are* you hungry for?

When I asked, I discovered new tools and solutions. I now see that when my life is in balance and I feel full from my work and the people I love, food is an afterthought. When I have those moments of loneliness and the need to fill a void, my logical mind tells me that food won't do the trick.

I take a breath and think about what will fill the void. Maybe I pick up my guitar. Perhaps I write. Or maybe I just sit and experience my real feelings, without the distraction of food to get in the way. Sometimes, I make the conscious choice to eat. Other times, I make the unconscious choice and find myself at the drive-thru of Jack in the Box, washing down curly fries with an Oreo cookie milkshake. Depending on the day, I may or may not beat myself up about it, but regardless, I don't fool myself into believing that I've filled the emptiness.

Remember that our objective is to love and accept ourselves as we are. We don't need to fix; we just need to fine-tune the true expression of ourselves. What I love about *TWE* is that for each type, it shows both the healthy and unhealthy sides. The goal is not to change types; it's to thrive within the context of who you are.

TWE helped me understand even better that a beach bum is not who I am. "Sevens know that they are most gratified by being focused and productive; they are contributing something new and potentially valuable to the world." I wrote in my notes, "You know when you're at your best so pipe down and start contributing more."

Exploring tools that lead to self-discovery means doing research, asking what has worked for people you respect, and dipping your toe in various waters. Maybe you think Myers-Briggs is a far superior tool than enneagrams. Great, then use it. Landmark Forum, men's weekends at the Sterling Institute, and the New Warrior Training Adventure from the Mankind Project are other options. (While I've yet to participate in any of those three, I've heard positive reviews.) There are many truths. Find the tools that lead to *your own truth.*

Whatever avenue you take, I hope you see the value of learning about yourself and gaining more awareness—even if it paints you in a bad light and is precisely what you don't want to hear. You'll know it's especially important if you are *afraid* to hear it.

Allow the Casting Agents to Show You Who You Are

My brother Andy received a scholarship in 1987 to play defensive tackle for the North Carolina Tar Heels. After a disappointing 5-6 season, Coach Dick Crum was replaced by Mack Brown, who would go on to win a national championship at Texas.

Coach Brown arrived in Chapel Hill and after evaluating his personnel, he saw exactly who his team was. In a word, slow. He knew that it was easier to put weight on a kid than make him faster. But rather than haphazardly change players' positions, he studied each of them to determine their strengths and weaknesses.

Defensive linemen get the sacks and glory, so when Andy got wind that he might get moved to offense, he braced himself for bad news. Even though Andy is 20 months older and was much stronger and faster than me, throughout our childhood, I beat him in any sport that required lateral movement like tennis, racquetball, or basketball. Coach Brown's keen eye for talent revealed why.

Fearing the worst, my brother was called into his new coach's office. Brown put on some practice film and told Andy that he loved his work ethic, strength, and technique. Then he pulled out his two big guns, each loaded with *because*—one of the most powerful words in the English language. "*Because* you are most effective moving straight ahead rather than side-to-side, you will be more successful on offense. *Because* you can compete for a starting job, we are switching you to offensive guard."

We feel safe around other alpha males. Brown's certainty, clarity, compassion, and courage transformed Andy's attitude about moving to offense. He walked out of the room more motivated than ever and ended up starting for three years at offensive guard. In fact, of the other five starting offensive linemen his senior year, only one (tackle Andrew Oberg, who was drafted by the Green Bay Packers) played his original position. And only one, 6'1" Andy, did *not* get a look at the next level.

Coach Brown transformed Brian Bollinger from a lumbering tight end to a lightning-quick guard, and the San Francisco 49ers chose him in the third round. Former quarterback Deems May moved to tight end and played eight years in the NFL. Defensive lineman Randall Parsons and Ricky Shaw switched to center and tackle, respectively, and both signed NFL free agent contracts.

◉ ◉ ◉

When we watch a brilliant theatrical performance, we are quick to praise the actor. What we don't see is the casting agent, who chose the actor and put him in a position to succeed. Wouldn't it be great to have Mack Brown watch life-film of you and clue you in on your weaknesses? *You say "like" all the time. You lose eye contact when you get nervous. Your breath reeks.* Again, we can't see our own blind spots and often don't even know our greatest strengths.

Let's not miss an important part of this story by giving all the credit to the coach. In fact, many players resisted position changes and some even quit the team. The ones who were successful had two primary traits: they were open to feedback and they took action.

I've learned that the best way to predict success is to watch people's feet. If they are moving and taking action, their odds of success skyrocket. Other leading indicators are lips and ears. Those talking the most are justifying old patterns and clinging to dated beliefs. Those whose lips don't move, but rather shut up and listen, have the most success.

If you're open to learning, the "casting agents," like Mack Brown, will find you. When they do, recognize them as prophets who can help you learn who you are.

Accentuate Strengths or Work on Weaknesses?

In the film *City Slickers,* Curly (Jack Palance) tells Mitch (Billy Crystal) the secret of life. He holds up one finger and says, "One thing. Just one thing. You stick to that. Everything else don't mean shit."

Mitch replies, "That's great, but what's the one thing?"

Curly answers, "That's what you've got to figure out."

Dirk Nowitzki's one thing was his exceptional shooting. When Nowitzki's marksmanship led the Dallas Mavericks to the NBA championship in 2011, a popular storyline was his personal shooting coach. Nowitzki had been one of the best shooters in the NBA for more than a decade, yet continued to employ a shooting specialist and practice incessantly. If he was already exceptional, why did he need to keep working at it? Plus, he was a mediocre defender. Would he have been better off having a defense coach?

Bill "The Sports Guy" Simmons, creator of ESPN's *Grantland* and author of the bestselling *The Book of Basketball,* says that you only need one exceptional skill to have a career in the NBA. Reggie Evans can barely catch, dribble, or shoot—three skills fundamental for even youth basketball—yet Evans (a poor man's Dennis Rodman, a *very* poor man's Dennis Rodman) has played 12 years in the NBA because of his rebounding prowess. Stuey Ungar was the greatest card player of all time. He was "savant-like" by virtue of the fact that he didn't own a toothbrush and couldn't run simple errands. Evans and Ungar succeeded by sticking to one strength.

Profitable business is about finding a skill in a niche where you excel and doing it over and over. Marcus Buckingham, coauthor of *Now, Discover Your Strengths,* advises you to "discover what you don't like and stop doing it." As a manager or coach, rather than spend resources fixing your employees' weaknesses, you'll get better results putting them in situations to utilize their natural strengths. The same goes for you.

I agree that both mastery and money come from repetition, though I disagree that it's also a recipe for fulfillment and happiness. What if your one thing makes you rich and miserable? Or poor and happy? Discovery and wonder come from the unknown. Art, as opposed to business, allows you to explore new things every day. But what if that which fills your heart doesn't fill your belly? If filling your belly is a struggle, then you either starve or work on it. If public speaking (or computer programming or social etiquette) is holding you back from success, you better find a way to earn money without doing it—or fight through the discomfort and improve your ability to do it.

Being a financial or landscaping whiz is not enough to carry your marriage, just as being remarkable at only making waffles or only telling bedtime stories is not enough to be a great dad. If your liabilities stand in the way of intimacy, they can override your strengths. If you're horrible at communicating, you're going to have a hard time being in any relationship. If it's worth enough to you, and you can see that it's holding you back, work on it. At the same time, if language is not your thing, don't try to pay your bills by writing poetry.

◎ ◎ ◎

Shawn hated salesmen. They always interrupted his dinner. Besides, as an educator, he was too intellectually superior to fall for their gimmicks. Fifteen years ago I told him that even though he called himself a teacher, he was also a salesman. I insisted that he had to sell the principal on his ideas, sell his students on trusting him, and sell their parents on his methods. He fought me tooth and nail until he saw less talented teachers having more success. The pain reached the level that he finally ventured out of his comfort zone. By studying sales, he got his career back on track.

Scottie is a cancer researcher whose one thing is oncology, yet he's learned that in order to procure resources for research, he must write grants, manage a staff, publish his findings, give presentations, and schmooze donors. He just smashed his *City Slickers* DVD and admitted that he needs to address his weaknesses.

You can do something you love even if it's your weakness. I'm inflexible in my hips and my voice, yet I spend a lot of time doing yoga and singing. I love the simple act of doing—without mastery—and those activities contribute to my life. I also recognize that it would be frustrating, if not impossible, if I tried to earn money doing them. If you heard me sing, you wouldn't be the first person to tell me not to quit my day job.

If you're confused and think I am playing both sides, mission accomplished. Remember that my role as coach is to give you the questions that make you pause and think. When you run into resistance in life, you must rely on awareness to make a smart choice. Is adversity telling you to dig deeper and push through the discomfort? Or is it a sign to find something else that better meshes with who you are? For every resourceful entrepreneur who hit a snag, nearly gave up, and summoned the strength to make a fortune, there is another obstinate one who ignored reality and wasted ten years of his life. How do you find the answer?

You ask questions:

1. What activities mesh with who you are and lead to the highest probability of enjoyment?
2. In your business, are you better off focusing on a strength or improving a weakness?
3. In your life, are you better off focusing on a strength or improving a weakness?
4. Are the things you're avoiding due to focus or fear?

When thinking about these questions, be sure to analyze rather than rationalize. Knowing who you are allows you to manage both your strengths and weaknesses and gives you the best chance at both success and happiness.

Which statements best describe who you are?

- I'm a morning/night person.
- I do best with/without structure.
- I like/dislike routine.
- I'm a contrarian/I believe conventional wisdom is wise for a reason.
- I lead with my heart even if it's irrational/I lead with my head and rely on facts.
- I'm not a self-starter and work best with deadlines/I'm self-motivated and hate authority.
- I need financial security/I like risk and having big upside.
- I trust in the universe/I'm a cynic and don't trust anyone.
- I like to plan ahead/I prefer being spontaneous.
- I'm more of a starter/finisher.

Use these statements to paint a clearer picture of who you are. Then ask if you're living in accordance with who you are.

You, Not the Label

Labels are great shorthand for other people. If you changed your name, would you still be the same person? If your top-five alma mater tumbled in the rankings, would you be any less educated? If you always introduced yourself as "Bob Jones, IBM," and you got fired, would you still have an identity?

One of the things I loved most about my community in Thailand was that no one knew my last name, much less bothered to Google or IMDb me to decide if I was worth their time. There were no labels to hide behind or extrinsic reasons for people to like me. The only criterion for hanging around me was if they enjoyed my company. It was about character, not characterization.

In *Fight Club,* Chuck Palahniuk wrote, "…you're not how much money you've got in the bank. You're not your job. You're not your family, and you're not who you tell yourself…You're not your name…You're not your problems…You're not your age."

You are *you.*

Our culture is so obsessed with branding that we've lost sight of the actual goods. It's one thing to hire a PR team to promote your identity; it's another to hire them to *create* it.

You *are* it.

Many of us have been taught to dress for success, but there's now a reverse hierarchy to formality. The more casual you can dress proves how confident and accomplished you are. When you know who you are, you have the courage to express your authenticity. LeBron James, at age 17 no less, took wardrobe courage to another level. As a high school senior, he had the cojones to show up at the Nike basketball camp wearing Adidas shoes. But King James did not stop there. Guess what shoes he wore to the Adidas camp?

I'll give you one hint:

Swoosh.

Now it's your turn to bring that LeBron-like swagger to the next set of questions.

QUESTION THREE: WHO AM I?
More Empowering Questions

1. Who are you?

2. What are you hungry for? What is your primary food?

3. What is the motto of the leading man in your movie?

◉ ◉ ◉

The questions are in this order for a reason.Now that you have answered the questions about who you are, you will be ready for the next question: Where Am I Now? If you're going to start removing gunk from your bell, you need to know where it is.

4

AWARENESS
Where Am I Now?

QUESTION FOUR

WHERE AM I NOW?

"All lies and jest, still a man he hears what
he wants to hear and disregards the rest."

—Paul Simon, *The Boxer*

When you're looking at a map at a mall, park, or museum, the first thing you want to do is orient yourself by finding those three magic words: *You Are Here.* If you want directions, what's the first thing your GPS needs to know? Where you are now. In life, it's not always easy to know where we are if for no other reason than, by definition, we can't see our own blind spots.

You won't know where you are unless you ask. That's why the GPS of life is empowering questions. Figuring out where you are now starts by *asking* where you are now.

There are constant signs that show you where you are. The first step in recognizing them is *wanting* to recognize them. That desire will grow out of understanding that these signs bring you more in touch with who you are and offer clues to get what you want. That's your *why* for gaining awareness. Daniel Goleman, author of *Emotional Intelligence,* said, "Star leaders are stars at leading themselves, first."

To lead yourself, start by asking where you are now. The second step is to actively look for signs. The third is to pay attention when you see them. Of course, these steps will do little good unless you act on your newfound awareness. Wang Yang Ming, the Neo-Confucian philosopher, said, "To know and not to do is not to know at all." While the focus of this chapter is determining where you are now, know that it's ultimately leading you to put it to use.

View Awareness As a Gift

The reason I observe others and do research is to gain the gift of awareness. Other times I gain awareness by asking people to be honest with me. And there are still other times I get it whether I want it or not.

My friend Joe went to kindergarten with my brother, which means I've known him since I was three years old. I ended up following in his footsteps by wearing #88 for our high school football team. Fifteen years later, we discovered that we had something else in common: male pattern baldness. Joe was smart enough to capitalize on Michael Jordan's gift to balding men all over the world by shaving his head. I wasn't as quick on the uptake.

For a couple years, whenever I saw Joe, he harassed me about my hair, or lack thereof. And when I say harassed, I'm being kind. Joe was relentless. As brutal as my friends can be towards each other, everyone agreed that Joe pulled off his shaved head perfectly. In between insults, Joe did manage to say that I had the perfect head for it and was confident I could pull it off too.

Mind you, I wasn't in complete denial. I was aware enough to follow my barber's advice and have it "cut short to make it look long." I was buying Rogaine in bulk and when I put it on my head, I yelled, "Grow!" So while I was concerned, I felt like my strategy was working well enough.

In September 2003, I had a speech in Palm Springs, California, and it worked out that I could meet Joe and a bunch of my buddies in Vegas beforehand. When I saw Joe from a distance in the lobby of the Palms Hotel, I braced myself for his verbal assault. No matter how insulting he was, there was no way I was going to shave my head. Besides, I didn't *need* to.

I was a bit surprised when Joe greeted me and didn't fling any insults. Instead, he reached into his wallet for his license. The picture was taken before Joe had shaved his head, and he was hanging on to his last bit of hair for dear life. He looked horrendous, but I didn't pay it any mind since I couldn't see what this picture had to do with me.

After Joe let the picture sink in, he turned to me and said, "This is you."

He paused for dramatic effect. "I know you don't think this is you, but this is you."

Another dramatic pause. "Shave your head."

He put his license in his wallet and walked away.

I didn't have time to tell him what I was thinking, which was, *"Whatever."* There was no way I was going to shave my head before my speech. If ever.

Two days later, after the speech, with new razor in hand, I went back to my hotel room scared to death. I looked in the mirror, thought back to Joe's license and knew he was right. Now there was no turning back. I lathered up my head, did all I could to keep my hands from shaking, and did the deed.

When I finished, I had mixed feelings. No warts, moles, or bumps, but then again, no hair. It took me a while to get used to it, but after about a week, I knew I had made the right choice. Even better, all the anxiety about losing my hair was gone. If only I had taken the money I began saving on Rogaine and bought stock in Apple. Here I am, more than 10 years later and I still love my shaved head.

Somehow when I looked at this picture taken right before I saw Joe, I couldn't allow myself to see how awful my hair looked.

G. Dinkin in 2003   G. Dinkin in 2013

I now see that Joe gave me the best gift in the world—the gift of awareness.

Let Go of Red Pen Syndrome

Do you remember that sinking feeling when your teacher handed back your paper with all those red marks? We've been conditioned to fear that red ink, which has led many of us to stonewall feedback. If this sounds like you, you may be a victim of Red Pen Syndrome.

On the other hand, if you had a role model, such as a parent or teacher, who understood the power of the word because, he explained that he pointed out your mistakes because he loves you and wants to see you improve. If you were lucky, you had a coach pat you on the back and tell you that he's getting on your case because he cares.

Dallas Mavericks coach Rick Carlisle lambasted O.J. Mayo after a bad game and explained why by saying, "I love O.J. as a kid, as a person…With him, I'm a little like a Little League dad. I want him to do well so badly that sometimes it gets the better of me."

Mayo's interpretation of his coach's feedback would determine his success. If he stonewalled Coach Carlisle's "red pen," he may have sulked. Instead, he accepted it as a gift of awareness, worked on his weaknesses, and had one of the best seasons of his career. Mayo embraced his coach's "red pen" to the tune of a $24 million contract.

◎ ◎ ◎

The *best thing* an unsatisfied customer can do for a business is speak up. Ninety-five percent of unhappy customers don't tell the staff, never return, but complain to anyone else who will listen. The same is true in life since most people are either too busy or too worried about offending you to tell you (but not others) how they feel. The five percent who do alert you to your weaknesses have given you the incredible gift of awareness—along with the opportunity to win them over.

In life, every criticism is a chance to deepen a relationship. In business, every complaint is a potential new source of revenue because an unhappy customer is telling you what he wants and why the competition (or your current offering) doesn't meet his needs. That's why the best managers *love* customers who complain and will pay for the privilege by offering rewards for filling out surveys.

Byron Katie's quote—that "the most spiritual practice is to hang out with people who criticize you"—bears repeating. Leading men demand criticism. Florida offensive line coach Tim Davis, at an event that Alabama head coach Nick Saban did not attend, called his former boss "the devil himself." Rather than fight back, Saban used it as a way to ask for awareness. "If I'm doing something to offend somebody," he said, "I'd certainly like to do whatever I have to do to fix it."

Davis lacked the alpha attributes to confront Saban like a man. Do you want to be the guy flinging insults behind someone's back or the guy asking how he can improve himself? Both the comment and the response show why, in 2013, Davis got a pink slip and Saban got a raise.

If you want to gain awareness, shift your thinking to view feedback as a gift. If someone else can help you identify where you are now, you are on your way to developing tools to get to where you want to go.

Five Ways to Learn Where You Are Now

Ask anyone why they're in a slump and they'll give you the stink-eye and tell you if they knew why they wouldn't be in a slump. So how do we determine where we are now?

1. Watch video or listen to recordings of ourselves.
2. Consult a third party (coaches, teammates, friends, coworkers, consultants).
3. Deconstruct your technique and go back to the fundamentals.
4. Slow down to become more aware.
5. Personal development training (who you are and where you are now go hand-in-hand).

After you see some examples, we'll return to this list for even more direction.

Self-Awareness Leads to Success Beyond Millions

Great poker players, athletes, and entrepreneurs study their opponents. The best of the breed also study *themselves*. Joe Navarro is an ex-FBI agent who specializes in poker "tells," involuntary actions that give away your hand. Antonio Esfandiari told Howard Stern that everyone, including him, has tells. That's why he and other world-class players such as Phil Hellmuth, Jr. (who collaborated with Navarro on the book *Phil Hellmuth Presents Read 'em and Reap*) ask Navarro for information about themselves.

Professional poker players understand the benefit of third party information. They use online forums like Two Plus Two to dissect their thought processes and solicit the strategic opinions of others. They reflect on their decisions and pick the brains of fellow pros. The best of the best also work on themselves.

Daniel Negreanu credits ChoiceCenter—where he took, in his words, "a 100-day course on emotional intelligence"—for a career year. He completed the program in February 2013 and went on to win $3.2 million in tournaments, World Series of Poker Player of the Year, and *Card Player* Player of the Year. In addition to his poker success, he credits the program for improving his relationships with his family and friends.

Nick Binger, another poker pro who took the course, wrote about his experience after a wave of criticism aimed at Negreanu for sharing what he learned. Binger, who has a background in chemistry, wrote that he "always hated pseudoscience and con artists," and approached the class with caution. A scientist at heart, Binger's measuring stick was quantifiable results.

He wrote that, "During the 3 month leadership period the group [of 48] lost 361 lbs. of fat, gained 51 lbs. of muscle, paid off $345K of debt, created $945K in new annual income, raised $280K for St. Jude Children's hospital, and 4 people quit smoking."

It's okay to be a skeptic. It's even better to be willing to confront your skepticism. If you've been looking for tangible benefits of finding out where you are now, read that last paragraph one more time.

What I found most interesting about Negreanu's experience was the venomous reaction after he shared it. Even by Internet message board standards, the slurs hurled at Negreanu were vicious and spiteful. I can understand why a person questions a program or says that it's not for him. It was the nastiness that surprised me.

We'll discuss in chapter six the importance of finding tools that uniquely suit you. If enneagrams, the ChoiceCenter, or men's weekends don't sound appealing, they may be a bad fit for who you are. Certainly I, the guy who embraces questions, am going to encourage you to find what best suits you.

I will, however, take you to task for devoting your energy to criticism. You would be better served getting in touch with why you feel the need to put others down. Then invest your mental real estate in tools you can use to heighten your ability to learn more about where you are now.

Speaking of self-awareness, I took notice of how the examples I chose in this section reinforced the stereotypes of masculine success. In my desire to show you the importance of building awareness, I called attention to money, awards, and fitness. I wonder if we would have been better served had I highlighted that Negreanu seems happier and that this work is about learning who you are and what fulfills you.

Let's get back to questions. Here are three more:

1. What truth am I afraid to face?
2. What could I work on to rise to the top of my profession?
3. What could I work on to make sure I enjoy being at the top of my profession?

Spotting the Lies We Tell Ourselves

My friend was smoking a cigarette on the beach when a stranger said to him, "Why are you trying to kill yourself?" He thought about it for a while but couldn't come up with a good answer. Whether it was the question or the pause, he has never smoked a cigarette since. He thanked this stranger for giving him the gift of awareness.

My former partner in our literary agency, Frank, told me that he observed that after a person gave me directions, I didn't say thank you. I protested that I'm not rude so that couldn't be the case. "No, you're not rude," he said. "You're just in such a hurry and in your own head that you're on to the next thing." Then he muttered under his breath, "Spaz."

It's natural that our first reaction is defensiveness. I know Frank to be observant and honest, yet I still became defensive. While I wasn't ready to receive his observation as a gift, if for no other reason than to prove him wrong, I began to monitor myself in these situations. Once I took notice, I watched myself rush off without thanking people. Frank was right, and I was able to change my behavior.

Frank and I built on this experience by creating a ritual that we used after every meeting. Our first debriefing question was, "Any gaffes?" If one of us made a mistake—lost eye contact, overhyped a project, had his zipper down— we let the other know. The first benefit was that it made both of us more aware. Second, it built a company culture that embraced constructive criticism. And third, it prevented resentment from building up since our concerns were addressed on the spot.

Mindfulness is the antidote for denial. The good news is that the truth only hurts once. The lies and denial hurt forever.

If you have a chronic back issue, maybe the truth (your truth) is that you have a crush on the chiropractor or the pharmacist who fills your prescriptions. Perhaps you like having a built-in excuse for missing work or that running group. Maybe you enjoy the sympathy you get for having a bad back. You might argue (because defensiveness is typically the first response to the truth) that no one wants to have a bad back.

Even you may not know what is happening on a subconscious level. Feigning illness to gain attention is so common that there's even a name for this psychological disorder: Münchausen syndrome. Those who can't figure out how to place the two little dots over the "u" call it hospital hopper syndrome or thick chart syndrome.

Since as many as 80 percent of us have suffered from back pain, it's a stretch to say that pain is only in your head. I, myself, have had back issues and felt frustrated that for all my mental gymnastics, the pain didn't go away. I'm bringing this to your attention because I want you to examine everything in your life and take nothing for granted. I understand that you may want more than anything in the world to heal your back. I'm also suggesting that the pain may be serving a *part* of you. If a boy only received attention when he was sick, he may equate illness with love and may seek to recreate these moments.

Deciphering the various parts of your subconscious will take some work, but if you're willing to be honest with yourself, you'll benefit from the hard truth about where you are now.

Why We Lie

The most common reason for lying is that the truth paints us in a negative light. Let's say you offer Billy a trip to Fiji. "I can't, dude. No cash," he says. You tell him that the entire trip is free. "The real problem is I can't get off work," he says. But a few days ago he mentioned that he has twenty vacation days that are about to expire.

Great salesmen turn liars into buyers. They do so by figuring out the true objection and solving it. If the real reason he won't go is a fear of flying, Billy may be too embarrassed to admit it and instead continue lying. If he doesn't want to go because he plans to steal your clients (or girlfriend) while you're gone, he'll keep lying. Unless you get to the real objection, you won't get to a solution.

The real trick to awareness is figuring out when you are lying to *yourself.* You may be so accomplished at denial that you miss seeing your own reality. You may tell yourself you don't want the promotion because the hours are too long, but perhaps you are lying because you fear that the truth will cast you in a negative light. The real reason is that you're afraid you're not qualified and will be exposed as a fraud. Or you're afraid that your parents or significant other will stop supporting you (and you equate financial support with emotional support) if they know you're earning more money.

Gaining awareness requires work. The question: "Where am I now?" is a challenging one. The way to find the solution is by asking questions and paying close attention to your answers.

Manning Up to Exceed Expectations

Dale Carnegie wrote the 1936 classic *How to Win Friends and Influence People.* The book, along with the training company he founded, remains popular to this day. My grandpa Harry was so moved by a Carnegie class that he said, "Dale Carnegie was the best course I ever took. Better than intercourse." As funny as he was, Harry's real gift was awareness. He ran a hosiery business in Baltimore, and when he went to ask for credit from a bank, he dressed impeccably so they wouldn't think he was desperate. When he went to collect money, he wore a coat with torn lining, lest his debtors think he wouldn't miss the money.

Harry's manufacturer was located in a dry county in North Carolina, and by bringing booze as gifts, he received favorable credit terms. Talk about walking in people's shoes and meeting their needs. Harry was quite the schmoozer, though he was also a leading man who kept his word—even if it meant owning up to a mistake.

If Harry agreed to pay his supplier in thirty days, it killed him when his cash flow wouldn't allow him to keep his word. The same men who refuse to ask for directions hide in these situations and kid themselves into believing that, as long as the other person isn't saying anything, it will go unnoticed.

Harry, on the other hand, would call well before the money was due and own up to the fact that he was going to be late. His suppliers rewarded his honesty by extending a grace period. Not only would Harry express his appreciation, he also told them the exact day he would send the money. Then he took it a step further by sending it a week *early.* By virtue of awareness and communication, Harry found a way to be late and exceed expectations! My grandpa didn't just put the X in EIX. He put the O *and* the G in original gangster.

It seems so obvious to man up, but I watch people hide all the time when things go wrong. If you're running late, all you have to do is text or call and you're in the clear. Leading men deal with the immediate pain of owning up to a mistake and do just that. Others will lie, justify, and do anything to avoid admitting to a mistake. Again, you earn the ease of a leading man when you walk in the shoes of others and take action.

Getting to that place requires awareness, which is born out of active listening.

Replace Mr. Fix-It With Mr. Active Listener

Watching two people talk only about themselves results in more whiplash than sitting in the front row of a Ping-Pong match. *Listen to me.* Listen to *me. Let me tell you about my day.* Let me tell you about *my* day.

This is the dynamic that Simon & Garfunkel were referring to in the *Sound of Silence* when they crooned, "People talking without speaking; people hearing without listening."

In addition to maintaining eye contact (put that phone *down*), when someone is talking to you, give them the stage. If a friend tells you he did 21 shots of tequila on his 21st birthday, resist the urge to steal the stage or one-up by saying, "Man, that's nothing. On my birthday…" Instead, shut up and stay focused on *his* story.

When I was 22, my girlfriend loved to recount every last detail of her day. Since I prided myself on my listening skills and knew better than to steal her stage, I actively listened. If she detailed a problem, I would listen without interrupting. Then when she came up for air, I would explain how she could fix the situation. It upset her and she would tell me that I wasn't *hearing* her. In turn, I became so defensive that I told her I could repeat every word she said. I had good intentions, but because my tools were limited, I couldn't see my own blind spot.

Shortly after breaking up, I read *Men Are from Mars, Women Are from Venus* and learned that Mr. Fix-it is a common affliction. Author John Gray explained that women want to be heard, and we connect with them by listening without judgment. While I meant well, offering solutions created problems in my relationship.

Growing up, most of my conversations with my best friend Bryan were about basketball. If he told me that his opponent pressed, he didn't want me to ask how that made him feel or nod and smile. He wanted my take on the best way to *beat* the press. Even now, when Bryan and I talk, we love helping each other *solve* things. While men tend to talk with an agenda, women talk to build connection. It took my masculine, logical mind years to figure out—while trying to understand a woman's point—that the point was to connect, not to fix.

When Michelle, my godkids' mom, rambles on and on, I'll let her go and only interject the occasional uh-huh or okay. When she finishes, I'll ask her if she was happy to vent or wants my opinion. Often she'll say the former, and I'll thank her for sharing and tell her that I love her. If Michelle asks for advice, and *only* if she asks, I offer feedback by asking questions. I don't offer a solution without being prompted.

Making Others Better Listeners for You

Whether talking with a man or a woman, in any context, give them the stage, genuinely show you care, and rather than wait for your turn to speak (sound familiar?), actively listen. If they ask what you think, ask them what they think. And off they will go, solving their own issue, grateful that you gave them the space to talk things out. If they press you for advice, you can tell them what has worked for others or for you. All the while, continue to emphasize that they will find the answers within as long as they keep asking questions.

The advice game is a lousy one, and its engine is ego. It is a sensational feeling when someone tells you that your guidance transformed their life. But what if the advice doesn't work? If you tell someone who they should marry, are you willing to take on the liability for a therapist and a divorce attorney? My friend L.Z. told me I could grow back my hair using moose mandible and my own urine. Do you want to take responsibility for *that* experiment gone wrong?

◎ ◎ ◎

When you want someone to listen to you, make sure they have the "bandwidth" to receive. Would you call up Santa Claus on December 24th and say, "Yo, Santa, I could really use a friend today. How does a three-Martini lunch sound?" Would you call your accountant buddy on April 14th and ask him to help you move?

Beyond those extremes, you can determine someone's capacity to listen if you begin a phone call by asking, "Did I catch you at a bad time?" The last thing you want is to start in on a rant only to be told that your friend's boss was in the middle of docking his pay for talking on the phone. When you start by asking about the other person's state, you make things easier for the listener. You will see that some friends can't focus at work, or home, or in the car, while others are looking to kill time in those places and can give you their full attention.

Steve Morse, owner of Milwaukee Lumber in Portland, Oregon, begins all his meetings with the acronym MERPS. He asks everyone in the room how they are doing mentally, emotionally, relationally, professionally, and spiritually. He knows that his message will only be received if the attendees are ready for it. When he started a meeting with a potential customer using MERPS, the guy talked about his substance abuse. Morse had the awareness to put aside his business agenda, turn into a trusted confidante, and help the man find a rehab facility. Imagine what might have happened if he was so in his own head that all he talked about was his company's impeccable service record?

It also helps to tell people what you want from them when a conversation starts. You could say, "I need a good ear" or "Hear me out for five minutes and then you can talk." If you only want to be heard, tell them that you're not looking for Mr. Fix-it. If you want honest feedback, emphasize that you have thick skin and ask them to be brutal.

In a chapter about awareness, it's no accident that we're spending a lot of time on listening. When you're asking empowering questions, you must learn to listen and find others who will show you the same respect.

Outlets and Risk-Taking Make You a Better Leader

Young Presidents' Organization (YPO) and World Presidents' Organization (WPO) are peer leadership groups organized into 400 chapters in 125 countries and are comprised of approximately 93 percent men. From bringing in speakers, to networking, to comparing best practices, the members I know, including Steve Morse, rave about their experiences. Many have told me that the most valuable aspect is having a forum to open up and share their lives. On ypo.org, it goes so far as to mention "the need for a 'safe haven' where issues can be aired in an environment of confidentiality."

Bear in mind these meetings take place under the premise of business. I'd guess that few of the members would sign up for group therapy. As relationships grow and trust deepens, they create a sounding board for both their personal and professional challenges. Keith Lemer, president of WellNet Healthcare Group and a member of the Washington, D.C. YPO chapter, told me, "There are few gifts greater than the ability to share your unvarnished truth with peers who only want to help and support you."

Without forums like YPO, when men get together, it's often to watch a sporting event. *Maybe,* in between commercials, a bit of real dialogue happens. Back in the day, clubs like Kiwanis, Elks, and Rotary, not to mention churches and taverns—often located in the same building—were the places men went to talk. Others would shoot the breeze on their porches or chew the fat at the racetrack or pool hall. These institutions for men have been replaced by coffee shops and sports bars where eyes are glued to screens and ears are plugged with headphones. Because we have few outlets, we miss out on opportunities to learn *where we are now.*

Finding an organization centered on your interests is an excellent start. Whether it's a fitness, business, or social group, you only need to check out Meetup.com or walk around with your eyes open. The magazine *Natural Awakenings* lists all types of groups including DC Contemplative Lawyers Group which begins with "20 minutes of guided meditation followed by guided discussion." If you're an overstressed lawyer who doesn't feel like anyone understands your plight, doesn't that sound like the perfect place to start?

You must go beyond simply showing up and start opening up to other men. The minute you become honest and vulnerable, your friends likely will reciprocate. Author Tony Schwartz understands the power of opening our hearts. In an article titled "What Women Know About Leadership That Men Don't," he explains how vulnerability makes us more powerful leaders. He writes:

> Empathy proved especially difficult for me whenever I felt vulnerable. My instinctive response was to protect myself, most often with aggression. I equated aggression with safety, and vulnerability with weakness. Today, I recognize the opposite is often true. The more I acknowledge my own fears and uncertainties, the safer people feel with me and the more effectively they work…
>
> In short, great leadership begins with being a whole human being.

Follow Tony's lead to share your entire self and watch the floodgates open. Take some emotional risks. The upside is that you will deepen your relationships, feel more connected, and give other men permission to open up about their lives. The downside is you may feel a little foolish, but if that person laughs at you or puts you down (which you know is a projection), you have at least uncovered the pretense of your friendship and can move on to other leading men.

I Love You, Man

When I was in high school, my friend Trey's dad said to me, "Greg, when you get to be my age you don't have any friends. Your friends are your wife's friends' husbands." It was hard to believe at the time, though I now know several married men who count me as their only friend. Here's a direct quote from the wife of a guy who used to be the life of the party: "Let us know when you get to town. It hasn't been the same without you. Donald went from one friend to zero."

According to the book *Season of Life,* the average man over 35 does not have one close friend to confide in. You can find the same statistic on men.ag.org, the website for National Men's Ministries, where it also says, "Men need teaching on how to develop and strengthen friendships and an environment where they can find genuine male friends." I wouldn't have believed that we needed to be taught this if I hadn't witnessed it so frequently.

Many of us are so busy competing with other men that we never learned to love and listen to each other. I ask (especially male) friends and the people I coach, "Who are your outlets? Who do you open up to? Who do you process things with?" Most mock me for ending sentences with prepositions. Humor hides and humor heals.

The film *I Love You, Man* was released in 2009 as art imitating life. In the opening scene, Paul Rudd's character proposes to Rashida Jones' character. Immediately, she calls all her friends to share the news. She then turns to Rudd, and when she asks why he isn't calling anyone, we learn that he has no close friends. The comedic film is about his search to fill up his side of the wedding party and illustrates how tough it is for men to form friendships. When he meets Jason Segal's character, the *bromance* is on, which is funny, in part, because it's so atypical.

Thankfully the John Hamburg-directed movie has given men the gift of humor to make it easier to say those three or four words that I'm happy to say first.

I love you.

Man.

◎ ◎ ◎

Think about your outlets, and whether you feel like you can be honest and heartfelt about your deepest feelings. My brother says that a true friend is one you can call at four in the morning and say, "Get a shovel." A lot of guys would comply but never talk about what led up to the situation, or how they feel about burying some dead dude. The strong silent thing has its limitations.

During a heart-to-heart with Charles, my first guitar teacher who has become one of my best friends, he asked me if it was *enough* for him to be a good dad, husband, and person, and if he could find fulfillment without "greatness." Charles is a Type-A, competitive guy with three kids under the age of seven. He's so exhausted making ends meet that he doesn't have time for delusions of grandeur about revitalizing his music career.

A coach's job is to hold up a mirror. The goal is to lead Charles, and *you,* to ask tough questions that allow you to see what fulfillment looks like to you.

Knowing Charles as well as I do, my gut tells me that a career that only pays the bills and hobbies that only provide escape will leave him feeling empty. Maybe he's not going to record an album this weekend. Perhaps he can't get up earlier to get to the gym every morning this week. Only he knows who he is and what makes him tick. Maybe he'll find that edge coaching his kids' teams or doing pro bono legal work and get his rush that way.

I guarantee he's thinking about it and asking questions. Are you? Are you honest about where you are now?

An Absent-Minded Maniac Discovers P-MILK

I've known Randy since second grade, and even though he was one of my best friends growing up, we lost touch until a few years ago when he came to visit me in Los Angeles. Before heading out to the Michael Franti and Spearhead concert, I started doing my "get-ready" dance. You know how you circle around making sure you have your keys, cell phone, wallet, and all your stuff. I thought this was normal, until Randy asked, "How come every time you leave the house you turn into a complete maniac?"

I told him that I'm forgetful and wanted to make sure I had everything. And besides, doesn't everyone do this? He laughed and said that, yes, we all need to gather our stuff, but I had turned it into a circus act. He then mimicked a lunatic running in circles, and I got the point.

With this awareness, I remembered a technique I had heard, but dismissed, called MILK. MILK is a mnemonic device for Money, Identification, License, Keys. It seems that ID and license are redundant, but identification can mean concert tickets, coupon, or gym membership card. Again, I didn't give it a second thought until Randy made me aware of how maniacal my circus dance was. Once he did, I added a "P" for phone and now use this tool several times a day. If you ever see me leaving my house, the gym, a hotel room, or an airplane, I'll be slapping my pockets and saying, "P-MILK."

A friend who travels abroad added another "P" at the beginning for passport and an "S" at the end for sunglasses. It's hilarious to see this jacked, weightlifter flex as he says out loud, "pee-pee-milks," but he'd rather get laughed at than forget his passport or sunglasses. Make this technique your own and let me know what you come up with. If it fits, add another C at the beginning for charger, converter, or compass and start saying C-P-P-MILKS.

Using P-MILK is a fantastic reminder that we only hear things when we're ready and paying attention. It's also a great example of being open to feedback and finding a tool that puts an end to a daily stressful occurrence.

Your Impetus for Change?

Having known me as an athlete growing up, Randy was eager to hear about how I transformed from a 300-pound, workaholic, spastic meathead living in New York City into a 200-pound, semi-spastic life coach living in Venice Beach.

He sat in my apartment and noticed the contrast from my childhood room that had been covered with posters of my idol Dr. J as well as Bobby "Secretary of Defense" Jones and George "Iceman" Gervin. He asked about my transformation, and sat captivated, waiting for my amazing tale.

"Well," I said. "My brother and my friend Tim did hot yoga, lost a bunch of weight, and said they felt fantastic. I figured I had nothing to lose."

I haven't seen Randy, a die-hard Washington Redskins fan, look this disappointed since L.T. broke Joe Theismann's leg.

"That's it?" Randy asked.

"That's what got me started," I said.

Randy looked confused and prodded me to pinpoint the cinematic moment when my journey began. I summed it up by saying that I was fed up being unhappy with my lot in life, that I finally got sick and tired of being sick and tired.

"That is the lamest story ever!"

I don't know if Randy had just finished reading *A Million Little Pieces* or *Eat Pray Love,* but he must have had something else in mind. Since the most dramatic stories are about people who hit rock-bottom—and those are the stories that turn into feature films and bestselling books—many people believe that you must suffer major hardship in order to gain self-awareness. Unfortunately, in most cases, this is true. The way I see it, however, is that if you believe you must hit a bottom, you just might lead yourself to one.

I remember telling my friend Ben that I felt lucky that I haven't experienced major trauma in my life. Ben's eyes got bigger than bazookas and his arms flailed. "No, you are *unlucky!*" he said. "It's not until you are drowning in the ocean and fighting for your last breath that you totally surrender."

Ben may be right, but do we need to manufacture trauma? Our experiences are what they are, and we have the power to choose the stories we tell and how we feel about them. You don't have to wait for tragedy to strike to clarify what you want and commit to living it. In this moment, whether you're on top of the world or down in the dumps, shine a light on yourself and find out where you really are. Your GPS device is, of course, empowering questions.

Questions Make the Awareness Police Obsolete

He doesn't get it. He has no clue. He's in denial. We've got to shake this guy and get him to see his blind spots.

You've already heard that a hallmark of masculinity is the ability to take criticism from other men. I hope this chapter reinforces the value of asking others for criticism and embracing feedback. I also want you to keep the focus on sharpening your own awareness, rather than being somebody else's wake-up call.

We have a responsibility to our loved ones to tell them when we can see what they are missing. I believe that the more you love someone, the more you should be inclined to ask tough questions. I've been on both sides of interventions and know that it requires courage to risk being ostracized in an effort to help someone. I would argue that we owe it to those who are closest to us to tell them when we think they are headed down a destructive path.

This is a delicate, slippery slope. I've spent far too many hours trying to make other people get it. The trap was thinking that "it" was some objective reality. The truth is that it was my reality. I wanted them to get "it" because it served me. Then there were other occasions where I shared my concern only for the benefit of a loved one. Before offering your opinion, your litmus test is to ask why you are doing it. If it comes from a loving place, go for it. If it's driven by self-interest, let it go and focus on honing your own awareness.

You see a friend whom you think is in denial, mindlessly chugging Southern Comfort in front of the TV. You may think this person needs to "deal," but maybe he knows he needs a distraction. At that time, ignorance may be bliss. Who are you to deny him that moment? And why do you think you know him better than he knows himself?

There are no easy answers in these types of situations. Often the best thing you can do is ask a question. If you can find a way to make your friend pause, and look inside, it might serve as a catalyst to get him off autopilot. Ask questions such as:

1. If I was in your shoes right now, what would you tell me?
2. Do you want to talk about what's going on?
3. What would the hero in your movie do when he felt like this?
4. What can I do to help you get out of your funk?
5. What good story doesn't have a little adversity? (Now let's see how the hero responds.)

You can also offer alternatives, without any judgment. "Hey, buddy, I understand that you may need to veg out all day and polish off that bottle, but if you're up for a hike, lunch is on me." If your friend is in a 12-step program, suggest that he call his sponsor. If alcohol isn't a destructive tool for him, you can say, "There's half-priced sake at Mao's tonight. If you're going to get tanked, it will be much more fun with friends around."

He might groan and say the last thing he wants is to be around other people. But he might, upon hearing the word sake, break into an Austin Powers' impersonation, stand up and scream, "Sock it to me baby!" With this spontaneous surge of energy, his fog has been lifted.

Just as you know what words trigger you, walk in your friend's shoes and think about what will trigger him. If I said to my friend Hubie, "Stop acting like a wuss," I can guarantee that, no matter how awful his mood, he'd come right back with a *Fast Times at Ridgemont High* reference. Next thing you know, we would turn into Mike Damone's character, and recite together, "You bought 40 dollars worth of film, Rat, and you never even talked to her. You don't even own a camera."

If you think this makes me sound both old and immature, you may be right. But this is how I talk to *some* of my friends. One goofy comment may be all it takes to interrupt a buddy's downward spiral. You know your friends best, and you know *yourself* best. We're going to talk about dealing with your own ruts more in the chapter on tools, so while you're thinking about how you can help a friend gain awareness, think about how you can do the same for yourself.

Remember that we are working inside-out. If you develop your own awareness, your interaction with others will improve. Since so much of what we say to others is our own projections, you'll feel less of a need to point out other people's issues and give unsolicited advice. It can be difficult to make someone get "it"—especially if that person is you.

Five Techniques to Develop Awareness

Let's get even more specific about the *Five Ways to Learn Where You Are Now.*

1. Watch a video or listen to a recording of yourself.

Find some way to "watch" yourself. If you're a musician or give presentations, film them. Same if you're a weight-lifter, chef, or cyclist. If you do something else, be creative and figure out how you can see yourself in a new light.

2. Consult a third party (coaches, teammates, friends, coworkers, consultants).

Ask people you know for feedback. Beg them for it. Take them to lunch or buy them gifts when they give it. Remind them to be specific, honest, and let them know that you have thick skin and are ready to hear constructive criticism. Also consider finding a mentor or hiring a coach.

3. Deconstruct your technique and go back to the fundamentals.

Start with the basics. If you're having trouble sleeping, examine your diet, caffeine consumption, and the lighting/condition of your bedroom. If you're struggling with your job, refocus on what led to success in the first place.

4. Slow down to become more aware.

You will find more clues when you slow down and actively look for them. Simply becoming aware and owning up to the fact that you're in a slump may be enough to discover solutions. Details become more prominent in slow motion, so slow down and take in what's going on.

5. Personal development training

We've listed many options. Find what resonates with you and commit to it. Remember that it must be *personal* and that a program only works when *you* work *it*.

Find Your Species Using Love Languages

Sex and relationship educator Reid Mihalko believes that we should "date our species" and contends that relationships work best when we give and receive love in a way that is compatible with our nature. He draws on *The 5 Love Languages* by Gary Chapman to make his point. The "languages" are physical touch, words of affirmation, receiving gifts, acts of service, and quality time. The book shows examples of well-meaning people who love their partner yet only learn to connect once they gain awareness from walking in their partner's shoes. Dale Carnegie summed up this concept brilliantly:

> I am very fond of strawberries and cream, but I have found that for some strange reason, fish prefer worms. So when I went fishing, I didn't think about what I wanted. I thought about what

they wanted. I didn't bait the hook with strawberries and cream. Rather, I dangled a worm or grasshopper in front of the fish.

Many people tell my friend Carol that she has the greatest boyfriend on the planet. It gives Mel pleasure to run her errands, clean her house, and give her two-hour massages. Mel's love language is acts of service. Even though he loves with devotion and passion, it does not *land* on Carol. It's as if he writes poetry in Swahili and Carol only can read Italian. Her love language is words of affirmation and since Mel doesn't speak to her in that language, despite the many acts of service he gives, Carol feels unloved.

I told Mel that he could save time and make Carol feel loved by using words of affirmation (rather than performing only acts of service). While he prefers to show rather than tell, *telling* Carol how much he loves her and how beautiful she is will land on her. Since his goal is to make her feel loved, he has to speak her language in order to be successful.

My mom also receives love through words. She may spend half the day cooking and waiting on my stepdad. In return for all her effort, he'll tell her, "That was the most delicious meal I've ever had. You really are something else, Erlaine." She'll bask in the sentiment, and I sit there thinking, "Who got the better end of this deal?" But credit her husband for loving her in a way she can *receive.*

A Good Pass Is One That Is Received

The way Carol's boyfriend Mel sees it, the most important quality of love is sincerity. He told me that saying "I love you" in a language other than English would be inauthentic and feel meaningless to him. He asked why the burden should be on the *giver,* and not the receiver. Shouldn't Carol be able to see that he is expressing his love the way he knows how and appreciate him for it?

Not exactly.

Walking in the other person's shoes is a two-way street. You need the awareness to see that even if you are not receiving love exactly the way you want it, your partner may be doing her best. She may spend hours creating the perfect ambiance for a home-cooked meal when you would prefer to eat Chinese food out of a carton while she rubs your shoulders and tells you how much she appreciates you. Although you may recognize that she made an effort to show love the way she knows how, you won't feel the love if it's not given in a way that lands on you.

I can still hear my former basketball coach Wilbert Givens yelling, "A good pass is one that is received!" If you throw a "perfect" alley-oop pass to a guy who can't jump and it sails over his head, who is at fault? If you throw a no-look bullet pass to a guy with bad hands, who is at fault? The guy who *threw* the pass gets the turnover. That guy, along with the guy who loves his partner in a way that doesn't land on her, gets sent to the doghouse. Getting angry about it is the equivalent of a comic getting angry at his audience. *I said this is funny! Now laugh, you imbeciles!*

You may think that Chris Rock and Louis C.K. are funny by being themselves. By just doing their thing, the thinking goes, people connect to their authenticity. If they kowtowed—if they, effectively, tried to speak in the love language of the audience—it would sound forced and they would stink.

Sort of.

Their material is authentic. What makes it work is that, by the time you hear it, it has been tested. For every funny joke, there were countless others that bombed. A comic knows that "funny" is defined by the receiver, not the giver. A joke works when the audience, not the comic, laughs.

Love "works" when the receiver feels it. That's why the responsibility is on the giver to be authentic *and* fine-tune the way he loves so that it lands on the other person. The very fact that Mel used the word "burden" rather than "responsibility" was part of his problem.

Imagine spending the entire weekend doting on your woman, then taking her out for a romantic dinner and reading her a heartfelt poem. Then imagine her saying, "If you really loved me, you would have bought me flowers." On one hand, she's ungrateful and lacks the ability to recognize the way you display love. On the other hand, if you had been paying attention and knew receiving flowers made her feel loved, why would you withhold that from her?

Wouldn't it make sense to focus on loving gestures that make *her* feel loved? Maybe the dinner was *your* treat, not hers.

If you buy her a Lexus and she hardly thanks you (but keeps complaining that you never take her on a picnic), you have every right to be infuriated. And the best place to direct this frustration is back on yourself. A leading man would have known that her love language is quality time, not gifts, and he would have saved a hundred grand and received the same result: for her to feel loved and for her to love you back. You both win when you walk in her shoes and choose the appropriate love language.

Keep in mind that although I said the responsibility is on the giver, that doesn't mean it's only on men. In a relationship, both parties need to pause and consider what makes their partner feel loved. If she's not considerate and aware enough to know what makes you feel loved, she likely isn't your "species" and is a poor match. We want to choose a woman who loves us the way we want to be loved. Getting there requires that you know your own love language—another form of awareness.

What's In It for Them?

When you pitch a business idea, is your focus on how you look or how the business looks to them? If *they* are the ones writing a check, you must present it in such a way that *they* comprehend.

Steve Jobs differentiated Apple's products based on the user experience. Rather than focus on technology, he focused on you—how you *interfaced* with the product. High-tech is high-crap if it's impossible to use. Jobs' obsession with design came from his desire to make sure the product/pass was received.

Take the time to think about what others want and the world will be yours. This is the ultimate payoff the leading man receives for awareness: do less, receive more, and increase the flow of love. And you can learn this. You *are* learning this *because* you are a leading man who knows where he is now.

◎ ◎ ◎

The question people want answered is: What's in it for me? That means you must stop to consider what will make them feel loved and/or what they consider a win. Then you have to figure out how to deliver it in a way that connects with them. All it requires is awareness, and it will set you apart because most people only think about themselves. They miss the simple logic that the way to get what you want is to help others get what they want.

Of the dozens of divorced people I've asked about their ex's love language, not one could tell me. Is it any wonder they're divorced? After asking him many questions, my friend Ace realized that his ex needed constant words of affirmation. Since he believes that "talk is cheap" and "actions speak louder than words," he went out of his way *not* to love his girlfriend in her language. The relationship was a nightmare. We deconstructed it and Ace learned that his disdain for his ex's neediness made him withhold the very things that would have made her feel loved. Now that he's with a woman he loves and respects—combined with his awareness that she, too, thrives on affirming words—the sweet words flow and their connection is deepening.

For Mel, there seems to be an easy fix. Just use words that make Carol feel loved. That's easy for me to say since words of affirmation are *my* love language (and my profession, no less). But if it feels unnatural, it may be difficult for Mel to use words. This is why I agree with Mihalko when he says to "date your species." Once Mel has the awareness, maybe he can find the words to make Carol feel loved. But if it's a constant struggle (as learning a new language can be), and it's exacerbated by him not feeling appreciated for his countless acts of service, they may be a poor romantic match. When your love languages are aligned, partnerships are more seamless, and thus, more sustainable.

Even Family Members Speak Different Languages

When Carol let me stay in her Manhattan loft, I could have sent her a present (gifts, obviously), taken her on a picnic (quality time), given her a hug (physical touch), or weeded her lawn (acts of service). Since I know that none of those will land on her like words of affirmation, I sent her a card with a four-line poem, which only took a few minutes to write.

Carol responded saying how much she loved it and that I can stay at her apartment any time. It taught me that while *The 5 Love Languages* is a great resource for couples, it's also an invaluable tool for non-romantic relationships, especially family.

Both my dad and brother receive love through quality time. Rather than send gifts or write heartfelt notes, I show up for special events. Like it or not, they're still getting bone-crushing hugs. If Andy tries to ward me off, I give him my best Chris Farley impression from *Tommy Boy* and declare, "Brothers don't shake hands. Brothers hug."

Sometimes you have to be a little smarter than the average bear to decipher a love language. Keep in mind that most of us have some combination of several. What's more, the way we give and receive love may or may not be the same. My friend Hal gives through acts of service, though his independent streak means he hates to receive that way. When you look around his house and office and see cards and notes displayed, it's apparent that he receives through words of affirmation. If I want love to land on him, I write him a letter. If I include a gift, it's much higher in thought than in price.

Since my primary love languages are words and touch, you can imagine that I want to hug my goddaughter, Maralyn, and tell her how much I love her 177 times a day. The hitch is that she can't stand either of these things. On one of her visits, I was convinced she didn't even like me. When she wanted to go to the store, I gave her some cash and sent her on her way.

"Aren't you coming?" she asked.

"I didn't think you wanted me to," I said.

This elicited one of those looks that said, "Uncle Greg, you are so clueless," before saying, "Put down that gross-looking green drink so we can go already." I was baffled, until I realized that Maralyn's love language is quality time. She and her mom will spend hours in front of the TV *without talking* and they'll both feel totally loved.

I tell this story to get you to think about how to love someone whose language is different from yours. How do I love Maralyn (because love is a verb) given her nature? Using words to convey how much I love her doesn't land on her. It affirms that in Maralyn's case, there is no substitute for quality time. It also reminds me that hugging her and telling her how much I love her annoys her. Sure, it kills me, but when I remember that my primary purpose is making sure she feels loved, I adapt.

What family members frustrate you the most? Why do you think that is? Do you know their love language?

If you have wonderful people in your life who treat you well, yet you don't feel nourished around them, it's likely you are speaking different languages. You know to call your buddy Vontaze when you need some encouragement just as you know *not* to call him when you need help building a shed.

If you find using the term "love languages" is a useful lens to examine your relationships, go for it. Even so, you already know who brings you up and who brings you down. You may not be able to explain chemistry, but you can *feel* it. When you gain this awareness, you will stop going to people for things who you know are not able, or not willing, to provide.

The takeaway is to date/marry your species. And when it comes to family and non-romantic relationships, know your species, figure out their love languages, and adapt so they can feel loved. A good pass is one that is received.

Do you stop to think about what others want? Do you "speak" to them in a language they can understand? And in all elements of your life, do you know where you are now?

QUESTION FOUR: WHERE AM I NOW?
More Empowering Questions

1. What's the one thing you can do right now to "look in the mirror" for a fresh vantage point?

2. What person do you trust the most to be honest with you? When is the last time you asked that person for an honest inventory of where you are now?

3. List one specific action you can take for each item on this list:
   a) Find a way to watch yourself.

   b) Consult a third party.

   c) Deconstruct technique and go back to the fundamentals.

   d) Slow down to become more aware.

   e) Personal development training.

4. List the love languages for at least two of the most important people in your life. Now write down what specific actions give love the best chance of landing on them. Also write down your love language(s).

◎ ◎ ◎

Knowing where you are is a prerequisite for knowing what you are thinking. Now that you have more awareness, you are ready for my favorite question—one that shows you how to enable your thoughts to propel you.

5

BELIEFS

How Do Thoughts Propel Me?

QUESTION FIVE

HOW DO THOUGHTS PROPEL ME?

"...it dawned on me that I have to change my inner thought patterns...that I would have to start believing in possibilities that I wouldn't have allowed before, that I had been closing my creativity down to a very narrow, controllable scale."

—Bob Dylan, *Chronicles Volume One*

New York City in the summer is hotter than a nine-day romance. Add the sweltering humidity and it's no surprise that city dwellers spend their summers trying to escape the Big Apple. Depending on budget, the getaway plans range from a subway ride to the public beaches in Coney Island to a limo ride to a mansion in the Hamptons. In between those extremes, there are "share houses" on the beaches of Long Island and the New Jersey Shore.

Anticipating the summer of 2005, I read dozens of ads on craigslist from share house owners. Maurice's pitch was the most interesting because he was more of a social engineer than a landlord. Since Maurice emanated his why, I signed up for nine weekends. Later that fall he approached me about a book on running a share house. At the time, I wasn't having any luck with women—and that's putting it kindly. I was working too much, partly because I didn't have any money, but mainly because I couldn't find anyone to go out with me. In a city with millions of single women, I seemed to be turning off all of them.

Maurice sent me his book proposal and I couldn't believe what I was reading. He wanted his house to be gender balanced and described his difficulties in recruiting men. He said there were tens of thousands of beautiful, fun, and smart women in New York between the ages of 27 and 37 (I was 34 at the time), but hardly any men who fit this category. He also said that most women echoed his sentiments about how few kind and creative men there were in New York.

His exact words weren't as relevant as what I took from them. My interpretation was that there were tens of thousands of amazing women in New York and most of them were *looking for a guy just like me.* Not only that, there was a massive supply imbalance in my favor.

From the moment of that realization, I was a magnet for incredible women.

I *did* nothing differently. My *actions* were exactly the same. I didn't start meeting women after I lost weight or saved money. I didn't buy a new wardrobe, join Hair Club for Men, or get calf implants. I only changed my thoughts, and in spite of being grossly overweight, with little disposable income in one of the most materialistic cities in the world, my dating life went from terrible to terrific in an instant.

I had reprogrammed my software.

By replacing a thought pattern on my mind's hard drive, I experienced the world differently. By simply believing that women were looking for a guy like me, it changed my perception which, in turn, became my reality.

The fastest way to transform your life is to change your thoughts. The foundation for this chapter is simple: *When you change the way you think about things, the things you think about change.* Again, the fastest way to transform your life is to change your thoughts. And it can be the easiest, fastest thing in the world to do.

It can also be the most difficult. Here's where things get tricky. Your belief systems about the ability to change belief systems hold the cards. There's a chicken or the egg question that we'll examine. Because what we believe is heavily influenced by axioms, here's the first of many in this chapter, courtesy of Henry Ford, "Whether you think you can or whether you think you can't, you're right."

Got Imagination? Steve Jobs and Russell Wilson Do

When my niece Jayme was five, we threw a raging tea party. We broke out the fancy china and sipped the finest teas from all over the world. Never mind that a fly on the wall would have seen tap water in plastic cups. After a while, we thought it would be fun to invite some of her friends. Suddenly we "heard" a knock. Jayme heard it. I heard it. And we both "saw" Avery walk through the door. This continued as Drew, Harry, Fanny, Asher, Grayson, Tillie, Ben, Sima, Ellie, Simon, and Sophie all joined us. Each time they knocked, we *heard* it and *saw* them enter. We served them tea and toasted to grandiose dreams. As our imaginations ran wild, the party took on a new life, taking us far away from Jayme's playroom.

Was this real? Could scientists prove that it happened? With two witnesses to the best tea party in history, could they prove that it did not?

How do we differentiate between a real experience and an imaginary one? Do our opinions about whether it *actually* happened, or about our *thinking* it happened, make a difference? Studies on visualization show that whether you physically shoot 100 free throws or mentally visualize shooting them, the benefits are the same.

We're constantly told to get more real, as if *real* can be so easily defined. The trick is to get more in touch with our imagination.

My friend Chi-Chi hates Sundays but loves Fridays so much that his favorite four letters are T, G, I, and F. On Fridays, his body is at the place he despises most, his office, but the mere thought of the weekend transports him to a happy place. On Sundays, when he could *be* in that happy place, instead of saying Thank God It's Sunday, Chi-Chi is consumed with stress about the week ahead. On both days, his *thoughts* call the shots, which demonstrates the link between imagination and reality.

His imagination is his reality. To change your "reality," all you need is a thought.

❂ ❂ ❂

Imagination schmagination, you say. Nothing gets done with thoughts. Put in the time. Hard work and persistence are the keys to success.

Before you dig yourself a hole with this line of thinking, consider how much money professional sports franchises spend on athletes' minds. Alyssa Roenigk of *ESPN The Magazine* reported that when high-performance sports psychologist Mike Gervais addresses the Seattle Seahawks, rather than offer tackling tips, he says, "Quiet your minds. Focus your attention inwardly and visualize success."

Quarterback Russell Wilson has individual *weekly* sessions with Gervais that include what Wilson calls, "imagery work" and adds, "I truly believe in positive synergy, that your positive mindset gives you a more hopeful outlook, and belief that you can do something great means you will do something great."

These words come from a 5'11" quarterback who many analysts thought would never play a down in the NFL, much less start a game. Russell Wilson became the only rookie in NFL history to start every game and finish with a passer rating over 100—more than 12 points higher than the next best, Matt Ryan. In his second season, all Wilson did was lead the Seahawks to a championship.

When he walked off the field after a 43-8 victory in Super Bowl XLVIII, the storyline centered on *belief systems.* The commentators relayed how his dad, the late Harry Wilson, used to say to his son, "Why not you?"

When you hear a question enough times as a kid, it can define your life.

What question do you ask yourself the most? How does it influence your thoughts?

❂ ❂ ❂

One of the themes from Walter Issacson's biography of Steve Jobs was the Apple founder's so-called "reality distortion field." His innovations sprang from *not* looking at things realistically. Rather than accept others' idea of reality, Jobs created his own stories and imposed his will on others to reprogram their expectations of themselves.

Issacson told Adam Lashinsky of *Fortune* the story about the time Jobs was working with Steve Wozniak (Woz) on the game *Breakout* for Atari. He told Woz, "You can make this in four days," and Woz said, "No, it's going to take four weeks." Jobs replied, "No, no, no. You can do it in four days." And Woz said, "Well, that was a reality distortion field, and I did it in four days.*"*

An imagination that trumped "reality" allowed Jobs to accomplish what others insisted was impossible. Everything seemed impossible before someone did it.

You can pound your fist about "facts" and argue that not believing in gravity won't allow you to fly. You can list as many examples as you'd like about why we need to be more realistic. Just ask yourself how fighting for limitations will propel you. Who ever achieved anything beyond mediocrity by playing it safe?

When filmmaker Brian Koppelman, best known as the cowriter of *Ocean's Thirteen* and *Rounders,* is criticized for encouraging artists to dream, he has an elegant response, "...the world is already out there dispensing 'reality,' discouraging the creative journey, tamping down enthusiasm, limiting opportunity. So I want to stand there in the face of that reality...And I want to help you get to the finish line any way I can."

Koppelman, Jobs, and Wilson recognized that your imagination and your affirming thoughts are the biggest factors in your success. You have the power to create the stories that serve you best.

It's True If You Believe It

To figure out what software is running on your computer, hit control+alt+delete, and the task manager will display a list. Tapping into your own software is more challenging. We all run thousands of thought programs simultaneously that were written by our parents and families, teachers and coaches, and "society" at large.

My second toe is longer than my first toe, and my mom told me it was a sign of intelligence. My friend Raffaella's mom told her it was a sign of beauty. My friend Jen's mom said it was a sign of royalty. Of course we all *believed* our moms.

Monte's mom told him that Albert Einstein was dyslexic so it had to mean that Monte's dyslexia was a sign of a genius. Einstein, along with Alexander Graham Bell, Leonardo da Vinci, Thomas Edison, and George Washington compose a formidable dyslexic starting five (though they routinely get beat in practice by John Lennon, Steven Spielberg, Richard Branson, Vince Vaughn, and Paul Oakenfold).

When I learned that my godson Reed has the same birthday as inventor and entrepreneur Elon Musk (Tesla Motors, SpaceX, SolarCity, and Paypal), I wrote to him, "Geniuses and pioneers are born on June 28." My friend Woody tells his kids that the brown spots on bananas are the sweetest and best part, and his kids fight over the brown spots. Imagine how different their reaction would be if he referred to those parts as bruises. Is what he's saying "real" or "true?"

It's true if we believe it.

Daniel Gilbert, Harvard professor and author of *Stumbling on Happiness,* says that perception "holds one of the deepest truths in psychology, which is that the mind generates reality."

Belief systems are also known as software, attitude, perspective, accepted wisdom, frame of mind, or emotional DNA. Fallacies are belief systems that have been debunked. If your software is in sync with your desired path, it will propel you. If it is not, it will sabotage your efforts.

We are conditioned and programmed (some might say "brainwashed") to believe certain things and to think in certain ways, which can be a good thing. The software, "Look both ways before crossing" serves to keep you safe. Other belief systems—such as "We're on this Earth to suffer" or "It's called a job because it's supposed to suck"—may not serve you. The key is to differentiate the two types. Once you've done that, you can write new software to reprogram your own hard drive.

Rejection is Redirection

Any comic will tell you that pain is the second best thing for his act. Only shame is better. Imagine how this outlook can transform the way you view adversity in your life. The late Nora Ephron was raised by writers who told her that bad experiences were opportunities for great copy. This programming by her parents led her to reframe suffering from "this sucks" to "wait until I write about this." Ephron's reframing resulted in three Oscar nominations.

Michael Parness—who went from a homeless addict to a multi-millionaire finance author—survived an abusive childhood by repeating to himself, "Your pain is not in vain." Citing Viktor Frankl's book, *Man's Search for Meaning* as inspiration, Parness says this one belief was enough to sustain him through hard times.

A leading man doesn't complain. When a situation goes against his expectations, he realizes that his attitude is what matters most. If the service is awful at a restaurant, he can choose to focus on gratitude, that he has the luxury of being with loved ones and having food to eat. He can laugh at it and turn it into a funny story. He can deal with it by talking to the manager. Or he can leave. Complaining is not in the toolbox of leading men. It's choosing to be unhappy and asking others for sympathy in a story that paints you as the victim.

Rejection is redirection.

That's the chorus I repeat when something seems to go against me. That website never called me back about distributing my videos. *Rejection is redirection.* The retreat center that is perfect for my budget and schedule is booked. *Rejection is redirection.* That woman shot me down. *Rejection is redirection.*

Please put your own spin on this. Michael Jordan made a commercial highlighting all his missed shots and losses and then said, "I failed over and over and over again in my life. And that is why I succeed." Yoga teacher Heather Archer says that when you feel like you're being rejected, it's actually the universe redirecting you to something bigger. Grammy Award-winning singer-songwriter India.Aire finds strength in the saying, "Every breakdown holds a breakthrough."

How do you react to adversity? What about criticism? I believe that people are either expressing love or crying out for love, which gives harsh words a different meaning. If someone criticizes me, my first reaction is that I must be doing something right. My attitude comes from believing that a coach only bothers to correct the star players.

A mental shift can reframe crisis and rejection into opportunity and redirection—if your imagination allows it.

Are Your Thoughts Your Own?

I'm torn between telling you reprogramming is easy (after all, what could be easier than changing your mind?) and admitting that it can be difficult. You already saw that my mentality about dating changed instantly when I read Maurice's proposal. You've also heard about people who have had near-death experiences. Once they realized they weren't going to live forever, their entire perspective changed and they saw the world in a new way.

When it comes to altering your beliefs, there is value in acknowledging what you might be up against. Thoughts become embedded in our minds when we hear them at a young age or from people we view as authorities. Even when we see or feel evidence that contradicts these beliefs, we hold on tightly.

I've seen and heard thousands of data points since I was a child that milk makes bones strong. From the charts on my classroom walls growing up, to the "Got Milk" campaign with famous athletes showing off their milk mustaches, it has been hammered into me so much that I believed it. Never mind that milk gave me gas and made me feel sluggish. So much programming was ingrained that, in spite of my discomfort, I continued to drink it.

I only began to budge when I learned that Americans drink more milk than any other nationality *and* have the highest rate of osteoporosis. My health coach, Amelia, told me that baby calves drink milk to turn into 800-pound cows. When she asked, "Do you want to be an 800-pound cow?" I budged a little more.

Are you getting the feeling that I'm brainwashing you about the perils of milk? You may be right. Also understand that my words only matter *if you choose to believe them*. The reason we're talking about milk is to show how pervasive attitudes take hold of us—and how they can harm us when we don't question them. It would be equally naïve for you to *stop* drinking milk if it works for your body.

The real question is: Are your thoughts your own?

"The conflict between what we're told we feel and what we really feel may be the richest source of confusion, dissatisfaction, and unnecessary suffering of our time." That quote from the book *Sex at Dawn* might be applicable to everything.

I made a choice about milk based on what works for me—not what others, with their own agendas, were selling me. But it took a mountain of evidence to get me to change a belief system that wasn't serving me. Now imagine how tough it can be if you're not even aware of your thoughts.

The reason it's worth challenging your beliefs—and asking if your beliefs are propelling you in the right direction—is that the returns are immense. One "aha" moment that leads to a shift in perception can change everything. And you don't need to be sluggish, near death, or at rock bottom to change what you choose to believe.

The Science Behind Belief Systems

Spa Samui, a health retreat in Thailand, has a library of books and films, and one sunny day in paradise, I watched Bruce Lipton's *The Biology of Belief.* Lipton, a Ph.D., earned his stripes for his pioneering research as a cell biologist at Stanford and the University of Wisconsin.

I couldn't stand science in school, yet I was spending two and a half hours on a tropical island watching a lecture about protons, membranes, and DNA. I was riveted. Lipton explained that a cell is made up of both DNA and proteins, but genetics research has focused on the DNA while ignoring the proteins. That's right; many scientists just flat-out ignored the proteins of the cell. That's like studying the biological properties of an egg and throwing out the yolk.

The Human Genome Project, and other gene research, has led many people to believe that humans are wired a certain way—that our genetic makeup, and not our choices, means that many aspects of life are beyond our control.

Scientists from this school of thought tell us that our DNA determines if we're going to get sick or depressed.

Lipton explains that our proteins are controlled by our environment. Our *perceptions* control the behavior and physiology of the cell, turning genes on and off. So while you may be "wired" for depression, your proteins, which are malleable, are the catalysts that turn on the gene. Therefore, even if you have the depression gene, your environment—which includes everything from nutrition, physical surroundings, and perceptions—determines whether it gets switched on. If it were only about the genes, you would be born with diseases. If it's about what turns the genes on and off, that could explain why some people who are predisposed to a trait exhibit it, while others never do.

After watching Lipton, I watched Dr. Andrew Weil explain that a significant part of the protocol for researchers to test a new drug is to give a placebo, a pill with no medicine, to a control group. Weil said that although researchers often look at the placebo effect as a nuisance to their research, it's precisely what they *should* be studying. Just thinking that something works is often all it takes for it to work. Again, your thoughts hold the cards. Deepak Chopra says, "We are the only creatures on Earth who can change our biology by what we think and feel."

The placebo effect reinforces the power of imagination.

The information from Lipton, Weil, and Chopra resonates because, long before I learned the fancy scientific terms, I knew the concepts were true. It started at age five when I read *The Little Engine That Could.* Whether saying, "I think I can, I think I can, I think I can," changes us on a cellular level isn't as important as knowing it works for me.

Are we here to suffer or is every day a gift? Is it called a job because it sucks, or is your job how you offer your gifts and provide for your family? Is rejection telling you to crawl into a cave or to fight for something better?

That's the beauty of belief systems. You get to choose and create the ones that work for you. You tweak and amend. Along the way, others will try to influence you. Your parents, the media, and society will speak their truths about their belief systems. You get to pick and choose to come up with *your* truth.

The "Secret" Weapon for a Book Deal

When a friend mentioned *The Secret,* I thought he was referring to *The Strangest Secret,* a 1956 spoken word record by Earl Nightingale that my brother gave me when I was 28. *The Strangest Secret* is that, "We become what we think about."

A film and a book called *The Secret* were released in 2006 with a similar message. The Law of Attraction states that like energy attracts like energy and whatever we think and feel in our inner world shows up in our outer world. The combination of timeless wisdom, brilliant marketing, and Oprah's endorsement brought the law of attraction to the mainstream. I knew it had hit the big-time when Charles Barkley said, "I'm thinking thin," during a TNT broadcast.

It wasn't long before I started hearing horror stories about *The Secret.* People ran up huge debts, reasoning that they were "thinking" about abundance and that the law of attraction guaranteed its arrival. Why not take a credit card advance when the law dictates the money is surely on its way? So what if they're not doing anything to earn money?

Remember that no program or "secret" works unless *you* work *it.*

◎ ◎ ◎

Aspiring authors are quick to point out statistics that fewer than one in a million authors gets signed by a publisher. Even though I had no experience or education as a writer, the enthusiast in me took over, and I believed I could overcome the odds. But after pitching *The Finance Doctor* and getting rejected by publishers all over town, I started to buy into the story that it's impossible to get published. Even when we start out with strong beliefs, rejection can lead us to reframe our story to rationalize our lack of success.

Frank was one of the editors who rejected my book. But unlike the others who wouldn't give me the time of day, Frank sent me a detailed letter full of criticism and suggestions. I received his "red pen" as a gift of awareness. I then made the wise choice to hire Frank as my editor and consultant, and I published the book myself.

After I released *The Finance Doctor* in September 2000, it seemed like all people wanted to talk to me about was *their* book—the one they had always wanted to write. Before long, I was the most popular volunteer publishing consultant on the planet.

Meanwhile, Frank, a life-long New Yorker, was on vacation at Del Mar racetrack, just north of San Diego. He thought it was paradise and decided to start a literary agency coupled with a move out west. Frank is a leading man who followed his heart and actualized his ideal day. When he first moved to San Diego, he went to the racetrack every day. Now he only goes every day it's open.

Frank recalled my background in business and sales, and on a lark, asked if I had an interest in working with him.

"What does a literary agent do?" I asked.

Frank explained that an agent finds authors and then calls publishers to sell their books.

Contemplating my recent string of unpaid gigs, the answer was easy. "Okay," I said, "Let's do it."

And so we did. Our startup budget of $200 each barely covered business cards and letterhead, but we were up and running. Before Frank left for San Diego, I met him in New York, where he had set up several meetings. What he didn't tell me was that it was a week of free gourmet! Editors from the most prestigious publishers like Doubleday, Random House, and HarperCollins were buying us meals at New York's finest restaurants. I couldn't understand why they were wining and dining two schmoes who didn't have a single client (not even Mr. Skin at this point) simply because we had hung a shingle. Frank explained that an editor's job is to acquire books and they depend on agents to send them material.

"They *need* material?" I screamed. "What about the millions of manuscripts they receive?"

"That's the slush pile," he said. "Most of it belongs there. Every editor

I know complains about how hard it is to meet his quota for acquiring high-quality books."

"So you're telling me editors get paid to *buy* books?"

"Well, not exac…"

I cut him off. Finding the right story to propel you is *not* about taking in all the information, which can lead to a paralysis of analysis. MBA graduates, in particular, know so much about what can go wrong in business that they often remain on the sidelines.

I could have listened to Frank explain that editors get paid for their discerning judgment, that they get paid both to reject and accept books. After all, we just devoted almost an entire chapter to active listening. But at some level I grasped a key question: How would that story propel my success?

Rather than become more realistic, take a cue from Steve Jobs' reality distortion field and latch on to the stories that propel you to build your own reality. In this case, it helped that my pants were tight from feasting on the expense accounts of publishers. Why else would they have been entertaining two rookie agents if they weren't dying for material? The *evidence* that I turned into a story made me believe.

Picture the graphic of me being programmed with a new software update, along with the caption, "Publishers, Who Get Paid to Buy Books, Are Dying for Good Material."

◎ ◎ ◎

I had a night to sleep on this new belief system. On our final day in New York we had a meeting with Pete, an editor at Crown, an imprint of Random House. Whereas before I believed that it's all but impossible to get published, now I believed that publishers are dying for good material. I was transformed from the hopeless author to Lloyd Christmas, Jim Carrey's character in *Dumb and Dumber,* who believed that one in a million meant, "So you're telling me there's a chance!"

Even though we didn't have any clients or other projects to discuss, I never mentioned *my* next book idea during any of our previous lunches. After all, I was nothing but a guy with no writing credentials who had self-published one book that hadn't sold more than a handful of copies outside of blood relatives. But with this new belief system percolating, before my shrimp cocktail arrived, I told Pete I wanted to write a book about using poker skills in business.

"Funny you should mention that," Pete said. "I actually brought up this idea at a brainstorming meeting and everyone loved it. We just need to find the right author."

Three months later I received a contract and a healthy advance from Random House. *The Poker MBA: Winning In Business No Matter What Cards You're Dealt* was published in May 2002. My only regret is that I didn't dedicate the book to Bruce Lipton, Earl Nightingale, and *The Little Engine That Could.*

One more time: The fastest way to transform your life is to change your thoughts. When you change the way you think about things, the things you think about change.

How to Reprogram Your Software

Just as it was once accepted that the world was flat, prior to 1954 it was accepted as fact that it was impossible for a human being to run a mile in less than four minutes. Yet on May 6 of that year, in Oxford, England, Roger Bannister ran a mile in 3 minutes and 59.4 seconds. In the next three years, 10 runners logged sub-four-minute miles. Their software was reprogrammed by evidence, which led them to believe they could accomplish what they previously had deemed impossible.

By now you get the concept. Let's get to work putting it into practice.

Four Ways to Reprogram Beliefs

1. Inquire. Question your beliefs continually.
2. Find examples of others who exemplify beliefs that propel you.

3. Provide evidence that supports your beliefs.

4. Sustain your beliefs through words, visuals, and other affirmations using the senses.

1. Inquire. Question your beliefs continually.

Byron Katie travels the world asking people four questions. I spent two days at her workshop, and the woman is a broken record, which I offer as high praise. She asks the same four questions, over and over, for any thought that pops into your head.

1. Is it true?
2. Can you absolutely know it's true?
3. How do you react, what happens, when you believe that thought?
4. Who would you be without that thought?

Katie reminds us that *we are not our thoughts* and that many of the thoughts running through our minds are not even true. At Katie's workshop, I watched a woman in intense emotional pain explain how her dad had screwed her out of her inheritance. Twenty minutes later, after being prompted by Katie to answer these four questions, the woman realized she had *invented* a story that made her miserable. Inquiry led her to a new truth, freed her from her misery, and she floated off the stage.

If you say or think, "I can't make money doing something I love," stop and ask these four questions. I use inquiry so often that I rarely get past the first question. *Bill never returns my calls. All politicians are corrupt. No one keeps his word anymore.* Whenever I have a thought like this, I stop and ask: Is it true? This one question can be enough to snap you out of a negative thought pattern.

2. Find examples of others who exemplify beliefs that propel you.

Watch a marathon, and you'll see people older and less athletic than you finishing the race. Your software will instantly be reprogrammed. Your mind can't help but register: If they can do it, I can do it. That's why we were so inspired by Jim Abbott, who was born without a right hand and still managed to pitch for 10 years in the major leagues (including a no-hitter).

Fans worldwide were inspired by Tyrone "Muggsy" Bogues who was only 5'3" yet had a brilliant 14-year NBA career. If you are 5'11" and running software that says you're too short to play professional basketball, seeing a 5'3" player will reprogram that belief. Likewise, Russell Wilson's Super Bowl title changes how we view the height of quarterbacks—and the power of visualization.

3. Provide evidence that supports your beliefs.

In *Learned Optimism,* Martin Seligman explains that a technique of cognitive therapy is to use evidence to help people change their beliefs about themselves. If a man talks about what a terrible dad he is, the therapist walks through all the evidence that demonstrates what a great dad he is—healthy kids, doing well in school, respectful, etc. The technique reprograms the faulty software by feeding the mind bits of information that it knows to be true.

Go back to that thought, "I can't make money doing something I love," and question it. Do you know any wealthy people who love their work? If so, you can see that your thinking is flawed. With that recognition, you let go of the thought and replace it with one that serves you. If it rings true, feel free to use this affirmation: *When I'm doing something I'm passionate about, it leads me to maximize how I serve people and how much money I earn.*

4. Sustain your beliefs through words, visuals, and other affirmations using the senses.

Both malicious leaders and loving coaches know the value of sounds and words to brainwash us. By using multiple senses, they get their message to seep into our thoughts. Fight songs, banners in locker rooms, inspirational posters in corporate offices, and t-shirts with catchy slogans all serve this purpose. The goal of branding is to influence consumers to believe a message. If you see and hear, "Built Ford Tough," and "Kraft is Cheese," enough times, you start to believe it. In *Lean In,* Sheryl Sandberg writes that Facebook uses slogans to foster a culture of risk-taking. Its corporate office has posters on the walls that say, "Fortune favors the bold" and "What would you do if you weren't afraid?"

Find ways to make your highest beliefs reach your eyes, ears, and heart to create the thoughts that propel you. If billion-dollar companies and malevolent leaders can use slogans, songs, and signs to brainwash others, you can find even more effective ones to brainwash yourself.

What pictures do you keep in your wallet, on your desk, on your fridge, and in your car? What words are you saying out loud or to yourself most frequently? What song is stuck in your head right now? The subconscious believes what it sees and hears.

Reprogramming Leads to Results

After watching *The Secret* in 2006, Jennifer Thompson created a mock-up *New York Times* Bestseller List with her book on green smoothies in the #1 position. At the time, Jennifer had little writing experience and a tiny fan base for her blog. She hung the mock-up above her desk, and every day when she sat down to write, she looked up and visualized her success.

Does this sound like New Age foo-foo dust to you? I'll spoil the ending by revealing that, seven years later, Jennifer signed a contract with a major publisher for a book about green smoothies.

Was this a coincidence? Some of Jennifer's friends (and all of the haters) thought so. Then again, they are the same type of cynics who cite the statistics that only one in a million authors ever get a book deal. Her book is not on sale yet, so it remains to be seen if Jennifer will make the bestseller list. I, for one, would not bet against her.

Jennifer's story is a perfect example about how the right beliefs and tactics lead to professional and financial success. Now let's take this to another level in order to create your own story about wealth.

Entitlement and Benchmarking

My mom used to say that any idiot could walk into a department store and pay retail, but it took real brains to buy a $100-shirt for 20 bucks. I have fond memories of our family driving home from outlet malls while congratulating ourselves on our savings. I also have warm memories of shopping with my dad at his favorite store, Syms, where "An educated consumer is our best customer." A powerful slogan can stick with us forever. Finding bargains reinforced our family's story that we were educated and thrifty. The downside is that it placed more emphasis on saving money than on making it.

My friend Hal calls being penny-wise and pound-foolish "misery economics." You run all over town to save a nickel on tuna fish or gas when you could be working on your next deal. Hal called me out for spending so much time saving money that I missed opportunities to make it. I was so attached to finding bargains that I loved to repeat gambler Titanic Thompson's quote that, "The key in life is not to *be* a millionaire; it's to *live* like one."

"Entitled" is one of the trickiest words in the English language. Like budget hawks, my mom used it in a negative context, with frequent rants about how kids think the world owes them something. Shaking her head, she would say, "I don't know where they get their sense of entitlement." As I grew older, I started to hear the opposite of my mom's sentiment, which is that we are all *entitled* to the life of our dreams.

The language in my home led to a negative view of entitlement. "Don't take anything for granted" and "Never show up anywhere empty-handed," were familiar refrains. My mom brainwashed me with these beliefs and now that I've had a chance to test them, I'm glad she did. In fact, I'm passing the torch by brainwashing my godkids with them.

My belief that no one owes me anything jibes perfectly with my belief that whether I'm writing a book, telling a story, or making a business pitch, I have to create value for the other person and earn my right to be there. But does that belief also mean that I'm not entitled to a happy life? Thomas Jefferson never said we were entitled to a life of happiness. He wrote that it's our inalienable right to *pursue* a life of happiness.

The word "privileged" is double-edged as well. Again, we choose what meaning we give to words, ideas, and other people's assertions. Ivy League is associated with diligence and intelligence, which are universally seen as positive traits. It is also associated with privilege and entitlement, which is why Harvard sometimes carries a negative connotation. In *Trading Places,* Dan Akroyd's character says, "He's wearing my Harvard tie. Like, oh, he went to Haaaarvard." That's all the audience needs to hear to hate him and root for his rival character, played by Eddie Murphy.

Then again, many Harvard grads are laughing all the way to the bank. Having a peer group with high expectations is a critical asset in shaping belief systems. We benchmark ourselves against our peers, and those closest to us affect how we view our potential.

Choose Your Top Five People As If Your Life Depended On It: Because It Does

When I was getting my MBA at Arizona State, I had friends in three of the top MBA programs: Stanford, Wharton, and Harvard. While my peers at ASU were figuring out how to pad a job offer by a few *thousand* dollars, my friends' peers were figuring out how they could start companies worth *billions* of dollars. My peers aspired to take on a lease of a luxury car. Those from the top schools aspired to take on *industries.*

Hal is a business magnate (with an undergraduate degree from a public university and without an MBA) and being in his presence is an exercise in brainwashing. He tells me all the time that there is more competition for the $10-an-hour job than the $10 million-a-year job. He believes it because he lives it. He sent his kids to public school and instead invested in influencing their imaginations, including pulling them out of class for Tony Robbins' events.

Robbins' mentor, Jim Rohn, said, "You are the average of the five people you spend the most time with." Hang out with a bunch of Dougy Downers and they'll bring you down, just as positive people will lift you up. *Life is contagious.* Write down the names of the five people you spend the most time with and see if they embody your goals and aspirations.

James Altucher turned his book *Choose Yourself* into a phenomenon and built on that momentum by starting a popular podcast. He credits much of his success to the company he keeps. Altucher, who is forthright about his social struggles, still goes out of his way to meet new people who inspire him. "When people with positive energy are around each other," he says, "more energy is created."

Altucher uses seven steps to create that energy—what he calls a Scene. The list below is excerpted from Altucher's blog by permission. I received that permission because I appreciate how much others impact our thoughts, and thus, made it a point to build a relationship with a forward-thinking author.

How You Build a Scene: Courtesy of James Altucher

- find the people whose work inspires you. Businesses, writings, art, whatever.
- come up with ideas for them. How can you help them?
- start doing your own work. Share with the people you like. Interact with the people who interact with you sincerely.
- try to meet the people who inspire you. Some of them are busy. Some would like to meet.
- go to conferences and meet the people who inspire you.
- every day work. Every day create. Every day share. The people you share with slowly solidify into your Scene.
- and then...repeat. Never stop helping.

Rumi, the 13th century mystic said, "Set your heart on fire and seek those who fan your flames." Ponder that thought while you answer these questions:

1. With whom do you benchmark yourself?
2. Did you choose these people, or are they part of a peer group you fell into?
3. Name the five people who will contribute most to keeping you living like a leading man.

Your Money Thermostat Is Set by Your Upper Limits

Effective selling is transference of feeling. Mr. Skin *believed* his service was a bargain and promoted it with passion because he would have paid 50-fold for it. When his business took off, his deep-seated beliefs that he was entitled to more (as were his customers) fueled his company's growth. Others would have sabotaged success.

Gay Hendricks believes that most troubles in life are "upper limit" problems. In *The Big Leap,* he describes his thermostat theory. Just as a heater automatically turns off when it reaches its set point, we turn off once we reach the upper limit that we set—or that was set *for us.* Hendricks says that our thermostat gets programmed in early childhood, before we can think for ourselves. He cites a statistic that within two years of hitting the jackpot, more than 60 percent of lottery winners return to their prior net worth.

Even world-class poker players are notorious for "leaks" in their bankroll. It amazes me that some of the most disciplined rounders, who make millions from their ability to calculate odds, piss away their money playing craps when they know the odds are against them. Other common leaks, and this goes for everyone, range from jewelry to drugs to electronics. I offer the same advice to poker players as I do to anyone who wants to hold on to money: Plug your leaks.

That's where the power of belief systems comes in. You can't plug a leak until you know what is driving it. And even if you plug one, another will appear until the thermostat has its day. If compulsive shopping is driven by feeling unloved, understanding how credit card interest snowballs won't plug it. Research on compulsive gambling reveals it's a form of self-punishment. Hendricks would describe it as an upper limit problem, and anyone can see that self-worth is at the heart of it.

Upper limits are often set by other people's projections. Isabella, a professional model who is insecure about her looks, constantly asked her mom if she was pretty. This divine little girl was seeking validation from Mommy and what she got instead was, "Pretty like the butt of a pot." Isabella's mom has a belief system that telling kids they are pretty leads to vanity. And she may be right. Her intention of keeping Isabella's ego in check was effective. Just ask her plastic surgeon and the pharmacist who doles out her anti-depressants. Parents and teachers who preach some variety of "don't get too big for your britches" imprint their upper limits on their children and students. As leading men, we have the power to imprint what we believe and to break through old, limiting beliefs.

Your belief systems about money were influenced by the axioms most prominent in your upbringing. You may have heard thousands of times that "money is the root of all evil." Maybe you were told the Bible actually says it's the love of money that is the root of all evil or that it's tougher for a rich person to make it to heaven. Either way, those are strong messages that influence your thermostat.

In his book, *The Trick to Money Is Having Some,* Stuart Wilde offered these fighting words: "All philosophies which teach that poverty is groovy, do so as a cop out. It keeps the non-performing members happy for they can live in the ego trip of thinking that somehow their lack of creativity and effort will be blessed at a later date."

Everyone has a take and unless you get clear on your own take, you might be mistaking someone else's truth for your own. Whose thoughts are you thinking right now?

Setting Your Own Thermostat

When you ask empowering questions, you replace the beliefs of others with beliefs that ring true for you. The first step in raising your thermostat is recognizing that you have a thermostat.

Start with these questions:

1. Do you have the power to change your thermostat?
2. Which people influenced your thermostat? How is that setting working for them?
3. Why do you want to change it? How will it improve your life?
4. What are you afraid of? How will your life change when you raise your limits?
5. Are you entitled to a privileged life? What about if you work for it?

As I said earlier, this can be the easiest thing in the world—or the hardest. Whether you think it's easy or hard, you are right. Once you've asked these questions, just as you would move the knob on a thermostat, do it for your life. In this case the cliché fits. It is as simple as lifting a finger.

Or is it?

You can work on your subconscious mind, but the real trick is believing it and *being* it. You simply can't think your way into being. The law of attraction states that your thoughts are made of pure energy and attract like energy. For all the techniques we've discussed, convincing yourself of beliefs is not always a linear, methodical process. To align your thoughts with your vision, it will require a conscious commitment.

It is up to you to decide if this is easy or hard. For now, let's give Wayne Dyer, author of *The Power of Intention,* the last word on this: "I have a little bit of a different take on *The Secret*. We don't attract what we want. We attract what we are."

Poker Is a Hard Way to Make an Easy Living. Or is it?

My dad, a retired accountant and a medium-stakes poker player, delights in saying, "I never steer you wrong." From the time I was eight years old, he played blackjack with Andy and me, teaching us basic strategy and emphasizing that you can't beat the house. To this day, he loves to remind us that Las Vegas luminary Steve Wynn says, "If you want to make money in a casino, own one."

My father's words led me to major in Hotel Administration with an eye on the business end of casinos. I interned at the Mirage when I was 19, and even though I was more attracted to the sucker end of the business (being the player, rather than the house), I managed to beat the toughest poker games in Vegas. My dad was so concerned that my success taught me the wrong lesson that he kept repeating the poker proverb that it's "a hard way to make an easy living." He told me that when M.C. Hammer's dad (*U Can't Touch This* and *2 Legit 2 Quit* were big in those days) quit his job to play poker full-time, he couldn't win. Even as I was proving to be a consistent winner, my dad kept explaining why it couldn't last.

For every cliché, there is an equal and opposite one. The early bird catches the worm, but the second mouse gets the cheese. Good things come to those who wait, but only what's left behind by those who hustle. I'm all for a good bumper sticker, but I'd rather you choose your beliefs than unconsciously live by the ones that others propagate.

Some people defend long-held beliefs to the point of absurdity (or insanity), rather than accept new, valuable information. The very survival of a belief system depends on continuing to find evidence to support it. My dad had a mountain of evidence to prove how hard it was to make a living playing poker because he looked for it—and missed seeing obvious examples to prove you can.

I now see he was projecting, but as a kid I viewed it as *the* truth, not just his truth. Even after years of success, my dad's words pushed down my upper limits. Let me rephrase: *Believing* my dad's words pushed down my upper limits.

Before I moved to Los Angeles in 1995 to play poker full-time, I had doubts about the decision. On the home-game circuit in Maryland, I played regularly with Jim Boyd, who had won tournaments in Las Vegas, and I wanted to know if a pro thought I had what it took. I had beaten the games in Maryland for a year, but it didn't undo all of my limiting beliefs. The culprits of seeking validation are *not knowing who we are* and *not believing in ourselves.* When I asked Boyd if he thought I could play professionally, I will never forget the incredulous look he gave me, which meant even more than his words, "Aren't you already playing professionally? I'd kill to have a piece of your action."

My dad's belief systems affected me—not so much that I couldn't win—but enough to push down my upper limits. It wasn't until I met Phil Gordon that one belief system would collide with another.

The Money Is at the Top

While promoting *The Poker MBA* in Las Vegas during the 2002 World Series of Poker (WSOP), I met gambling legend Amarillo Slim and ended up collaborating with him on his award-winning memoir, which was published by HarperCollins in the US and Random House in the UK (publishers need material!).

Frank and I followed that up by building a niche representing poker authors just as the game was exploding into the mainstream. One of our authors was Phil Gordon, co-host of *Celebrity Poker Showdown,* and a world-class poker player and entrepreneur. Phil is a leading man who teaches poker using my favorite technique: empowering questions. Little did I know the impact he would have on my thoughts.

Phil's mental approach to poker goes far beyond knowing when to hold 'em and when to fold 'em. While editing his manuscript on tournament poker, one concept kept surfacing: *The money is at the top.* Because most people want to win *something,* they play fearfully once they are close to any prize money. Phil explained how smart, aggressive players take advantage of those playing it safe, giving themselves a chance to make the real money—which goes to the top three spots. I didn't realize it at the time, but Phil was reprogramming my software.

Prior to 2006, the most I had ever won in a poker tournament was $7,000. When Frank asked about our plans to attend the 2006 WSOP, I told him it wasn't worth it. The poker book market was saturated, making it a poor investment of time and money to search for more poker authors. Frank reasoned that it was more of a reward than an investment, and I ultimately agreed.

Since I had finally erased $50,000 of credit card debt, I timed our trip so, in addition to networking, I could play in the $1,000 7-Card Stud Hi-Lo event. As I had done any time I left New York, I sublet my apartment for $900. Because, in my *mind,* I had already earned back the buy-in before the cards were dealt, it altered my mindset as the tournament progressed.

On July 24, 2006, the tournament started with 788 players. Back in 1995, after Boyd's validation, I had worked as a "prop" player at the Bicycle Casino and was paid $25 an hour to play poker with my own money (The casino uses props to keep as many games going as possible and increase their rake). I played quite a bit of 7 Card Stud Hi-Lo and became a solid, but not world-class, player. Over the next 11 years, I had played the game fewer than a dozen times. Let's just say no one pegged me as one of the favorites to win. Many opponents viewed me as dead money. As expected, I was rusty and hemorrhaged chips from the start.

On our first break, I went to the pool for yoga and breath work. It became my ritual for every break. I felt the physiological benefits, plus I reasoned that I was gaining an edge over opponents who were smoking and eating junk food. My actions influenced my beliefs and reinforced that I was more disciplined than my opponents.

I hunkered down and as the rust wore off, I accumulated chips. When we quit in the wee hours of the first day of a three-day tournament, we were down to 99 players and I had the eighth most chips. All I had to do was finish in 70th place, and I would earn $1,793. I was in a position to wait for other players to bust out and be assured of winning my money back, plus $793. But in my *mind*, I had already recouped all but $100 of my investment. Because I had paid off all my credit card debt, I felt even freer.

You are in a stronger negotiating position when you come from a place of power—and that power comes from your *perception* of the situation. If you need the money, you'll be scared and tentative (which are, after all, feelings) and your adversaries will pick up on it. Even though I felt free, the temptation to lock in a modest slice of the prize money was strong, just as Phil had explained.

And then my new software kicked in—the screen "New Update" flashed in my mind—and there was Phil Gordon screaming, "The money is at the top!"

I made a conscious choice to avoid finding out the prize money for any place besides first. The only number I knew was $172,091—the winner's share.

Just as Phil had described in his book, others began playing scared. I sought out the players who were running the "move up in prize money" software instead of "the money is at the top" software, and I attacked. At the end of day two, with nine players left—and only eight coming back the next day for the final table—fear ruled most of the other players. My mental computer, on the other hand, was running *the money is at the top.* I continued to attack and knocked out Dan Heimiller, who finished ninth and took home $7,888. Heading into the final table, I was the chip leader.

On day three, I played aggressively from the start. Unfortunately, the cards didn't cooperate, and half my chips disappeared within the first hour. I did manage to stay alive as four players were eliminated. The good news: I was guaranteed $49,479 for fourth place, while third paid $65,971, second paid $102,542 and first paid $172,091. The bad news: I had the fewest chips. The worst news: I had failed to block out all payouts besides the one for first place.

The reward for moving up one spot was more than $16,000. *Maybe if I sit back and don't play any hands, someone else might lose their chips.* That software ran for about a second (a second too long?), then *the money is at the top* software clicked in and I continued to play to win. I knocked out Mark Bershad, said a silent thank you to Mr. Gordon, and we were down to three.

Two previous WSOP winners, Pat Poels and Jeff Madsen, were my remaining opponents. If you had asked me, at that moment, to rank the table, I would have said Poels was the best, I was second, and Madsen was third. For the next two and a half hours, none of us blinked. Television condenses an entire tournament to an hour or two because it's like watching paint dry: raise, fold, shuffle, deal; raise, fold, shuffle, deal. Finally, Pat and Jeff got involved in a big pot, and Jeff was all-in. If Pat won the pot, I was guaranteed an additional $37,000. Pat would also have more than twice as many chips as me.

After Pat took down the pot, I was six figures richer than when the tournament began.

The Delusional Moneymaker

In 2003, a 27 year-old from Tennessee paid $39 and won a satellite tournament online that earned him an entry into the $10,000 main event of the WSOP. A man who had never played in a live poker tournament in his life was suddenly staring down Johnny Chan, back-to-back main event winner who was immortalized in the film, *Rounders.* This rank novice, Chris Moneymaker, lived up to his storybook name and took down the poker elite on his way to becoming World Champion.

Moneymaker made $2.5 million and made an even bigger impact on the psyches of untold numbers of other fledging poker players by making them believe they could do the same. He said that, during the tournament, something clicked in his mind and he *believed* he could win. Given his inexperience, he was deluding himself about the upper limits of an amateur—so much so that he won first place.

Delusional might be an even trickier word than entitled or privileged. We label dreamers as morons and imbeciles, only to redefine them as visionaries once they succeed and we witness the results. How many people do you think told Michael Dell, Larry Ellison, Bill Gates, Steve Jobs, and Mark Zuckerberg that they were delusional to think they could drop out of college and build multi-billion-dollar technology companies? My estimate is about as many who are scratching their broke asses wishing they had invested in them.

◎ ◎ ◎

What about my tournament? Where was my upper limit? A few hands earlier, I believed that I was the second-best player behind Pat Poels. Then it was down to the two of us. I read him for a bluff when he raised with a queen showing and re-raised him with my pair of nines. I was right that he was bluffing. Unfortunately, my hand never improved, he caught another queen, and at three in the morning, I was eliminated.

I was devoid of emotion, as I had been the entire tournament. As I turned to walk away, a reporter from *Card Player* magazine asked me for an interview. I asked him to give me a few minutes, and I walked over to one of the abandoned tables.

Then I put my hands on my face and bawled like a baby. For five minutes, tears streamed out of my eyes like water from a fire hydrant. Was I happy? Sad? Relieved? Overwhelmed? After three days of displaying no emotion, it all flooded out of me. Then I collected myself and walked over to the reporter. He asked, "How do you feel?"

For the previous seven years, I had vacillated between broke and $50,000 in debt. With a $100 investment, I entered a poker tournament three days earlier and had just won $102,542. So, of course, I didn't have to think much about my response.

"Disappointed," I said, with tears in my eyes.

In retrospect, I was most disappointed in my *thoughts.* One could argue that my thoughts wouldn't have changed the cards that were dealt—but they absolutely would have changed the way I played them. It's not so much that I made tactical errors; it was more that I lacked a game plan—I didn't have an *idea*—for how to beat Poels. At least I had learned a lesson from Moneymaker to convince myself—even *delude* myself—that I'm the best player in every tournament I enter.

You may have been told thousands of times to be realistic, that you're not entitled to anything, and to keep your expectations in check. Now consider if all those projections are working for you. Ask yourself if you would be better off being delusional, raising your sense of entitlement, and increasing your upper limits. After all, those three thoughts may be the most significant elements to becoming a *moneymaker.*

Stories Are Organized Beliefs: Tell the Ones That Propel You

Facts are what happened. Stories are how we remember and explain them.

Fact: I earned $102,542 for second place at the WSOP. Story: I succeeded because…

- I improved my health and had more energy and mental clarity than my opponents.
- I got my finances in order and didn't need the money.
- I was open enough to assimilate Phil's message that the money is at the top.

Because it was exactly two decades from the time I first played poker, I could have used these facts to reinforce the adage that "overnight success usually takes about 20 years." Our minds grab on to events and organize them in ways that support our belief systems—whether or not those belief systems support us. If I had a negative view of myself, or the universe, I could reframe the same facts in all sorts of stories:

- I lacked the confidence to finish first.
- A glimmer of success will make me feel even worse when I go broke again.
- Even a loser like me can catch lucky cards.

Those with disempowering belief systems can find a way to turn anything into bad news. The story I choose is that I made 100 grand because I took a holistic path and asked empowering questions to reprogram my beliefs and improve my habits. My inner state of abundance created an opportunity—one that I was able to seize due to my discipline and emotional intelligence—that led to external abundance.

Doesn't it make perfect sense for a holistic coach who writes a book about empowering questions to craft such a story? By asking questions, I made my business profitable, paid off my debt, hired Amelia as my health coach, sublet my apartment, and showed up for the tournament not needing to win. And the universe rewarded me. Or did I just catch lucky cards for three days?

We can view experiences from whatever lens we choose. There are many facts about your life. You'll process them better by asking these three questions:

1. What stories are you telling yourself about the facts in your life?
2. What stories are you telling others?
3. Are the narratives that you repeat over and over propelling or sabotaging you?

Lottery Winners and Paraplegics are Equally Happy: Say What?

For all the talk about raising our upper limits, let's avoid the trap of thinking that money solves all of our problems. I believe that our minds play the biggest role in our wealth, but anyone who quotes his "net worth" in dollars and cents has a limited view of his own value. The Peace Pilgrim, who walked more than 25,000 miles with no possessions, was on to something—especially now that airlines charge for checked luggage—when she said that everything you don't need is a burden.

After my WSOP score, I didn't buy one new toy. It wasn't out of restraint. I didn't want anything. I've always viewed money as freedom tickets and viewed waste with disdain. When I returned to New York, I was still a slave to my inbox and found running the agency to be a grind. I wasn't any more or any less happy.

This might surprise you, but it makes perfect sense to psychologist Daniel Gilbert. In his TEDTalk, he says, "The fact is, a year after losing the use of their legs and a year after winning the lotto, lottery winners and paraplegics are equally happy with their lives."

In other words, if I had gone to Vegas and lost my legs instead of winning a hundred grand, Gilbert believes my happiness would have returned to its set point within a year. But I had *beaucoup dólares* and war stories to tell! I was the lead story on "Page Six" of the *New York Post,* which opened new doors. At a charity poker event in the Hollywood Hills, I played at the same table as *Old School* and *Hangover* director Todd Phillips, WSOP champion Jesus Ferguson, and Leonardo DiCaprio. I soon learned that cash, publicity, and even A-list name-dropping made *zero impact* on my happiness. Going all-in on his position, so to speak, Gilbert adds, "If it happened over three months ago, with only a few exceptions, it has no impact whatsoever on your life."

Gilbert was saying that what we *do* and *have* doesn't change how we *are*. What determines our happiness is the lens through which we view life (a fancy way of saying imagination), which is why Gilbert says we can "synthesize happiness." As for the poker windfall not making a difference, Gilbert was right. My life (if not my ego) was exactly the same as it was before Vegas. Having broken through my money limits, I still had work to do on my life limits. I chose to keep my mom's belief system that we're not entitled to anything. But I also started to believe that if I worked on it, I could live the delusional existence I was crafting for myself.

It's time to get even more tactical so that your thoughts propel you.

How to Reprogram a Belief System

List one *limiting* belief for each of the following:

- Money: (example) Money doesn't grow on trees.
- Health: (example) It's too expensive to eat healthy.
- Purpose: (example) Anything you do, after a while, is going to feel like a job.
- Relationships: (example) All relationships get stale and are unsustainable.

Now take each limiting belief through four steps:

1. Inquire. Ask yourself if the beliefs are true and if they're serving you. Reword them so that they support your mission and are true. You must believe what you are saying.
2. Find examples of others who exemplify beliefs that propel you.
3. Provide evidence that supports your beliefs.
4. Sustain your beliefs through words, visuals, and other affirmations using the senses.

Example:

Money doesn't grow on trees.

1. Is that true? Technically, yes, though if you own mango or avocado trees, you might think it does. Reword: I earn more than enough money to feel prosperous *because* I am talented, I work on my craft, and I am dedicated to providing value for others. Ask yourself if you really believe this? Keep revising until the statement is both true and propelling you.
2. List successful people in your field who are prosperous.
3. For evidence, make a statement that's true. *If this fits...* When I worked that job I thought I had to do, I earned a decent paycheck but always felt stressed, tired, and worried about money. When I did X, I always felt hopeful and had a better outlook about money.
4. Affirm using the senses. On my fridge, mirror, and screensaver, I see: I can earn more than enough money to feel prosperous because I am

talented, I work on my craft, and I am dedicated to providing value for others. I repeat this three times whenever I take a shower.

◎ ◎ ◎

Is changing your thoughts easy or hard? You decide. Either way, leading men commit daily to making sure their thoughts propel them.

QUESTION FIVE:
HOW DO THOUGHTS PROPEL ME?
More Empowering Questions

1. List belief systems that propel you using statements that you believe and that include the word because for:
   a. Money:
   b. Health:
   c. Purpose:
   d. Relationships:

2. List the five people you spend the most time with. Now list the five that most embody the life you want. How will you make those lists the same?

3. Rewrite your ideal day beyond your previous upper limits as if you are entitled, privileged, and delusional.

◎ ◎ ◎

If your mind is in the right place and you are working hard to no avail, perhaps you need to sharpen your saw, find a new saw, or find an approach that has nothing to do with a saw. In other words, you need to find the *tools* that uniquely suit you.

6

TOOLS

Which Tools Uniquely Suit Me?

QUESTION SIX

WHICH TOOLS UNIQUELY SUIT ME?

"Never ask a barber if you need a haircut."

—Warren Buffett

The mind is a powerful tool. So is a self-propelled lawn mower. Which tool would you choose to mow a field of knee-length grass? Would you try to chop down a tree with a butter knife? Do you prefer a tricycle or a Tesla to cover 111 miles?

This chapter is where you chose from the vast buffet of tools to create your very own toolkit. The best part about a buffet is that you have choices. The worst part is that you have choices. Try to taste everything and you end up overwhelmed. Try to do what works for others and you end up sick. Consider the conversations between people at a smorgasbord.

- The meatloaf is better than grandma's. *I'm a vegetarian.*
- The almond bark is mouth-watering. *I'm allergic to nuts.*
- The sausage is off the hook. *I'm kosher. And I don't roll on Shabbos.*

Determining the best choice of tools (and food) depends on who you ask. When people tell you what to do, those people are projecting what works for them—often without asking questions about what works for you.

Leave it to the great Abraham Maslow, author of *The Farther Reaches of Human Nature,* to put it in perspective. Maslow said, "It is tempting, if the only tool you have is a hammer, to treat everything as if it were a nail."

Tools rarely work if forced upon you. When Phil Jackson, who coached 11 NBA championship teams, wanted to motivate Michael Jordan, he asked questions instead of barking orders. In his book, *Eleven Rings*, Jackson wrote, regarding Jordan, "...I simply pushed him to think about the problem in a different way, mostly by asking him questions...When I let him solve the problem himself, he was more likely to buy into the solution and not repeat the same counterproductive behavior in the future."

The past five chapters have taught you how to be a detective for yourself. Now that you know why you are asking, your ideal day, who you are, where you are now, and how belief systems propel you, you have clues. Most importantly, tap into your inner alpha and remember that no one knows you as well as you do. With this knowledge, you're on your way to answer this question: Which tools uniquely suit me?

We're going to get specific about making the leap to action—action that is specifically tailored to your life. Finding the right tools requires effort, but there are ways to minimize the investment. Listen to the podcast that your friend keeps raving about. If a coworker has started a program that is working for him, go to the introductory talk. Take the free sample. Dip your toe in and find out what works for you.

This chapter will make that process seamless. It will also reinforce that a tool is only effective if you commit to using it. Think of the old Shaolin monk in the 70's TV show *Kung Fu* saying, "I can only point the way, Grasshopper; you must walk the path yourself."

Keep in mind that choosing the right tools is not always about common sense. For example, if you want to lose weight, an obvious tool would be to go on a diet. But when we stop eating, our brain sends a signal to our body that we are starving. And in a famine, our body stores fat and conserves energy. That's why going on a diet is often counter-productive and rarely works.

The larger point is that we have to experiment to find what works for us. We're going to talk about nutrition and exercise in this chapter—two topics that often leave us frustrated. While both are critical, we're going to learn how to block out those who only think they know us and hone in on the tools that uniquely suit you.

Friends Don't "Should" on Friends

My clients' success skyrocketed when I substituted the word why for the word should. *"Should-ing"* implies that you know more than the other person. *"Why-ing"* implies a genuine desire to learn what makes you tick. It allows you to reflect and come up with your own discoveries and solutions.

Even people with warm hearts, good intentions, and nothing to sell will suggest that you "should" use the tools that worked for *them.* If they're nagging you by telling you what you should do, say, "Stop *shoulding* on me!"

My friend Mary Beth posted on Facebook, "Does anyone have a remedy for a pinched nerve in your neck? I am in some major pain right now!" Twenty-seven responses included:

- Chiropractor
- Stay away from a chiropractor.
- Jack Daniels and Coke…double shots.
- Alternating heat and ice.
- No heat. Only ice.
- An x-ray to see what's going in your cervical vertebrae. Oh, and no headstands :).
- It's a call to stop and slow down.

Keep in mind that none of these well-meaning people had performed an exam. They didn't know Mary Beth's health history, lifestyle, resources, or the cause of the pinched nerve, yet they all had suggestions for tools to fix an undiagnosed problem. And that's okay, because it's Mary Beth's job to figure out her own truth. Soliciting feedback is different from blindly following it. All the while, the one voice you must keep listening to is your own.

State, Story, and Strategy

Picture the performers backstage before a play or the athletes in a locker room before an Olympic event or a championship game. Some wear headphones to listen to music or an inspirational sermon. Others chitchat to stay loose and keep their minds off what's about to happen. Others are silent and inwardly focused. One way or another, everyone is taking an action to get in the right *state*. State is your frame of mind, your outlook, your degree of focus. It's the difference between a group that's fired up and one that's flat.

Directors and coaches offer words of wisdom. They want you to buy into the belief that you are going to be successful. "You have been preparing for this moment your whole life," or "I believe in you." There may be posters on the wall such as, "No pain, no gain," or "Winners never quit and quitters never win." The performers/athletes will be repeating mantras to themselves such as, "You can do this." In short, everyone is taking an action to create the right *story*.

The last point of preparation is more tactical. Performers rehearse the most challenging moves. Coaches diagram X's and O's. Key points of execution are reviewed and emphasized. All involved are taking an action to focus on the *strategy*.

State. Story. Strategy.

I learned this at the four-day *Unleash the Power Within* workshop with Tony Robbins, who emphasized state because of the power of emotion. If you are in a state that you can conquer the world or that life is beautiful, your odds of success skyrocket. If you're exhausted, you will struggle with the easiest of tasks. Robbins asks rhetorically, "What's wrong in your life when you are totally in love?"

We've covered the concept of story enough to know the importance of belief systems, though Robbins points out that your story is not fixed. It changes based on how you feel. When you're in love and full of energy, your story about the world is different than when you're hung-over or battling a migraine.

Robbins also says that if your state and story are strong, you will figure out the strategy. Your degree of awareness and choice of tools will expedite the process, but even if your initial strategy misses, your empowered state and story will lead you to find the correct one. The Wright Brothers had a flawed strategy for flying for years, but their state (enthusiastic) and story (they believed it was possible) led them to persevere.

Think about each day of your life as a performance or a championship game. It's the biggest event of the year. Curtains back, lights on, and you are the leading man—every day. That's why you prepare by putting yourself in the best possible state. You stack the odds in your favor by using the tools that are most effective for you.

I understand that many of you just want to get out of the house to beat rush-hour traffic, and you'll stop reading if I suggest a nine-minute, much less a 90-minute morning ritual. No matter what your routine, find ways to solidify your state, story, and strategy every day. If it has to wait until your lunch break, that's okay too. For mapping out your strategy, it may be more effective to do it the night before, so that your morning routine requires looking at, rather than creating, your to-do list.

Now let's get more specific about how to find tools that facilitate your own winning way.

Tools for Creating the Right State

Think about how much effort you put into the tools for a romantic vibe. You put on cologne, pick a restaurant with a sensual ambiance, and add a seductive tone to your voice. You choose the right substances, like champagne, chocolate, and oysters. You go to a dive bar and throw down shots to lower inhibitions or to an art museum and sip tea at an outdoor café.

For all the health concerns about smoking, it endures because inhaling and exhaling nicotine instantly changes your state. So does dancing or exercising to music. Try singing while jumping up and down and see if you can feel depressed. Or put on your favorite music, inhale deeply, and have a sip of your favorite drink. Then sit on your butt, watch the news, and drink spoiled milk and notice the difference.

The Six State Creators
- Sound (Music or Your Own Voice)
- Movement
- Breath
- Substances
- Scent
- Thoughts

Is it any wonder there's a coffee shop on every corner in America? The smell alone can change your state. Caffeine is an instant state-changer. Throw in some sugar and chocolate (mocaccino anyone?) and things really shift. Since there is so much judgment around sugar, coffee, smoking, watching the news, and drugs, you may be waiting for me to tell you how to choose tools without the side effects.

Keep waiting.

Use as much trial and error as it takes to find the tools, especially in the morning, which put you in the right state. I happen to love coffee (don't panic, I drink organic) and there's a ton of research that it is great for you, as well as a ton of research that it is not. The most important bit of information is how it works for you.

Treat each day like a leading man. What's one day, you ask? String the days together and you get…your *life*. Obtain the right state by finding the morning routine that's worthy of a leading man. It might be as simple as setting a coffeemaker with a timer so the aroma will motivate you to get out of bed. Maybe you play a song on the piano or sing in the shower. Whatever it is, find a ritual to create the best state for your day. Reference the six state creators above.

Also do your best to spend at least 30 seconds on your story. Close your eyes and take one deep breath while envisioning your day. Write morning pages (check out *The Artist's Way* by Julie Cameron) or in a gratitude journal. Or stare in the mirror and declare, "I rule!" You could watch a short YouTube clip or a TEDTalk to get you in the right frame of mind, or listen to something in your car or on the bus that gets your head right.

Your strategy will be very specific to your goals. When you are in the right state and have the right story, you will find the right strategy.

Prescribe Tools for Yourself As You Would for Others

Our agency thrived when I lived in New York and Frank lived in San Diego. If I needed Frank's input before 8 A.M. PST, I would call and ask if he had his coffee yet. If I needed him to focus, I'd give him 10 minutes to brew and drink before getting down to business. If we were in the middle of a creative conundrum, and Frank said that he needed to go to the gym, I acquiesced because I knew that was his best tool for thinking.

We tend to be good at knowing what tools are best for others. *Make sure Grandma takes her meds!* Now I want you to think about what you need. Since we can't see our blind spots, we're often not as good at choosing the right tools for ourselves. How many people do you know who tell you they're a wreck when they don't get enough rest, yet continue to neglect their sleep?

As a parent or babysitter, you experiment to find the tools that expedite putting kids to sleep. You use the pacifier, the blanket, the back rub, and the dim lighting. If you're a coach who wants your players to perform, you remind them to stretch, ice, massage, hydrate, watch film, visualize, and practice like they play.

Phil Jackson was referred to as the "Zen Master" because he was obsessed with finding the *unique* tools for each of his players. Before a long road trip, he gave every player a different book, ranging from *Song of Solomon* for Michael Jordan to *The Way of the Peaceful Warrior* for Craig Hodges to *Beavis & Butt-Head: This Book Sucks* for Stacey King. Jackson's brilliance lay in understanding that the tools were *different for each player.* If Jackson could find unique tools for 12 men, you can find them for one—the one you know better than anyone.

You've done all this work for a reason. You know who you are and why; now it's time to channel that into *what* to do and *how* to do it.

Finding Your Anchoring Action

Since we've talked about cultivating feelings rather than objects, you have to be creative to find the right tools. For example, if you want to feel more grounded, walk outside barefoot for five minutes or stand in the grass barefoot while you visualize, meditate, or sing. If you want to feel intellectually challenged, use a site like Lumosity, do crossword puzzles or Sudoku, or play chess or Scrabble. If you are hyper-competitive, want to be intellectually challenged *and* keep your stress low, day-trading or playing online poker may be destructive tools. But bridge or chess might be perfect.

Gratitude, love, passion, and a quiet mind are four intangibles that I want to cultivate. How would you go about designing a tool to generate these intangibles? This gets to the seemingly oxymoronic question of how to work on *being by doing*. Fortunately, the answer was right in front of me.

My friend Hajjar wrote "The Gratitude Song," which is simple to play on guitar and is composed of four questions:

1. What can I say to give thanks for this day?
2. What can I do to let my love shine through?
3. Who can I be if I live my passion free?
4. What beauty can I find in the quiet of my mind?

By asking the questions combined with movement (singing and strumming), I tap into all four of these feelings. Often, as I'm singing about what I can say to give thanks, I'll simply say, "Thank you." When I ask how I can let my love shine through, it reminds me to make that apology, feed a stray dog, or be more patient. When I ask about living my passion, it motivates me to work and serve.

This tool is so powerful that I have made it my *anchoring action*. Every single day, I play and sing this song. If I don't have access to a guitar, I sing a cappella. It's such a potent tool because it can be done in less than three minutes, it ties directly to how I want to feel, it nourishes both mind and spirit, and it instantly impacts my state.

What anchoring action will work best for you? What one thing can you do daily to bring you to your happy place? What's the one action you can count on to put a smile on your face, a spring in your step, and allow you to see the world with fresh eyes?

◎ ◎ ◎

Think about the things you do reflexively every day. You check your stock portfolio, your email, and see how many people retweeted your post. Because these results are outside of yourself, they lead to a large variance in your feelings. And that's fine; life has its ups and downs. With your anchoring action, there are no external factors. You create a happy place that's yours and yours alone. Not only does it ground you in how you want to feel, but it also balances the facets of life that you can't control.

When you see the list of people who practice transcendental meditation (TM), it reinforces the power of personal time. Filmmaker David Lynch writes about TM in *Catching the Big Fish,* and Howard Stern talks about it on his show. Ray Dalio, Jerry Seinfeld, Ellen DeGeneres, Arianna Huffington, Martin Scorsese, Brian Koppelman, Russell Simmons, Bill Walton, and Jeff Bridges (The Dude!) also credit TM for their success. I attended an introductory talk and the speaker said that Oprah and Dr. Oz hired him to train their entire organizations in TM. Who would have guessed that rather than rushing to the fast lane to find success, the real trick is not only to pause, but to stop altogether?

We'll build on your anchoring action even more in the next chapter about habits. For now, remember that the most critical daily tool is the one that connects you to how you want to feel.

Choose Tools That Can Be Measured and Sustained

How exactly does one measure meditation? I've never been one to quiet my mind and float for hours, much less minutes. I did, however, feel bad that I wasn't keeping the promise I made to myself, which created evidence that

I lacked discipline. Given that meditation is ambiguous, I committed to something measurable instead—seven deep breaths every morning.

Since the last line of the Gratitude Song is, "What beauty can I find in the quiet of my mind?" I repeat it several times and then go right into my seven breaths. Some days it leads me to visualization or tapping. Some days I may actually sit still for ten minutes. And other days, I'll just take seven deep breaths and enjoy the double satisfaction of serenity and evidence of my discipline.

When you choose your anchoring action, pick something finite and sustainable. I'd rather you commit to writing one paragraph than one page, reading one page than one chapter, or doing 11 push-ups rather than 1100, as long as it is something you are able to accomplish daily. When you choose something attainable, you increase your odds of consistency and build confidence from small wins. Moreover, you give yourself the opportunity to build on it. It's the same rationale as meeting a business contact for coffee rather than lunch or a blind date for a drink rather than dinner. A shorter time commitment lowers the barrier to entry and increases the odds of consistency.

Playing one song often turns into playing guitar for several hours, because picking it up is often the hardest step. Keep in mind, however, that if it were a choice between several hours or nothing, there would be many days I would choose nothing. Since we now see how actions support belief systems and vice versa, I'd be giving myself evidence that I don't follow through on my promises. When you commit to something doable, you continually build evidence that you keep your promises to yourself and have discipline.

What is your go-to activity that sets the tone for your day? What anchors you in your truth? What provides evidence for the belief systems that propel your success?

Every day you'll keep coming back to this action, so pick a good one. It could be as simple as preparing homemade hot chocolate every morning, while you firmly plant your feet on the ground and give thanks. Or maybe you take a freezing cold shower and scream, "Yippee ki-ay," for two minutes. Movement, music, and breath are great places to start.

Five Questions to Choose Effective Tools
1. What has worked for you in the past?
2. What do you enjoy enough to make it sustainable?
3. What creates the greatest ripple effect in the rest of your life?
4. What "moves the needle" the most with the least effort?
5. What anchors you most in the feelings you want to create?

Ferrari Versus Honda: Ayurveda and Metabolism

It's nearly impossible to lead an exceptional life without taking proper care of your body. I've experienced what it feels like to carry around 300 pounds as a carbohydrate addict, and I know how much better I feel when I move and maintain my body. Since we spent the entire previous chapter on our minds, let's spend the next several pages on our bodies.

If there was ever a system of medicine designed for a leading man who seeks tools uniquely suited for him, Ayurveda is it. Having originated in India thousands of years ago, it is regarded as the oldest form of healthcare in the world. It starts with the premise that we are all different. The word "dosha" is equivalent to "our nature" and the three doshas are: Pitta (fire), Kapha (water), and Vatta (air).

The more I studied health and nutrition, the more I saw how we were led astray by diets that fail to incorporate our ancestry, lifestyles, and tastes. Ayurveda, like Dr. Joseph Mercola's nutritional typing, and Dr. Peter D'Adamo's diet for your blood type, highlights that we have to choose tools that are aligned with our nature. While this premise holds for everything, it's especially critical for nutrition and health.

Much of the literature for men is about how to speed up our metabolism. That's great if you want to get ripped, but it comes with a downside, one that makes sense when you consider the difference between a 12-cylinder Ferrari and a four-cylinder Honda. The one with the bigger engine is built for speed and power and looks menacing. You could go on a diet of Red Bull, cigarettes, and cocaine to boost your metabolism. Then you, like a Ferrari, would break down and cost more to maintain.

If your only goal is longevity, you would lay off the stimulants. When you learn that the slower metabolism of Kapha doshas allows them to live longer, healthier lives (even though their watery constitution means they don't look as sleek), you see the benefits of a Honda. Those who drive a *three*-cylinder car are so convinced they made the savvier choice that they call it a *Smart* car.

We have to keep coming back to *why* we want a faster metabolism and six-pack abs. Even if research shows that a certain diet "works" for losing weight, it may not consider the long-term impact on your health. Biff may look impressive at the beach, but that doesn't tell you how his liver will function in 50 years. At a minimum, you now have another perspective that making your body Ferrari-like has its downside. My friend Hal summed it up by saying, "I'd rather date a Ferrari. I'd rather marry a Honda."

There's a constant debate in nutrition circles about how often we should eat. One theory is that small, frequent meals (as many as six per day) ramp up your metabolism, keep your blood sugar stable, and prevent overeating. The downside is that constantly revving your engine taxes your organs, impairs digestion, and increases the odds of overeating because you have to stop eating six times a day. I've also seen research that it makes *no* difference how often you eat. Besides, all those theories mean nothing unless you figure out what works for you.

Ayurveda shows you how to balance your doshas using a whole body and mind approach. If, *by nature,* you are hot-tempered and fidgety, cooling foods and relaxing music are going to serve you better than jalapenos and heavy metal. If your head is in the clouds, grounding practices, like walking barefoot and eating root vegetables, will bring you back to earth. Figure out who you are, experiment with what leads to the results you are seeking and put it into practice. And while I encourage you to seek out information from multiple sources, run it all through the filter of *you.*

◉ ◉ ◉

It's no surprise that many of the belief systems about health are derived from axioms. "Eat breakfast like a king, lunch like a prince, and dinner like a pauper." But just as there is a corollary to every axiom, the same goes for health. Intermittent fasting, which recommends skipping breakfast, was all the rage in 2013.

While *The China Study* was being hailed as the definitive, peer-reviewed truth that animal protein is evil, there was a growing "paleo" community with its own research (consistent with that of the Weston Price Foundation, as well as Mark Sisson, author of *The Primal Blueprint*) that extolled the virtues of animal products. If we can't even agree on the frequency of meals, whether to eat breakfast, and if animal products do more harm than good, what can we agree on?

Sugar. Everyone will tell you that sugar and refined carbohydrates (as well as processed foods) are bad for us. On this point, "everyone" happens to be right. There's quite a list of foods to avoid after sugar—artificial sweeteners, anything genetically modified or containing animal hormones and antibiotics, hydrogenated oils—though Dr. William Davis, author of *Wheat Belly*, makes a compelling argument that wheat (not just gluten, the protein in wheat, but all wheat) should be near the top of that list. After hearing him speak and observing how I felt when I gave up wheat, I'm a believer. But don't take it from me, Dr. Davis, or anyone, besides yourself. The research can guide you, but only trial and error will lead you to determine what works for you.

Beyond sugar, it's tough to find a consensus on much else. Sure, everyone agrees we need to stay hydrated, but even the right quantity and quality of water (spring, distilled, alkaline?) can set off a debate. As you might expect, I will tell you that the key is to start from the inside out. As we learned from *Man 2.0.,* hormones play a big role, and as we are learning from Mark Hyman, Leo Galland, Frank Lipman, Donna Gates, and other pioneers in functional medicine, gut health may play an even bigger role. Don't get me started on the perils of antibiotics and the importance of fermented foods. Besides, it may take the focus off the theme of this chapter: experimenting to find the right tools that work for you.

We can agree on two things related to health. One, minimize consumption of sugar. And two, you are unique, and only you, can find the proper fuel for your body.

The Biggest Nutrient Bang Leads to Longevity

The one commonality linked to living longer is calorie restriction. The more you eat, the more your organs have to work and the faster they expire. Of course, the other extreme is not eating enough to feed those organs. The majority of the health problems in the Western world result from simultaneously being overfed and undernourished. We have diseases of the "too much" variety (diabetes, heart disease, hypertension), yet for all our consumption, because the food is void of nutrients, we lack the fuel that feeds our brains and our bodies.

Dr. Joel Fuhrman, author of *Eat to Live,* offers a simple formula: H=N/C (Health = Nutrients/Calories). He believes that "Adequate consumption of micronutrients— vitamins, minerals, and many other phytochemicals— without overeating on calories, is the key to achieving excellent health."

In *The Omnivore's Dilemma,* activist and journalism professor Michael Pollan explores the corruption of food by describing how companies have *engineered* it to increase demand. When food is processed to remove the fat, fiber and micronutrients—the very things that make us feel full—and addictive chemicals are substituted, companies sell a lot more of their products. It's not by chance—rather it's the work of brilliant/evil food engineers—that you can eat a whole bag of potato chips and feel hungrier than before you started.

Fuhrman created the ANDI (Aggregate Nutrient Density Index) scoring system to show what foods give you the biggest doses of nutrients, vitamins, and minerals per calorie. Leafy greens like kale, collards, and watercress have the top score of 1,000. Carrots are 458, strawberries 182, white bread 15, and French fries 12. Not surprisingly, cola is in last place with a score of 1.

The simplest nutrition advice I can offer is to consume the most nutrition with the least amount of effort on your body. At a base level, view food as fuel. If you only make one change to your diet, drink more water and eliminate soda.

Opt Out of Normal With Nutrients

After six months in Thailand, I rode with my brother and his family from Charlotte, North Carolina, to Myrtle Beach, South Carolina. Having heard all the conspiracy theories about how the "system" wants us to be sick so we keep consuming its crap food and pharmaceutical drugs, I noticed that on almost every corner in America, there are three fast food restaurants and one pharmacy. Are you not seeing a correlation? Don't forget to grab them Tums with that KFC Double Down.

Turn on the TV and there's Larry the Cable Guy talking about how he can stuff his face and not get heartburn because of a magic pill. He's standing in front of a Colossal Corn Dog stand, saying that he is not just an actor; he actually uses it. As Dr. Michael Noonan pointed out in the *Bangor Daily,* "The message is subtle but clear—eat whatever you want, as much as you want, and let the drug take away the pain of these poor food choices." And it will. Antacids are an effective tool for heartburn—at least in the short term.

Antacids also increase your odds of osteoporosis, digestive issues, and irritable bowel syndrome. Somehow we look at the health crisis as a mystery, a riddle that has yet to be solved, when it's obvious that washing down poisonous food with poisonous pills is a reliable recipe for disease. The only reason we may miss it is that we have *normalized the abnormal.* Because most "normal" people eat a standard American diet (the fitting acronym is SAD), it leads us to believe it is okay. Never mind that "normal" behavior is making sick, fat, medicated, and exhausted the new normal.

As processed food becomes the norm all over the globe, the abnormal health issues that plague Americans are becoming prevalent worldwide, as well. There were 4,429 KFC restaurants in China in 2013, and Diane Brady reported in *Bloomberg Businessweek* that "the company sold chicken fattened on illegal drugs" and "the ice cubes at a KFC...Beijing outlet had 13 times as much bacteria as water from a toilet bowl." Mmm-mmm, finger lickin' good! Despite this news, 700 more stores were set to open in China the following year. The word is out about the perils of fast food. The "normal" folks continue to ignore it.

Is there a *hidden* conspiracy to keep you hooked on processed food? There doesn't have to be. All the exposés, documentaries, and even the mainstream press have divulged what's in our food, yet we keep eating it. Even the fast-food joints post their ingredients. There's no conspiracy because there doesn't have to be. Because we are addicted to processed foods, we continue to eat this crap with full knowledge that it makes us sick—and then turn to poison pills for temporary relief so we can eat more.

Is our health crisis a mystery? If we started putting 12 and 15 octane fuel in cars that require 87, they would break down and we would know exactly why. Yet we continue to treat our cars better than our bodies and speculate as to why they don't perform better. Eating food full of toxins and lacking nutrients is the equivalent of putting soda in our gas tank and then wondering why our car won't run.

Before I step off the soapbox, it is worth noting that because many of today's foods, and our environment, are *extremely* toxic, it is no longer enough to be *somewhat* healthy. To be a leading man, you can't afford the sugar crashes, the cravings, the heartburn, the sick days, the sluggishness, and the cost of bad health. Just as many *food* problems are actually *life* problems, many *life* problems are actually *food* problems. If you're undernourished, starving, stuffed, or fatigued, you're in the danger zone for tantrums, careless mistakes, and miscommunication. It's fundamental: You must feed your body phenomenal food if you want to live a phenomenal life.

Entrepreneur, author, and innovator Dave Asprey spent 15 years and more than $300,000 to "hack" his own biology. He lost 100 pounds without cutting calories and raised his IQ by 20 points. What I appreciate most about Asprey's approach is that he appeals to our sense of adventure and desire to test our edge. His "Why" goes far beyond losing weight or living longer. "Health is cool," he said at the Longevity Now conference (where I loaded up on his "Bulletproof" products), "but isn't kicking ass cooler?"

I've given you some clues on where to gather more data. Build on this information with your own experimentation to find the right tools that suit your unique body and lifestyle. There's no conspiracy—and no sense complaining about one—when you realize that you are not the masses, and you determine what is normal.

Getting Real About Our Health Challenges

My "Why" for that rant was to fight off any sort of victim mentality. My goal was to assure you that if you set your mind to it, you can maintain optimum health. Then again, I have every advantage to sustain first-rate health—access to quality food and the education to find the tools that work for me—and I still struggle. I did lose 100 pounds, but I gained 50 back, and I have to keep asking questions to get it off again. On that very drive to Myrtle Beach, I ate a fried seafood platter and French fries from Captain D's, which my brother and sister-in-law have not let me forget.

For all the talk about a coach forcing you to "reach," some support is in order. I acknowledge that the deck is stacked against you. The food *culture* is toxic. Processed junk food is pervasive. I went to my nephew's baseball game and saw the kids with sports drinks full of food coloring and high fructose corn syrup, only to be given a soda when the game ended. At the neighborhood swim meet, one of the dads showed his team spirit by handing out candy. The snack bar wasn't much better.

In fact, I went to Costco with my sister-in-law, Leslie, to pick up provisions for the pool snack bar. You're probably expecting me to tell you I was appalled, but instead I'll remind everyone that we have plenty of choices. In fact, I buy organic kale from Costco. My friend, who is a caterer and private chef for health-conscious clients, does the majority of her shopping there.

Costco is neither the problem nor the solution. You are.

Leslie worked within the system to change the culture of those swim meets. She added organic fruit, organic carrots with hummus, and a grilled chicken salad to the menu. She said, "Everything was a big hit! We typically ran out of each item at the meets." She also said that they tried to offer a healthy hot dog, but the kids thought they were horrible so they stuck with the regular hot dogs—and she didn't fight it. Leslie's effort combined all the elements of taking initiative, making healthier choices, and diplomacy. You have all those tools at your disposal, as well.

Short of living on a biodynamic farm in a cocoon that doesn't exist, it is tough to be healthy in today's world. Dr. Mark Hyman, author of several bestselling books including *The Blood Sugar Solution 10-Day Detox Diet,* cites research that sugar is eight times more addictive than cocaine. He also writes that "discoveries in science prove that industrial processed, sugar-, fat-, and salt-laden food is biologically addictive."

Biologically addictive!

Because the food is so cheap, tasty, convenient, and brilliantly marketed, we keep consuming it. The only reason we miss that it's poisonous is because we see all the other "normal" people eating it. Only the weird, *abnormal* ones abstain, but today's reality is that the only way to maintain your health is to live outside the norm.

We've already discussed how you are the average of the five people you spend the most time with. This assertion may be even more apropos for your health. If the five people closest to you think ketchup is a vegetable, it will make an already tough task tougher. You do things—eat, socialize, exercise, set goals—with people. Naturally, the things that you do with others are going to become your tools and habits. Why not spend time with those who practice habits that make you feel your best?

After a seven-day fast in Thailand, my friend Jonathan said he felt 10 years younger. The day before he left, he carried on about how hard it would be to maintain his regimen in New York—where happy hour, lavish dinners, and bottle service at clubs were his *only* choices for entertainment. "You live in New York frickin' City," I told him. "I guarantee every weekend there are a dozen healthy pot lucks and hundreds of free cultural events—not to mention some of the top libraries, healthy restaurants, and workout studios in the world."

He got the point, and thought long and hard about his circle of friends. I told him that the healthier I get, the more nutjobs I hang out with—and I've never had better company.

Here are some questions to sit with:

1. Who in your life will help/hinder you in your quest to live an ideal day?

2. What does the leading man in your movie do on a night when his buddies are determined to destroy themselves?

3. If you have friends whose sole form of entertainment is self-destruction, how much time do you make for them in your life?

4. What are your tools for stimulation, exhilaration, and companionship?

5. What tools will you choose that are consistent with an abnormally healthy guy?

Integrate the Four P's of Detox

To have healthy teeth, you have to brush and floss daily *and* go to the dentist for a deeper cleaning every six months. You make your bed daily, wash the sheets weekly, and clean the comforter quarterly. You pick up what's on the carpet daily, vacuum once a week, and steam-clean annually. You must also develop consistent detox actions for your body—the basic ones daily and more thorough ones at various times throughout the year.

There are four ways your body removes toxins: pee, poop, perspiration, and pranayama (breath). Dr. Hyman calls these the quadruple "P" and says, "Every moment of every day your body is relying on the quadruple 'P' to mobilize, transform, and excrete toxins." Detox is a book in and of itself, and a good place to start is http://drhyman.com/blog/. Type "detox" in the search box and you'll find several informative articles.

If you're not sweating enough, find a steam room, sauna, a hot yoga studio, or do a workout that makes you drip. My brother bought a FAR infrared sauna for $999 that's easy to assemble and plugs into a regular outlet. Deep breathing will remove toxins from the lungs. If a spaz like me can commit to seven deep breaths daily, so can you.

To pee more, drink quality water. A good rule of thumb is half an ounce of water for every pound. If you weigh 256 pounds, drink 128 ounces. That's a gallon of water a day. For those who don't speak American: If you weigh 116 kg, drink 3.79 liters of water a day. If you're sweating a lot, you'll need even more. For poop, in addition to drinking plenty of water, fiber-rich foods like vegetables are critical. Chia seeds and/or flaxseeds (which also contain

Omega-3 fatty acids) help, as well. Ginger, cayenne, lemons, cilantro, celery, and garlic are all "cleansing" foods that promote detoxification.

Like your teeth, carpet, bedding, and car, you have to create the daily rituals, as well as the "deeper" cleaning rituals each month, quarter, or year. Fasting can be a great tool, but it's more complicated than simply not eating and I strongly urge you to do your own homework. Just know that when you give your organs a break, they work better and you look and feel better. The same goes for your mind. This explains why the leading men I know build vacations around their health. A meditation retreat, a multi-day hike such as the Camino de Santiago, a surfing trip, a biking excursion—these are the activities that allow you to function at your best.

◎ ◎ ◎

For all of the emphasis I put on health, believe it or not, I strive to put *less* energy into food choices. The more stringent you are, the more food dominates your life. Plus, if you have a rigid diet, it makes it harder to socialize. The trick to avoiding poor food choices is to *feel full*. From an emotional standpoint, that means having a full life. When you get joy from your ideal day, food will seem less important.

From a physiological standpoint, you feel full by giving your body the nutrients it requires. Make a big smoothie in the morning with spinach, berries, protein powder (the less processed the better), coconut oil, and chia seeds or flaxseeds. Put half in a container for your work fridge and make that, rather than what's in the vending machine or break room, your afternoon snack. In three minutes, you have made two affordable, nutritious meals that give you a solid foundation for feeling sated.

If you're going to an event where you'll be tempted with unhealthy choices, show up full. It helps to keep healthy snacks nearby—raw walnuts in your glove compartment, hardboiled eggs in your work fridge, a protein bar or meal supplement in your gym bag. If you have time, grab a salad or a healthy meal before you arrive. If you don't have any restrictions, you'll feel free to have what you want, and since no fruit is forbidden, you'll end up nibbling. A few wings and beers while watching a game may be fine. It's the few *dozen* that get you into trouble.

In a normal world, you only need to be a little atypical to be healthy. In today's toxic world, you have to be abnormal to feel and look great.

How to Be Abnormally Healthy in A Toxic World

1. Feel full physically by eating nutrient-rich foods. Include Omega-3 fatty acids (chia seeds, flaxseeds, or fish oil), as well as fiber, vegetables, and protein.
2. Feel full by drinking adequate water. Find an eco-friendly water bottle you love to make carrying water with you convenient.
3. Feel full from life by getting your "primary food": relationships, physical activity, career, and spirituality.
4. Have go-to healthy snacks handy in your cupboard, car, backpack, and office.
5. Show up for social events feeling sated. When you feel full and are unrestricted, you end up enjoying reasonable amounts of food without the guilt.
6. Make detox a part of everyday life. Find tools that help you to sweat, breathe, pee, and poop.

Making Fitness Work for You

It's the sickest workout ever! It will kick your ass.

No it won't. It will only kick your ass *if you do it.* Going through the motions or not showing up at all won't get it done. Moreover, you will only benefit if you do it consistently. When it comes to new fitness toys and trends, it's less about what's out there and more about what works for you. Rather than tell me about your new app; tell me about your new *effort.*

Don't get me wrong, if technology—like an app or a heart rate monitor—

increases your awareness and allows you to work out more efficiently, then it's a great tool. Tim Ferriss' *The 4-Hour Body* is a valuable read, but it doesn't do any good unless you are committed to putting it to use. If watching *SportsCenter* keeps you on the treadmill longer, then do it. If going for a walk with your lady after dinner becomes a ritual, you've discovered an effective tool—maybe even your anchoring action.

You've heightened your awareness so you know whether you need to leave the house to get a great workout or whether you have to stay home. If it's the latter, get that P90X video or make space for a pull-up bar and a jump rope. If you thrive from competition or camaraderie, get out of the house. If a CrossFit class pushes you in ways that you wouldn't do on your own, you have found the right tool.

When my friend Adam visited Santa Monica, I told him about Yogaglo, a studio with free classes from some of the best teachers in the world. Yogaglo sells subscriptions for video-streaming and offers free classes to increase their visibility. Adam shrugged, and because I felt he was missing out on something, I was tempted to *should* on him. I let it go because I respected that he knows himself better than I do.

A month later, Adam called me raving about Yogaglo. I don't know if it's because he's a germaphobe, a homebody, a value shopper (it's only $18/month for unlimited streamed classes) or an efficiency expert who can't stand wasting time commuting, but he never liked going to yoga classes. He did, however, love yoga—in the comfort of his living room. And just when Adam started to sell me on the benefits of the subscription, he realized why it's a horrible tool for me. I need to get out of the house more, I derive energy from others, and I have a thing for yoga teachers. This reminded both of us that no one knows us as well as we know ourselves.

The key to exercise is to find something that you enjoy enough that you will do it consistently. For your health, sanity, vanity, and productivity, it is mandatory because it impacts all facets of life. According to researcher James Prochaska, "Exercise spills over. There's something about it that makes other good habits easier." As you would expect, after a workout, you are more inclined to make better food choices. What may not be as obvious is that exercise increases your productivity at work, leads to less stress, and reduces use of credit cards. Prochaska explains that exercising just once a week triggers a change in *everything*. Your job is to figure what kind of exercise best suits you.

We've beaten the individuality horse to death because tools are only going to work and turn into sustainable habits if you figure out for yourself what suits your unique life.

Tools for When You Are Down: Text or Feel?

Louis C.K. explained to Conan O'Brien why he won't let his kids have a mobile phone. "I'm not raising children," he said. "I'm raising the grownups that they're going to be. So I have to raise them with the tools to get through a terrible life." He went on to say that a human being would be well served to develop the ability to do nothing but sit and face the emptiness and loneliness of life.

Comics masquerade as prophets so don't let the humor distract you from the message that it's a *learned* reaction to reach for tools outside of ourselves the minute we feel sadness. We're willing to endanger ourselves and others by texting while driving, because we want a distraction from our thoughts. Smartphones only accelerate the process of asking for validation and relying on others to make us feel anything other than our own pain.

"The thing is," Louis C.K. said, "because we don't want that first bit of sad, we push it away with a little phone or a jack-off or the food." He also shared the payoff for allowing ourselves to be still enough to experience the sadness:

> Just be sad. Just let the sadness, stand in the way of it, and let it hit you like a truck... Sadness is poetic. You're lucky to live sad moments. Because when you let yourself feel sad, your body has antibodies; it has happiness that comes rushing in to meet the sadness. So I was grateful to feel sad, and then I met it with true, profound happiness. It was such a trip.

We're either expressing love or crying out for it. Start noticing what others (and more importantly, you) write on social media and in text messages and you'll see that most of the time we are crying out for a diversion to avoid feeling anything. The next time you feel sadness, worry, or pain, pause and resist the desire for distraction. Sit with it. Be with it. Feel it.

To Avoid Depression: Drink or Think?

The choice of how to best handle adversity—particularly the bigger problems in life that lead to depression—may surprise you. One option is to go into your cave, contemplate your problems, and then think about them some more. The other is to get drunk, start a fistfight, and drag race. Which do you think is the better choice? To simplify, get out a scorecard and keep track of your choices for "thinking away" or "drinking away."

In *Learned Optimism,* Martin Seligman explains that women suffer from depression more than men at a ratio of 2 to 1 because they ruminate while men find distractions. In other words, thinking about the problem can make it worse. That's a point in favor of "drinking away."

This might lead you to conclude that reckless behavior is a better approach. Never mind the other guy's face or the people with whom you share the road. Besides, once you come down from your buzz or adrenaline rush, your problem—not to mention the gutterpup in your jail cell—is still there. Score one for "thinking away" to even things up.

Just as your imagination is your reality, the majority of the time the problem *is* your mind. That's why taking your mind off the problem is the solution. That's another point in favor of "drinking away." But don't fill up that beer funnel just yet.

Alcoholics Anonymous has an adage that there's no problem a drink can't make worse. For others, a drink or three may be the perfect remedy. That's why the key to choosing a distraction is to make sure it isn't destructive *for you.* If shopping makes you feel better and you are flush with cash, go for it. If, however, you are depressed about being in debt and unemployed, leafing through a Zegna catalogue may be a bad idea. It's the same with comfort food. A vat of macaroni and cheese might be the perfect remedy to cheer you up.

It only becomes destructive if the very thing you're stressed about is clogged arteries or man boobs.

The main argument against distraction is that avoidance can turn a simple problem into a train wreck. Taking your mind off piles of laundry might attract buzzards. Disappearing for a week after a fight with your partner could be the coup de grâce that gets you kicked out of the house. Thus, chalk one up for "thinking away" to knot us at two-two.

The trick is to differentiate between dealing and ruminating. Complaining or worrying while going in circles is ruminating and leads to depression. Checking in with yourself, recognizing your patterns, and choosing the right tool is dealing and leads to a winning way.

Checklist For When You Feel Down or Depressed:
1. If you can do something to fix or ease the problem, do it immediately.
2. If the problem requires strategic thinking, take the time to come up with a plan.
3. If there's no action required, sit with it and feel what you're feeling.
4. Find a harmless distraction.

Getting drunk and fighting may be better tools for warding off depression than ruminating, but it doesn't mean they are your best tools. Instead, the next time you're down in the dumps, find the right mix of strategic action and non-destructive distraction. Better yet, follow Louis C.K.'s lead, put down your phone and engage in the experience of being human.

To make that experience the best one for you, find the tools that uniquely suit you.

QUESTION SIX:
WHICH TOOLS UNIQUELY SUIT ME?
More Empowering Questions

1. What is the anchoring action that you can do daily, anywhere in the world, for the rest of your life? This may be the most important element of this book.

2. I put myself in the best state every day by starting my day with:

3. The best tools in the morning for me are:

4. The best tools in the evening for me are:

5. The best tools for me when I'm down in the dumps are:

◉ ◉ ◉

Good work not allowing anyone to *should* on you. Since you chose the tools, now you have to put them to use. All the detective work you have done will only pay dividends if you commit to acting on it consistently. Every day, you create the right state, story, and strategy. Once these actions become habits, the focus of the next chapter, you become a leading man.

7 **HABITS**
What Habits Produce Effective Results?

WHAT HABITS PRODUCE EFFECTIVE RESULTS?

"You want to touch the heavens, you want to feel the glory and euphoria, but the trick is that it takes work. You can't buy it, you can't get it on a street corner, you can't steal it or inject it or shove it up your ass, you have to earn it."

—Anthony Kiedis, lead singer of the *Red Hot Chili Peppers*

Three frogs are on a lily pad and one decides to jump. How many frogs are left?

Hint: *deciding* to jump and *jumping* are not the same.

There are still three frogs on the lily pad.

You have put tremendous energy into figuring out who you are, what makes you tick (and why), and now you have the tools to put it all together. If you're that frog who has only *decided* to jump, you'll still be stuck in the same place. Don't make me quote our boy Wang Yang Ming again. Fine, you talked me right into repeating, "To know and not to do is not to know at all."

By this point in the book, you know your winning way. Now it's time to execute. It's tempting to steal Nike's catchphrase and write, "JUST DO IT. The End." Instead, we're going to examine how to build habits that will sustain you on your path. It's not enough to learn the tools that uniquely suit you. You must put in a consistent effort to make them habits.

Why It's Called Commencement

In *Good Will Hunting,* Matt Damon's character (Will) sabotages success. Over the course of their therapy sessions and budding friendship, Robin Williams' character (Sean) finally gets Will to see that "it" (the beatings his dad gave him and his mom) wasn't his fault. Because Sean builds his trust and takes him through a process, Will eventually believes him. Will's reprogrammed software changes the way he views the world and this breakthrough affects every part of his life. Through hard work, he finds his own winning way. Right now, you may be in the exact same place in your life as Will was in the movie.

Everything that Will experiences feels realistic, and we believe it when he takes off to drive cross country and open up his heart to the woman of his dreams. We'd be willing to bet that he'll find a job in Silicon Valley and make millions now that he's broken free from his upper limit issues. In real life, that *could* happen. The difference between fantasy and reality is Will's *habits.*

The fantasy is that once he breaks free and sees that "it" wasn't his fault, that he's enough, that he's entitled to being loved, his work is finished. The reality is that unless these thoughts are *consistently* fed, he will stop believing them. The mind is like an engine that needs fuel. Fearful and sabotaging thoughts will arise. It is how Will deals with these thoughts that will determine his life. What he does daily—with his body, mind, and spirit—will create his world. Sure, the work he did was life-*altering,* but it will only be life-*sustaining* if he feeds it daily.

Graduation is called commencement because when you think you are at the finish line, you are actually only at the beginning. If you fall prey to the Guru Trap, you mistakenly believe that you have seen the light and your work is over. Just as you know that even the most satisfying meal only lasts a few hours, know that your beliefs and attitudes have to be fed constantly. All of the questions you've answered, all of the time you've spent getting to know yourself, has been important. Now is the time to put it to use through habits.

Habits Create Evidence, Which Leads to Beliefs

I structured my TEDTalk as a debate about whether our actions or beliefs lead to success. Larry, an entrepreneur and health crusader, argues that it's all about actions. Ever the pragmatist, he says that it's much easier to change your actions than thoughts, and not only that, changing your actions will then change your thoughts.

Larry confused me a bit until he offered an illustration. He said to go to a beautiful place, reach both arms out to the sky, smile, then take a deep breath and try to feel depressed. Then sit on the toilet, scrunch up your face and hold a roll of toilet paper in each hand and try to feel sexy.

The simple act of forcing your face muscles into a smile releases endorphins and causes us to feel better. This brings us back to the chicken or the egg question. Do our thoughts lead us to the right actions? Or do our actions lead us to the right thoughts? Ultimately it's our habits that influence both.

My childhood friend Tank didn't like the fact that he was a slob and felt trapped bartending in Arizona. To get out of his rut, he could have visualized his sparkling clean apartment or gone to a therapist to analyze his childhood.

Tank came up with a different plan. Every morning, right when he woke up, for one year, he pledged to make his bed. That's it. His one anchoring action was to spend two minutes making his bed. It was small enough that it was doable, so he did it every day. He then started believing that he was a neat and disciplined person because he had the evidence right before his very eyes. When you lack the evidence to believe in yourself, you must *create* the evidence.

Tank said, "My biggest regret was spending ten years of my life sitting on a barstool getting drunk and talking about how I wanted to travel around the world and teach English."

He told me this while we were sitting in his clean apartment in Budapest, where he teaches English—and lives like a leading man—in part because he has 80 fewer pounds to lug around.

One small, *daily* habit propelled Tank to reprogram his software. *In The Power of Habit,* Charles Duhigg cites research to explain why:

> Making your bed every morning is correlated with better productivity, a greater sense of well-being, and stronger skills with a budget. It's not that a family meal or a tidy bed causes better grades or less frivolous spending. But somehow those initial shifts start chain reactions that help other good habits take hold. If you focus on changing or cultivating keystone habits, you can cause widespread shift.

Belief systems fuel actions and actions fuel belief systems. Finding your anchoring action—something as small as making your bed or singing a song—can be the catalyst that reprograms your software. When it becomes a habit, your thoughts and actions work in concert and the impact extends to all areas of your life.

How You Do One Thing Is How You Do Everything

The One Thing by Gary Keller is an entire book dedicated to the impact of one habit. When you narrow an endless list of tasks down to the most important item, it gets accomplished and everything else falls into place. There is an entire chapter on dominoes, which sums up the importance of your anchoring action. "…Find the lead domino, and whack away at it until it falls…You do the right thing and then you do the next right thing. Over time it adds up, and the geometric potential of success is unleashed."

The impact of one small thing can be seen in cities. The "broken windows theory" was invented by social scientists James Q. Wilson and George L. Kelling to explain the power of perception and momentum. A building with broken windows becomes a catalyst for escalating acts of vandalism. By repairing the windows, setting up that one domino, people begin to treat the building with care. We're inclined to litter on a dirty street or put dirty dishes in a big pile in the sink. But once the street and the sink are clean, it is more likely that your next action will be to keep them clean.

Musician and actor Tom Waits said, "The way you do anything is the way you do everything." This explains why Jerry Rice, who many argue is the greatest football player in NFL history, was so meticulous about the way he got dressed. How you do one thing is a symbol of how you do everything. If you are present and conscious while putting on your socks, there will be a "ripple effect" in all facets of your life.

For this very reason, on first dates, I've noticed women will try to sneak a peek to see how much I tip. They assume that if I'm generous with the server, I'll be generous with them and others. Same if I'm cheap. They are also evaluating how we treat the parking attendant and the busboy—and for good reason. They know the way we do one thing is a solid indicator of how we do everything. A former girlfriend told me one of the things she liked about me most was that I took my car in for routine maintenance. While it wasn't the most flattering compliment I've ever received, it made perfect sense for her to view this one thing as a sign of dependability.

Cultivating one good habit creates a ripple effect and extends to everything you do. Tank's one domino was making his bed. Mine is one song. What's your domino?

You Start by Starting, Not Stalling

Ronnie "Woo-Woo" Wickers is such an iconic Chicago Cubs fan that the late announcer Harry Carey called him "Leather Lungs" for his ability to shout non-stop for hours. When I lived in Chicago in 1998, Ronnie's voice dominated Wrigley Field. "Sammy. Woo. Sosa. Woo. Sammy. Woo. Sosa. Woo." Again and again and again. When Ronnie Woo-Woo turned up at a spring training game at HohoKam Park in Mesa, Arizona, my friend Stuckey asked him how he got there.

"Step by step," Ronnie said. "Step by step."

Simple wisdom only gets complicated when we get into our heads instead of taking action. Hockey legend Wayne Gretzky said you miss 100 percent of the shots you don't take. I was thinking about Gretzky and Ronnie Woo-Woo when I heard a friend go through his typical litany of excuses for not getting in shape:

- There's no sense working out until I start my five-day boot camp.
- I won't have any time to look after myself until work slows down.
- I can't get in shape until I save enough money for a personal trainer.

Sometimes I want to grab him by the ear and scream, "Go for a walk!" In sales, you learn to differentiate between an *objection* and a *stall*. Not being able to do pushups because you have a broken arm is an objection; not doing them because you don't like the song on the radio is a stall.

In his book *The Monk and the Riddle,* Randy Komisar identifies a form of stalling that he calls the "deferred happiness plan." Here are a couple of examples:

- I want to fall in love, but I can't start a relationship until I pay off my student loans.
- We're not going to travel until the kids are in college.

Another stall is to put the power in someone else's hands. For example:

- As soon as my boss takes me off this project, I'll focus on having fun again.
- If my parents/spouse/kids/mother-in-law/bill collectors weren't always nagging me, I'd have time to work on my portfolio.

We can label every one of those stalls with two letters:

B and S.

If you want results, cultivate habits that lead to the results. I understand you may have to work a job that pays the bills. That doesn't give you a reason to cop out and forego what you love to do. In *The Way of the Superior Man,* David Deida nailed this concept:

> Don't believe in the myth of 'one day when everything will be different'...Do what you love to do, what you are waiting to do, what you've been born to do, now. Spend at least one hour a day

doing whatever you simply love to do—what you deeply feel you need to do, in your heart—in spite of the daily duties that seem to constrain you.

In addition to the other BS excuses, focusing on the outcome—the fear that it won't turn out as planned—often stops us before we start. Instead, focus on the action. Finishing a project is fulfilling, but you can't finish what you don't start. Starting something new gives you a rush because you must first let go of the fear of failure. Continuing the activity becomes the evidence that you are on the right path. Completion of the project brings you full circle and provides the motivation and confidence to try something else new.

Every aspiring author I met (and I'm talking 100 percent of them) who mentioned a fear that their idea would be stolen has never written a book. Not one. They had already chosen an excuse (complete with a victim-to-be story) not to start—and they never did.

Writers constantly ask me for advice. I start by asking them why they want to write a book. Many will say that they want to share their knowledge with the world. Others mention creative expression. Some say they want to build a fan base so they can make a fortune.

I tell them all the same thing: start by starting.

It's free to start a blog, and it accomplishes all three of the goals listed above. My friend Caroline did just that and called me six weeks later with big news: A publisher had read her blog and offered her a book deal.

Why?

She started by starting.

Paying Yourself First and Crowding Out the Negative

To start by starting means that you take action—any action—towards what you want. When you pay yourself first, you turn the important elements of your life into effortless habits.

In his book, The *7 Habits of Highly Effective People,* Stephen Covey suggests creating a quadrant to see if you're making valuable use of your time.

While you must deal with what's truly urgent, leading men make time for the important, but not urgent, activities that others put off. Here is what the chart looks like:

	Urgent	Not Urgent
Important	Helping a choking victim.	Skill and spiritual development.
Not Important	Answering a ringing phone.	Randomly surfing the web.

We invariably spend too much time on activities that fall in the bottom left quadrant. It's common for businesses to get so caught up putting out fires that they don't find time for strategic and creative planning. Then they end up falling behind their competitors, which leads to overpaying consultants to rescue the business, or not having a business at all.

A UC Irvine study points to the importance of staying out of that urgent, not important quadrant. The study claims that after a distraction, one as simple as responding to a beeping phone, it takes 25 minutes to get back to your original task. In a *Fast Company* article that explains how Smartphones can decrease productivity, Lyst CEO Chris Morton says, "We don't actually do the important things we need to do in our lives because we are obsessively checking [email]."

Leading men know when to turn off the phone, step away from the mundane, and commit to specific times and rituals for the non-urgent, but important, parts of their lives. One strategy is to figure out your biggest priority and do it first thing in the morning. Morton keeps his phone off the first hour of every day and devotes that time to yoga, meditation, and planning tasks while eating breakfast. Another tool is to do what you enjoy least the minute you arrive at work or return from lunch. The "get it out of the way" approach can be an effective strategy for both productivity and peace of mind.

Paying yourself first is a habit you can apply to most facets of life. For investing, have your monthly savings automatically withdrawn from your account (or paycheck) into a savings or a brokerage account. This makes savings an effortless habit. Once the money is gone you'll hardly miss it. Aside from avoiding the drudgery of writing down every expense and putting your energy on what you don't want (overspending), it allows you to focus on what you do want (savings).

Use the same approach for food. Crowd out junk food by first giving your body the nutrients it needs every day. Throwing a bunch of healthy foods in a blender or juicer is a great way to limit cravings. Filling half your plate with broccoli leaves less room for pork rinds.

Rather than making a list of all the things that suck your time, list the things you *will* do. If you're committed to finishing that business plan, spend 20 minutes on it before opening your web browser. If you want to spend more quality time with your kids, commit to the habit of reading a bedtime story. If you want to keep up with friends, make it a habit to send three postcards every Friday before you arrive at the office. A handwritten note continues to increase in value in our electronic world.

This goes back to choosing tools that can be measured. You can't measure a time-suck, but you can measure how long you spend on your business plan. There's no box to check for surfing the net endlessly, but there is one for reading a bedtime story. It becomes a win all the way around. When you pay yourself first, you enjoy the time in front of the TV (or obsessing over fantasy stats) more, because you carry a feeling of accomplishment, rather than guilt.

We've touched on how it may benefit you to weed out your toxic friends. The problem is that the very process of weeding out brings toxicity to the forefront. A more effective approach is to figure out who you do want to hang out with. Once you create a habit of spending time with the people who bring you up, there won't be enough hours left to spend with those who bring you down. The toxic folks (like the toxic food, debt, and websites) will get crowded out. Schedule weekly or monthly jam sessions, walks, hikes, movie nights, charades, and other events you enjoy with the people you enjoy the most and they'll become lasting habits.

The Habit Loop: Cue, Routine, Reward

We form habits for a reason. Something happens—we get bored, angry, or nervous—which is our cue. Then we take an action—biting our nails, munching on Flamin' Hot Cheetos, sending a nasty tweet—which becomes our routine to get a reward. The reward is the feeling that comes from taking this action. If our brain likes the reward, it becomes a habit.

The Power of Habit explains that you don't break habits; you replace them. It's why people who quit smoking often gain weight. The cue is stress. The action is to smoke. The reward is relieving anxiety and feeling better. Take away smoking and you replace it with something else. In the absence of a helpful or at least a neutral action, we chose another destructive action, like eating, that gives us the same dopamine rush.

Ever have a friend who can't stop talking about how his ex dumped him or how his boss screwed him? A well-meaning response would be to tell him to get over it, to stop obsessing, to let it go. But you don't break a thought pattern, just as you don't break a habit. To get that annoying song out of your head, rather than tell yourself to stop obsessing about it, replace it with another song. Since the subconscious only processes what it *does* experience—sound, sight, feelings—thinking about a negative only perpetuates more of it. To get over something, you have to focus on another positive thought.

By now you have worked on the root causes of negative thoughts and have the awareness to make better choices when you are triggered. When you get that cue, instead of biting your nails, take a walk. Instead of sending a text, take a breath. Instead of cutting crystal meth, cut the rug with your dynamite dance moves.

When I lose a tough hand in poker, I stand up and take a deep breath. If I lose two, I take a walk. These are two habits that force me to pause before my next action. Losing players deal with frustrating hands by playing like maniacs and end up pissing away their money. We're all faced with the same cues and seek the same reward—feeling better—though we chose different actions to attain that feeling.

If your cue is an incendiary email from a colleague, reply with a nasty email and you will feel the instant reward of relief. When I write that nasty email and hit send, it feels fantastic to get the frustration off my chest. My secret is that I only send it to *myself.* This allows me to receive a reward without the negative ramifications of starting a feud. It has become a powerful habit.

Rasheed Shows Us the Limitations of Knowledge

When former NBA champion Rasheed Wallace was triggered by the refs, he relieved his pain by lashing out, but then received technical fouls. Rasheed's reward was the instant gratification of venting his frustration, which hurt his team. More disciplined players take that same cue as a trigger to work harder. By foregoing short-term gratification, the ultimate reward is helping their team win.

Don't you think Rasheed's coaches were hip to the science of habits? Pure logic dictates that all they needed to do was create a reward—a monetary bonus, a day off from practice, his favorite meal after the game—for running down the court after a bad call. If only they could have gotten him to pause, it would have given Rasheed time to see that lashing out is a poor choice. There already were major costs for his actions —free throws and possession for the other team, as well as fines for criticizing officials.

Yet six years into his career, Rasheed (whose teammates reportedly loved him and was so revered for his intelligence that he became an NBA assistant coach upon retirement) broke the record with 41 technical fouls in one season. Both consequences and rewards were established, yet he couldn't break a destructive habit. Rasheed holds the all-time mark for most career technical fouls with 317. In other words, he *never* learned to replace a bad habit.

If you want to geek out on the research, *The Power of Habit* is an excellent place to start. In addition to fascinating studies about neuroscience, there are stories about Tony Dungy, Michael Phelps, Starbucks, Target, and AA. The reason we're only touching on the science is because creating the life you want is not an intellectual process. Students who dissect the most case studies often work for those who put the time into building, rather than studying, habits.

My friend Shawn, who is a teacher with a PhD in education, turned

Rasheed-like every time his principal talked down to him. His fellow teachers made bets on whether he was going to have a heart attack or beat the crap out of the principal first. Rather than hand him a scientific journal, I offered a tool that would force him to pause. I told him that when his boss demeaned him, he try replacing white-knuckling with saying "carbuncle" under his breath. Instead of going ballistic, it made him smile. With the benefits of awareness and an effective tool, Shawn was able to receive the same positive reward without the cost. It became a lasting habit.

Studies show that choosing a specific cue, like running the minute you get home from work, increases the odds of sticking with a workout plan. Tank makes his bed first thing in the morning, and it's now as automatic as taking a leak. My brother goes right to his elliptical machine the minute he hears his alarm. Michelle's cue to work on her design portfolio is her kids falling asleep. My friend Reggie lives in an apartment with thin walls, so lunch hour is his cue to go home to jam on his drums.

Notice how all of these successful habits coincide with a cue that you develop. When you schedule, you perform. When you perform, you earn rewards—and develop effective habits.

Use the Calendar For Cues to Build Effective Habits

Do you need to be reminded to sleep in on Sundays or see fireworks on Independence Day? Holidays and special dates on the calendar anchor us in habits. Think about all the rituals that go along with Christmas—from shopping, to picking out a tree, decorating it, wrapping presents, and caroling. Those can be positive habits if they are *your* choices and bring you closer to how you want to feel. If, on the other hand, the holidays make you feel stressed because you spend too much money or too much time with people you can't stand, develop habits that deliver the rewards you are seeking.

Many of us let Hallmark dictate when we should buy flowers or get smashed on champagne. I recommend telling Hallmark to go "have sex with" itself. Then build habits that suit your vision rather than someone else's bottom line.

The calendar can be your friend. My friend Lou gets upset every time he talks to his dad, but he wants to let his dad know that he still loves him. His cue is paying his rent every month. His routine is sending his dad a postcard at the same time he mails his rent check. His reward is feeling okay about his role as a son without getting upset. Since he has coupled contacting his dad with a chore tied to the calendar, it has become second nature. Sure, they're not exactly Ward and Beaver Cleaver, but the habit has elevated the relationship from disheartening to agreeable.

Sundays are for family. Saturdays are for long runs. Friday night is date night. The second Tuesday of every month is poker night. A full moon is a signal to get your freak on. The end of every quarter comes with a retreat or an offsite strategy meeting. Find a way to make the calendar work for you.

The office also has rituals, many of which revolve around food. Wednesday is pizza day. Friday night is Happy Hour. Last one in the office has to buy bagels. If these rituals are working for you, then dig in, by all means. But if they're making you bigger than a double-wide, turn Wednesday into picnic day, or a cookie break into a wheatgrass shake.

Meals are the perfect cue for habits. Saying grace is a way to connect food with a gratitude ritual. Here's the one I use, courtesy of Thich Nhat Hahn, the Vietnamese Zen Buddhist monk, author, and peace activist: "In this food, I see clearly, evidence of the entire universe, supporting my existence." The reward is a feeling of gratitude.

Also try using humor as a way to build habits. Okinawa, Japan, is known for health and longevity, in part, because its residents built the habit to stop eating when they are 80 percent full. Conversely, the state of Oklahoma has one of the highest rates of obesity and diabetes in the U.S. My friends Adam and Vanda have a ritual they use at the end of their meals to remind them of the perils of overindulgence. When they're contemplating another helping or ordering dessert, they ask, "Okinawa or Oklahoma?" This question, along with their laughter, is a cue to pause and reflect. It often leads them to the reward of feeling satisfied and light rather than guilty and bloated.

◎ ◎ ◎

Corporations work hard for you to build habits that support their goals. But do you choose habits that support your own goals or are you letting them program you? The owner's manual for your car tells you to change your oil every 7,500 to 15,000 miles, yet companies created marketing campaigns to do so every 3,000 miles. They have also inundated our senses by putting that sticker on our windshields, which we have to look at *every second* we are driving. With these simple actions, they have programmed us with the habit of changing our oil every 3,000 miles.

If companies can come up with a strategy to become more prosperous selling something you don't need, you have the power to create habits that make *you* prosperous. If the trash gets picked up every Wednesday, make it the day you also give one item away to charity. If you have a housekeeper every other Friday, every other Thursday night is your time to try a new recipe and invite friends over for dinner.

Every time you pay your cable or mobile phone bill, put an equal amount into your savings account or toward your favorite charity. If your bills get paid automatically (see how crafty corporations are at creating habits to clean out your wallet?), then pay yourself or make the donation when you get the email confirmation of your payment. If you get quarterly reviews at work, make that the time you revisit your ideal day and your belief systems.

Imagine saying a word of gratitude every time you logged on to your computer or every time you sent a text. Or coming up with a joke to keep from stuffing your face. What other habits can you tie to your own rituals or life calendar?

Habits Keep Your Tank Full and Your Woman Happy

After a tune-up and oil change, you replace your air filter so the engine is operating at peak efficiency. You fill up with premium gas and drive 400 miles. When you check the gauge and see you are low on fuel, you would never say, "How could I need gas? I already filled up today!"

This reminds us of the Guru Trap. We go to a workshop or have a session with a coach or therapist and think that we're good. We're healed...forever! Yet we would never make that same mistake with food and fuel. We know we have to continue replenishing. And how do we replenish?

Habits.

Comedian Steven Wright said, "I don't walk my dog anymore. I walked him all at once." We laugh at the absurdity of this statement, yet sometimes we forget that we have to walk *ourselves* daily. An apple a day may or may not keep the doctor away, but eating 30 apples on the last day of the month guarantees you'll need a doctor.

Cultivating love is also a daily habit. Three dates in, you're madly in lust and the gestures come naturally. You open the door, buy flowers, write poems, and worship every bit of your woman's body. You do this every day for a year, and you are both living in bliss. Then one day you decide to ignore her. She turns sour. One frickin' day! Hadn't you filled the tank enough over the past year to keep it full? In a word: no.

I think of women like flowers. They're beautiful, they smell great, and they brighten up the world. Our job is to make sure they get sunlight, water, and nourishment. Watering your plants regularly is a habit; watering your loved ones needs to be as well. It's the goodnight kiss, telling her how great her legs look in heels, saying I love you, editing her cover letter, giving her the weekly massage, planning the quarterly getaway, that keep love flowing. You'll get conditioned to make the gestures just to see her smile or receive the same back in return.

Love is a verb.

Success is a habit.

This is why your anchoring action, along with the rest of your rituals, is so critical. The things you want in your life don't accumulate automatically. You have to continue creating them every day.

◎ ◎ ◎

Hal doesn't even like poker, but he's been attending the same monthly poker game for 19 years and will not miss it unless there's a life-threatening circumstance. It's a penny-ante game, so while the financial stakes are low, the bonding stakes are high. The average guy over 35, without one close friend, doesn't stick to these types of rituals. This is a social and bonding anchor for Hal, just as four-hour bike rides on the weekends are a physical and spiritual anchor. He is a leading man because he knows what tools work and has used them to make effective habits seem effortless.

What differentiates Hal is his commitment to weekly, monthly, and yearly rituals that meet *a vast spectrum of needs*. Hal fasts at Spa Samui twice a year with an entourage, and even foots the bill for some. This meets his needs of physical renewal, deepening relationships, and contribution to others. He takes his kids to Tony Robbins' events for purpose-renewal, father-son bonding, and expanding his network of winners. He also writes down exactly what he wants his year to look like.

I once said to Hal, "You've already made it. Why not stop now?"

"I made it because of my habits," Hal said. "My habits will continue to make me."

Is 10,000 Hours the Entire Story?

Actor Will Smith said, "Talent you have naturally. Skill is only developed by hours and hours and hours of beating on your craft." In *Outliers,* Malcolm Gladwell offers many examples to illustrate that becoming an expert usually takes 10,000 hours of practice. He describes how Bill Gates had access to a computer in his teens and all those hours helped lead to his success.

I have been playing guitar for 17 years, and people tell me that I'm pretty good—for a beginner. The reason is in the math.

How to be a Mediocre Guitar Player After 17 Years
- 17 years
- 20 minutes a day/six days a week
- Two hours a week

- 104 hours a year
- 1,768 total hours

I haven't even put in 20 percent of the time needed to be a virtuoso. Unless I start practicing more, it will take me 80 years to get to 10,000 hours, which means I won't be an expert while I'm alive.

Am I comfortable leaving you with the notion that success is all about the hours? You should know by now that this is only a jumping-off point to ask more questions about habits.

Less Can be More: The Irony of Productivity

Woody Allen is famous for saying, "80 percent of success is showing up." If you combine this quote with Gladwell's premise of 10,000 hours, you have bought into a belief system that all you need to do is put in the time. Yet we know that going through the motions is a recipe for mediocrity.

I've played poker with people who have played 100,000 hours and still stink. The young guns are dominating the game because they *work* on their game. What often gets overlooked is putting in the time the right way. To be an expert, showing up is not enough. Doing something the lazy way only builds the habit of laziness.

In his book *How to Win at the Sport of Business,* NBA owner and *Shark Tank* investor Mark Cuban said, "…I had to make sure I wasn't lying to myself about how hard I was working. It would have been easy to judge effort by how many hours passed while I was at work. That's the worst way to measure effort." Phil Jackson embraces Coach Al McGuire's philosophy that, "If you can't get it done in eight hours a day, it's not worth doing."

The irony of Woody Allen's output is that he only works three to five hours a day. Other filmmakers stay up all night and produce less quantity and quality, so clearly it's not only about time. It's building the habit of putting in the hours along with the right intensity, belief systems, and tools.

Here are three questions to ask about making the best use of your time:

1. Are you lying to yourself about effort by falling back on how much time you put in?
2. Are you implementing the tools that provide the greatest impact?
3. What is your recipe for productivity and how do you make it a habit?

The Seinfeld Calendar

The story of how Jerry Seinfeld built a habit by creating a visual tracking device changed our vocabulary. What used to be called a wall calendar is now simply known as a Seinfeld Calendar. Software developer (and former comic) Brad Isaac had the chance to ask Seinfeld his secret of success, and he told him that the key to writing better jokes was to write every day. That was obvious. The real gem was how he created a visual that fostered consistency and turned daily writing into a sustainable habit.

Seinfeld hung a big calendar that included every day of the year in a prominent location on his wall. When he finished writing, he drew an X with a red marker on that day. Whether he was motivated by the pleasure of seeing those X's or the pain of seeing a gap, having the calendar stare him in the face worked for him. On the website lifehacker.com, Isaac remembers what Seinfeld told him:

> After a few days you'll have a chain. Just keep at it and the chain will grow longer every day. You'll like seeing that chain, especially when you get a few weeks under your belt. Your only job next is to not break the chain.
>
> 'Don't break the chain,' he said again for emphasis.

The genius of this technique is that it removes the focus from the difficult task of writing and shifts it to the reward of having a chain of X's. When Monte decided to improve his vocabulary, he pledged to learn three new words for 60 straight days. He downloaded an app called Day One to track his progress. Seeing the mark on his phone (blue shading rather than a red X) each time he learned the words created the same incentive Seinfeld received from his calendar. The fear of breaking that chain of blue led him to complete 60 consecutive days.

When Monte and his fiancée Melinda were going over their New Year's resolutions, Monte came up with a new spin for a reinforcing visual. First, they agreed to make their exercise regimen specific and measurable. Monte had to log three miles—either walking or running, on the treadmill or outside. Melinda had to complete 30 minutes of exercise. If she missed her class at the studio, she could use one of her videos.

They hung a Seinfeld calendar on their kitchen wall and bought a green marker and a blue marker. When Melinda completed her workout, she marked one half of the X in blue. When Monte finished, he marked the other half in green. Their incentive to workout daily is to keep the multi-colored chain going. They don't have to nag each other to exercise. They let the calendar serve as a reminder. It has become the perfect blend of encouragement and accountability.

When I sold office products for Lanier Worldwide, a huge "trip board" was prominently displayed in the office. This visual showed our monthly sales and let everyone see where we stood on our goal for the company's incentive trip. The ego boost of the entire office seeing your success, or the shame of them seeing that you were below quota, were strong motivators. Having to look at that board every day (or was it looking at us?) served to build habits.

What tracking devices will you use to increase your success?

Five Steps to Develop a Habit

1. Get clear on the feelings you want to create or the things you want to attain.
2. Use your awareness, along with your five senses, to appreciate the full benefits of committing to this habit.
3. Rewrite your software by using the word because to propel your thoughts and reinforce your why.
4. Choose a tool that is sustainable and pick a prescribed time.
5. Create a visual tracking device.

Putting It All Together to Create Habits

Now is the time to go back to your ideal day and commit to the habits that create it. If you want to wake up feeling refreshed, what evening habits will you choose? If you want to own that beach house, what will you do *daily* to make it happen?

Many people set goals or make resolutions with good intentions. Few succeed. Here's a look at the common pitfalls as well as how to put everything together to form powerful habits.

Old way: I'm going to stop getting down on myself and acting like a loser.

Notice that his focus is on getting down on himself and being a loser, which gives more fuel to the subconscious to perpetuate these negative feelings. Even worse, there is no action that will lead to a resolution. It's all about willpower, and more importantly, it doesn't offer positive actions to replace the negative ones. Moreover, it's so ambiguous that there is nothing to measure. It's a recipe for defeat. Here's a better approach:

Chosen Feeling: I feel happy and loved and have more fun when I am grateful.

Awareness/Senses: When I get frustrated, I focus on the negative. When I get my head in the right space, I feel more powerful and I see the world differently.

Software: I can feel this way because I'm a solid guy with a ton to offer.

Tool/Time: I write down three things I'm grateful for while boiling water every morning.

Tracking Device: I have a Seinfeld Calendar in my kitchen that I mark every day with a red X when I accomplish my action.

Old way: My resolution is to stop running out of money and having to stay home and work while my friends are on vacation.

This thought focuses on what he wants to stop doing (running out of money and staying home). Unlike a habit, there is no action that takes him to where he wants to go. He's cooked before he starts. Here's a better approach:

Chosen Feeling: I feel confident and in control when I have savings. I feel excited and motivated to work out when I have a vacation planned.

Awareness/Senses: When I get down on myself, I piss away money to feel better—and it only makes me feel worse. When I stick to a savings goal, I feel disciplined and abundant.

Software: I can feel this way because I make enough to save and I've done it before.

Tool/Time: I will automatically transfer $400 from my monthly paycheck to my brokerage account.

Tracking Device: I put a poster of the Great Barrier Reef on my bedroom wall. Each month, I add a sticky note with a kangaroo below the poster.

Old way: I will stop being such a slob and being judged by others.

Notice that the focus is on what he wants to eliminate: being a slob and being judged. See that the software runs so deep that a behavior (sloppiness) has turned into an identity (I am a slob). Like most lousy resolutions, there is no positive activity and nothing to do to make it any better. Here's a much better approach:

Chosen Feeling: I choose to feel organized and act "as if" I have my life in order.

Awareness/Senses: When my surroundings get messy, I beat myself up, and I judge myself. With less clutter in my home and office, I can find things more easily and think more clearly.

Software: I feel this way because I'm capable of anything I set my mind to, and because it takes so little effort for such a big reward.

Tool/Time: I will put away all the dishes every night before I go to bed.

Tracking Device: I will send a text to Bill with a picture of Mr. Clean every night. He'll do the same for his anchoring action so we can keep each other accountable.

One anchoring action may seem too simple, yet the research is clear that tremendous momentum can be generated by following through on one simple promise. As you learned from Tank, making his bed was a vehicle for a revamped life. Former CEO of Alcoa, Paul O'Neill, applied the broken windows theory and made safety his primary focus. With an unwavering approach to improving safety, significantly fewer accidents occurred. This led to a ripple effect that transformed the entire company. One domino, leading man. One domino.

Here's one last trick: Choose a period of time that feels doable. I know we talked about choosing an anchoring action you'll do the rest of your life, but it may take some trial and error to find it. A year, or a lifetime, may feel like an impossible goal and only one day won't create a habit. Perhaps one month is the perfect sweet spot.

Committing to one action every day for the next month will provide both your conscious and subconscious mind with evidence that you finish what you start, keep your promises, and take action to accomplish goals. That evidence will allow you to reprogram your software—the thoughts running through your mind that end up controlling your actions—and give you a foundation to build upon for the rest of the year and beyond.

Habits make everything else work. Stephen Covey said, "Sow a thought, reap an action: sow an action, reap a habit: sow a habit, reap a character: sow a character, reap a destiny."

Your life is your habits. In a chapter about action, words are cheap. It's time for you to act.

QUESTION SEVEN:
WHAT HABITS PRODUCE EFFECTIVE RESULTS?
More Empowering Questions

1. Every day, I commit to the anchoring action that I listed in Chapter Six. Now I'm going to be even more specific about my anchoring action.

   Chosen Feeling:

   Awareness/Senses:

   Software:

   Tool:

   Tracking Device:

2. Once a week, I commit to _____ at _____ time because _____.

   I track this habit with _____.

3. Once a month, I commit to _____ at _____ time because _____.

   I track this habit with _____.

4. Once a quarter/year, I commit to _____ at _____ time because _____.

   I track this habit with _____.

5. Special dates for me are X and they coincide with these habits. List three:

   a.

   b.

   c.

◎ ◎ ◎

We're almost at the finish line. It's time to review the seven questions, and maybe even learn some better ones.

DINKIN'S
7 EMPOWERING QUESTIONS

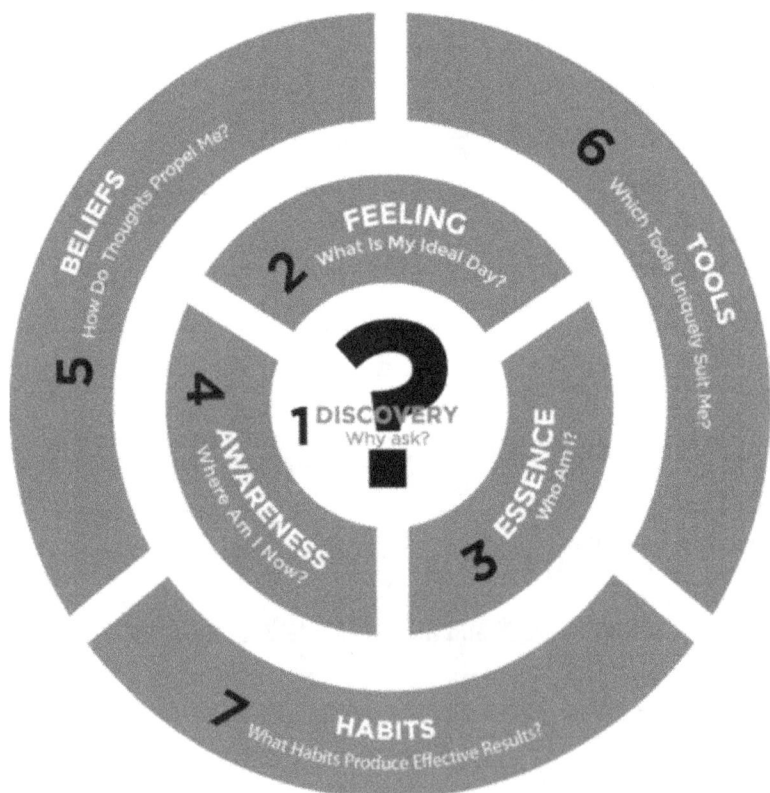

BELIEFS
How Do Thoughts Propel Me?

5

FEELING
What Is My Ideal Day?

2

6

TOOLS
Which Tools Uniquely Suit Me?

4

AWARENESS
Where Am I Now?

1 DISCOVERY
Why ask?

?

3

ESSENCE
Who Am I?

7

HABITS
What Habits Produce Effective Results?

YOUR MOST POWERFUL QUESTION

"Yes the answer lies within; so why not take a look now.
Kick out the devil's sin; pick up, pick up a good book now.
YES THE ANSWER LIES WITHIN!"

—Cat Stevens, *On the Road to Find Out*

You thought we were done with questions?

So did I.

Marianne Williamson is a spiritual author running for a U.S. Congressional seat in 2014. At one of her campaign events in Los Angeles, I had no shortage of questions for her. Since I'm more interested in personal development than politics, I asked her for suggestions on how to get my message out.

"I don't think about how to get the message *out*," she said. "I focus on getting the message *in*."

That hit me so hard I nearly fell out of my flip-flops. I had grown frustrated coaching a guy who focused on material possessions, who kept trying to manage the behavior of others without looking at his own. He was seeking answers everywhere but within, and for all of my questions, I wasn't reaching him. When I paused to ask myself why I was frustrated, I saw that I was projecting: *I* was looking for answers outside of myself.

When I backslide in parts of my life, I rely even more on questions. After being prompted by Williamson, another powerful question emerged: How do I get the message in?

The night before Halloween in 2013, I walked into The Love Dome, a multi-purpose studio in Venice, California, for pot luck, not realizing that a workshop was going on. For the previous month, I had been visiting family on the East Coast and was not only out of shape, but also worn down emotionally.

I had planned to be in Los Angeles for a week to gather my things before going back to Thailand. I knew that no matter how out of balance life got, Spa Samui would rejuvenate me. What I also knew, but didn't want to admit, was that seeking geographic solutions to problems was a lifelong habit that wasn't serving me. I've moved so often that every time I talk to my mom, she asks, "Did you know where you were when you woke up today?"

◎ ◎ ◎

Xochitl Ashe was leading the workshop at The Love Dome and her demeanor, along with the candles and incense, prepared me for a touchy-feely evening. She said that we are often reminded of the virtues of being more child*like,* and I could feel the Kumbaya and group-hug coming. Then, to my surprise, her tone shifted as she explained the difference between child*like* and child*ish.* She defined childish as opposing reality and not being with what is. Parking tickets, taxes, and dirty laundry aren't wished away by childish fantasies.

Like any great teacher, Xochitl put the onus on us and hit us with a powerful question. "How are you being childish?" she asked.

I wrote:

1. Procrastinating on my website
2. Not writing every day
3. Feeling slighted by the people who aren't showing up for me
4. Lacking consistency in my daily habits
5. Running away

Her question was a powerful gift of awareness, and I knew the reward would only come if I acted right away. I made another list to remedy the first four items. Number five, running away, remained at the front of my mind, even when I tried to bury it. Fortunately, my habit of questioning made me feel like I would eventually find my answer. In the meantime, I stocked up on healthy foods, which naturally crowded out the junk. I returned to my seven daily breaths and continued to play "The Gratitude Song" every day.

Deciding about Thailand was a difficult choice, especially since my plane ticket was paid for and expired in December. I had been thinking so much about the need to feel more grounded and how habits, not geography, would determine my fate. I was inspired by Seth Godin, who says that his key to publishing books is based on a simple premise: *he ships.* He finishes and "ships" by hitting "send" on his computer. He doesn't worry about being perfect. He sets a cutoff date, and he ships. Period.

I set Thanksgiving as a deadline to finish this book and started writing every day. I emailed my Web designer that night and we finished gregdinkin.com in short order. Rather than devote energy to the people I felt slighted by, I followed my own advice about crowding out toxic people and made plans with the people I enjoy. By recommitting to the people and activities I love, there was little time or energy to be upset with anyone. I fixed the bike that sat broken for months (procrastination is childish behavior at its finest) and started riding every day at sunset. I also called Aaron to schedule regular guitar lessons.

Leading Men Challenge Each Other

Since life is contagious, I reconnected with the friends who uplift me. Roberto and I dug into our coupon stash and had a *bro*mantic afternoon of juicing, go-karting, and organic Vietnamese food. Roberto is married. To a woman. He was an all-conference football player in college. He can probably kick your ass—though he's more likely to hug it out and tell you that he loves you. Man.

As I fall back on humor to diffuse how unmanly a bro-date can sound, I am reminded that many of us are so hung up on appearing tough that we close off opportunities to open our hearts and thrive. My female friends tell me how they challenge and nurture each other. They get together to create vision boards and bond over activities that develop emotional intelligence. Other women I know label these get-togethers as "book club" and drink wine and gossip. No matter the activity, they meet each other's needs for support and understanding. This needs to start happening more among us men.

Roberto and I talked about everything from the Lakers to upper limits. When real conversations become a habit, our guards come down and we connect. But even for me and Roberto, it would be hard to say, "Yo dude, let's get Ricky and Joey and Bobby and Jimmy, grab a case of Kombucha and work on our vision boards Sunday night. Screw the Packers game. I picked up some killer kale at the farmers market, and I'm bringing my Blu-ray of *The Secret* so we can watch it on the flat screen with surround-sound."

I can predict word-for-word what my friend Jimmy would say: "I'll be there in my new Lululemon outfit after my Pilates class and my pedicure. And I promise to remember to leave the seat down."

We'd have a healthy laugh, but we'd have a healthy (and wealthy) *life* if we had done the vision boards and created tracking devices for our anchoring actions. Just ask Seinfeld. Or ask Daniel Negreanu, who felt comfortable enough in his masculinity to post his vision board for 2014 on Facebook.

If you know a guy like my friend Noah, who is not afraid to look you in the eye and tell you that you're coasting, you are lucky to experience real friendship. I paid Noah homage by challenging Roberto about his effort to land a TV writing gig. Roberto displayed true masculinity by listening and taking it to heart. He then asked me, "If you're so committed to being grounded, why would you go to Thailand now?"

Wherever I went, I kept running into empowering questions. And leading men.

Is It the Question or the Pause?

After asking us how we were being childish, Xochitl told us that whenever we have a choice to make, asking one simple question would reveal the answer.

The question to ask ourselves is: What would somebody who loves themselves do in this situation?

She explained that since ego takes over when we talk about "I," using the word "somebody" allows us to step outside ourselves and make a choice consistent with self-love. A question that came up in the group that night boiled down to how to balance self-care with self-discipline. If you're feeling run-down and have been pushing yourself too hard, yet promised yourself to be up at 6 A.M. on Sunday for your 10-mile run, what then? The best answer is *your* answer, and it could vary from day to day. At least ask:

What would a leading man who loves himself do?

◎ ◎ ◎

Before I had a chance to share this brilliant question with Monte, he called me raving about a tool that was yielding powerful results. Whenever he finds himself in a tense moment, before taking action, he asks, "What would the person who *I want to be* do in this situation?"

I told him that Xochitl said that using the third person (he instead of I) takes the ego out of it. Before I could convince him of this logic, Monte said that personalizing the question makes it work for him. We debated the merits of both approaches until we realized that how the question is worded may be irrelevant. The power comes from asking a question to get you off autopilot and saying *something* to answer it. For the same reason we say "because," being forced to think of a reason results in conscious, effective choices.

Whether it is saying "carbuncle" under your breath, or asking "Okinawa or Oklahoma?" find tools that force you to slow down. Rasheed didn't erupt at referees because he lacked the perfect question. His outbursts were a result of never finding a tool—*any tool*—that led him to stop and reflect before reacting.

Before you put the needle in your vein, yell at the airport attendant, or stonewall your partner, do something that gets you to pause. Breathe. Pinch.

Smile. Yawn. Ask a question. Find a word that makes you laugh. Say because. Say something. Say *anything* that gets you to pause.

Pick at least one question you can use in any situation. Here's a list to give you some ideas:

- How would a leading man execute in this situation?
- What would the guy who makes his family proud say?
- What would the world's most generous man offer?
- How would a guy building a billion-dollar company react?
- What would the hero of the movie I'm directing declare?
- What would The Dude/Zen Master/O.G./Ghandi/Tebow do? (Use the shorthand of W.W…D and insert the initials that work for you).

Monte learned that when he asked a question, he automatically took a deep breath. This gave him all the time he needed for his higher self—rather than his adrenaline—to take over. Before he learned to pause, he would choose unconscious actions or destructive habits that he learned from watching his parents.

Once you gain the awareness to see that a situation is making you stressed, you have the power to make effective choices. When you take the time to ask a question that best suits you, you act based on your vision, rather than someone else's programming.

Super Bowl champion Russell Wilson's dad taught him to ask, "Why not you?"

What is your one go-to question?

The Best Detectives Get From Point A to Point B

Most books about success focus on getting from point A to point B. The expert maps out the exact steps you need to take, and if you follow them, you'll succeed. In three of the realms I know best—personal finance, nutrition, and writing books—I learned why maps alone rarely suffice.

When I wrote *The Finance Doctor,* I believed that the answer to financial success was based on information. The proper knowledge, along with the structure of an eight-step "prescription," was all anyone needed, and some people did, in fact, achieve results from the book. Yet my lack of awareness about the power of belief systems meant that I didn't address the subconscious and the core causes of failure.

If someone is running software that says he is unworthy of having money or that rich people are sellouts, he will get lost even with the best financial map. If he lacks the awareness to know that excessive shopping is a substitute for feeling loved, knowing that credit card debt multiplies faster than a pack of rabbits in heat isn't going to change his behavior.

I learned similar lessons from my own experience reading diet books. Eat less. Exercise more. Use your willpower to fight late-night cravings. I followed various maps for 20 years but could never reach my ideal weight. I worked hard. I was open to new ideas. I had plenty of willpower, so much so that I fasted for 15 days and even completed a marathon. So why couldn't I lose the weight? And why do 99 percent of dieters fail?

When I was a literary agent, new clients told me they had always dreamt of writing a book but didn't know where to start. I explained that I would be their guide and the first thing I sent them was a "Process" document that outlined the 20 steps from idea to post-publication marketing. Having that map led many to fulfill a dream. When it didn't happen, I would rack my brain to figure out why. They had the desire. They had the diagram. And they had a motivated coach. I'd beat myself up about it for months and Frank would always say the same thing, "Some people are lazy. Get over it."

I knew it wasn't that simple, but it took me years to figure out why. I now tell the people I coach that our job is to be detectives. We search for what has been getting in the way and what will propel them to reach their goals. It's not only the how, but also the why. It's not only the actions, but also the thoughts. It's not only the grand vision, but also the daily habits.

Disempowering belief systems can be challenging to overcome. It's easy to say that someone has a fear of success, but that doesn't go far enough. If a prospective author is running "being more successful than my spouse will disrupt our marriage" software, the words of the most inspiring coach won't make a difference. Someone running the program "at my core I'm really a fraud," will find a way to sabotage the process.

It requires a detective's mindset to uncover these beliefs, especially if they are buried so deeply in the subconscious that even they may not be aware of them. Writers who were aware of their weaknesses and were "strong" enough to admit them had the most success navigating their obstacles. If a potential author said he didn't have the time to do research, I suggested an intern or negotiated a research budget. If he said he needed a deadline, I would give him a deadline. If he said that he didn't know how to write, I would find him a ghostwriter. The common denominator for success was EIX. The authors who were vulnerable enough to vocalize their flaws and execute the solutions got results.

The right tools are important as well. A recording device helps those with writer's block get the words out at the moment inspiration strikes. Creating habits with built-in leverage works too. If a writer didn't allow himself to eat lunch or check his email until he wrote a single page, he would have a 270-page book after nine months—and afternoons off along the way.

Remember state, story, and strategy. My 20-step process for authors covers strategy, but without the proper health habits, a writer might not be in the proper state to generate anything. Walnuts are considered brain food; Whoppers not so much. Even the most energetic artist can turn apathetic when his blood sugar crashes and food allergies take over his biochemistry.

I still find Frank's contention that some people are lazy to be incomplete. People who are lazy in some aspects of life can end up surprising us with their work ethic in other circumstances. Is it because they got inspired? Scared? Or did they find the tools that suited them?

If you find yourself in a slump or a rut, keep coming back to these seven questions. Life is a moving target. Your ideal day keeps changing. Find the belief systems, tools, and habits to change with it.

7 Questions to Arrive Happily

These seven questions will increase your odds of attaining any goal. More importantly, they will boost your chances of being satisfied once you arrive.

1. Why do I want to do this? Will success bring the core desires I am seeking?
2. What does my daily schedule look like? How do I want to feel along the way?
3. Does this project mesh with who I am? How will it lead to what I'm building?
4. How will I know when I am on the right track? What checks and balances (and people) will I put in place to prevent blind spots?
5. Are my belief systems in line with my goals? How will I program my beliefs daily to keep propelling me?
6. Do I have the right tools to optimize efficiency? Am I open to trial and error so that I keep experimenting until I find the right ones?
7. What habits produce effective results? What anchoring action is the most critical domino?

These seven questions are similar to the ones you have answered in each chapter. I reworded them to be specific to a goal or project. Like our seven original empowering questions, as you'll see in the diagram on the next page, each one can be reduced to one word.

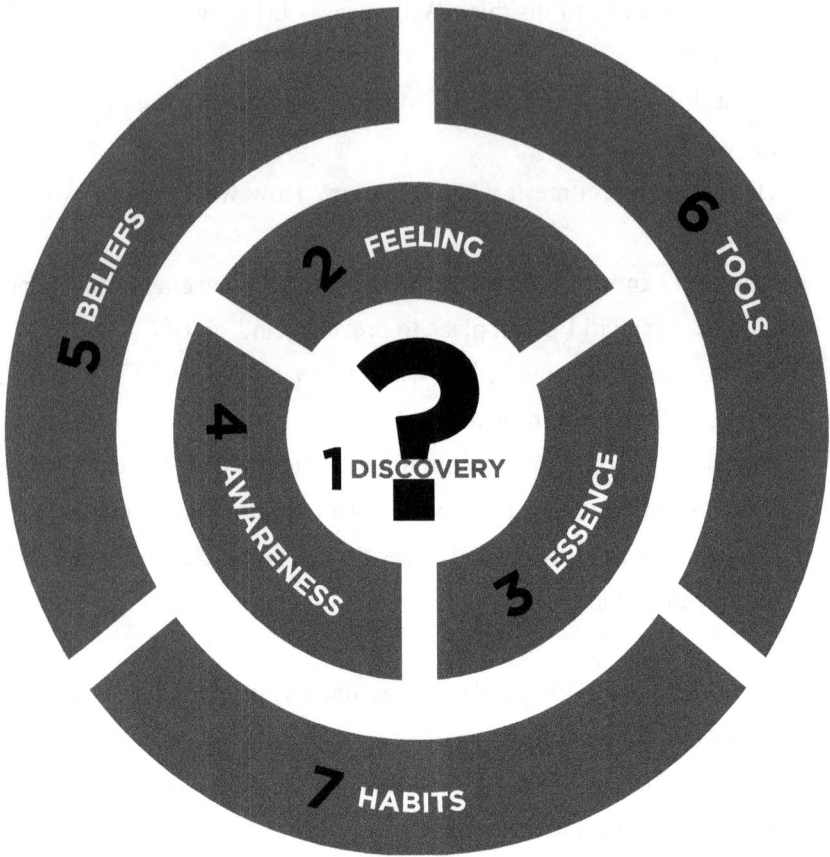

The Hollywood Ending

When my godson Reed saw the clear map that would pave his way to college, he stepped up his effort and improved his grades dramatically. I worked with him on his essays, kept my promises, and modeled the type of man that I want him to be—and want *me* to be. He received a guaranteed transfer to Cornell as long as he earns a 3.0 in his first year at another college. Equally important, the process that led to his acceptance built his confidence and brought us closer.

My masculine yearning to provide has been an incentive for me to earn more money. I've pledged that Reed will graduate college without any debt. *Living like a millionaire* now requires that I have enough money to contribute to my godson's education. They say kids teach you more than you teach them, and I'm grateful that Reed forced me out of my comfort zone and inspired me to increase my upper limits in all aspects of life.

I also love my friends for modeling true masculinity. Now that many of my relatives and buddies are fathers and husbands, I have the privilege of witnessing leading men firsthand. I visit their homes and watch how they listen, show affection to their wives and kids, and say those three words that were so difficult for men of previous generations to say: "I love you."

Doug Zeigler, a former college basketball player and father of four, wrote a column entitled, "Yeah, I Kiss My Sons…So What?" and declared, "The stoic patriarch dad is out; the hands-on dad is in." His column was published by The Good Men Project, a website that uses the tagline, "The Conversation No One Else is Having." While it's a great hook, the reality is that men *are* having the conversation.

The same guys who shared with me the pain they felt from what their fathers lacked—as well as the ones who lacked a father—are stepping up big-time. Yes, we are bound to recreate our childhood wounds and perpetuate abuse and dysfunction—*if* we fail to pay attention. The men I know *are* paying attention. With tears in my eyes, I humbly offer thanks for their examples.

◎ ◎ ◎

Before my ticket to Thailand expired, I asked: *What would a leading man who loves himself do?* Running away was childish. Realizing that the answers were inside of me, I made the choice that I wouldn't leave Los Angeles until *The Leading Man* was in print. As I worked hard to get the message out, I stayed focused on getting the message in.

I recommitted to the tools that are most effective for me, and my momentum continued to build. Was the decision to stay the one domino that was driving my success? Or was I being propelled because I was acting like an adult and a provider?

Have you thought about the ending to your movie yet? Have you asked what it looks like for you to return with the elixir and ride off into the sunset?

Here Comes the Bride

I don't know if your leading man has a love interest, but there's definitely one in my movie. On our first date, at a karaoke bar, I could see right away that Charlotte was smart, beautiful, healthy, and kind. I told her how Aaron, my guitar teacher, had taught me to play the song "Kiss Me" by Sixpence None the Richer. She actively listened as I explained that Aaron chose it to show me a new strum pattern as well as the chord C7, but that it was a horrible song for my vocal range.

"I'll sing it for you," she said.

Little did I know she was a professional singer, and she nailed it, as much with her voice as with her presence. I've always said I'll know her when I see her, and there she was, right in front of me. Charlotte had a Southern name to go with her sweet Southern voice, and her own perfect blend of solid values and starlet sexiness. My imagination took me to fantasyland.

I grounded myself with a breath, and we talked about what I should sing. Like any good muse, Charlotte suggested I stick with something in my range, and I put in a request for *Ring of Fire* by Johnny Cash.

After we ordered appetizers, she said, "I'll pay for my food."

"No you won't," I said, holding her gaze.

She tried to reason with me. "You said we were meeting for a drink. Not food."

"And your point is?"

Certainty. Clarity. Compassion. Courage.

No game. No script. No macho BS. Embodying the alpha requires nothing of the sort.

Consciously, she was being polite. Below the surface, she was testing me.

I passed with flying colors. And she won points for not being so entitled that she, an actress who could easily have been spoiled by success, expected me to pay. She earned even more for receiving the offer with appreciation.

Charlotte softened and became even more beautiful. Even though we had known each other less than an hour, my presence allowed her to melt into a safe resting place to unfold. None of this had to be said, but we both felt it.

Before we cut to the wedding scene, and *your* grand finale, let's catch up with some of our friends.

Mr. Skin and Our Cast of Characters

Mr. Skin extended his empire with mrman.com and boldly introduced his new website by saying, "The time is right, the buns are tight, and Mr. Man is the complete package. To all my wife's friends, just email me for your free password!" You don't think he took hell from his buddies for creating a website for celebrity male nudity?

Mr. Skin knows who he is and with "I know you are but what am I?" in his arsenal, he continues to laugh all the way to the bank. He does so while his son gobbles up grounders and awards on the baseball diamond. Papa Skin, older and in better shape than the rest of the dads, has been there to coach and support, because he asked the proper questions 15 years earlier, when he was a comfortable, though not quite leading, man.

In November 2013, Deepak Chopra published a book about weight-loss and well-being. He titled the book, aptly enough, *What Are You Hungry For?* It's a question I continue to ask myself. When I get too deep into thought, I remind myself that *researching* happiness and fulfillment doesn't create it. In that spirit, remember that this book only promises a foundation. You have to build the house (and raise the roof, jabroni) by asking the questions and living the answers.

Since we're the average of the five people we hang out with most, we have to surround ourselves with other leading men. I recently had lunch with Darius, the Wall Street executive, on a day that he was up at 5 A.M. to swim. He was as fit as ever and had just engineered the biggest acquisition in his company's history. He was often exhausted, and at times overwhelmed, though as I predicted, he said that he thrived from the *dis*comfort.

⊚ ⊚ ⊚

At 6'3" and 165 pounds, my godson Reed has the looks and metabolism of a Ferrari. In keeping with the Ayurvedic premise that fast-revving engines lead to health issues, Reed started feeling sick from the cafeteria food at college. One day he sent an email with "Uncle G approved?" in the subject line. There was a picture of my brands of chia seeds, supergreens, and protein powder.

Talk about the law of attraction! By some miracle, my actions had permeated into his subconscious. All those choices I thought had gone unnoticed, and here was an affirmation from the universe that my habits were having a positive influence on my godson. With this miraculous story percolating, I asked Reed how he chose those brands.

He wrote back, "I saw you brought those products over the last time you were here."

So much for the astonishing coincidence. Duh. But I like this story even better. What a remarkable affirmation to see Reed buying the exact same products he saw me using. He had learned to pause, show vulnerability, and ask for direction. I was proud to see that Reed's response to adversity showed that he had EIX in spades.

The spectacular stories continued to pour in. Remember when we talked about the American Illusion—how the goal of so many men is to earn enough "F-you" money to buy a yacht and eat and drink like kings? Well, Monte's company announced it was going public, and he was poised to make a boatload. I had a hunch he was yacht shopping when he sent me this email, "Looks like we are in the process of IPO. Maybe I will go with you to Spa Samui for a month and detox after I cash out!"

Monte exemplifies how our consciousness and ideals are shifting, and the data backs it up. Silent retreats were one of the top travel trends in 2013, and a *New York Times* article titled "This is Las Vegas?" reported that wellness tourism is a $438 billion market. The list of men finding answers—by asking empowering questions—continues to expand.

The Leading Man Experiences a Beautiful Day

You've seen enough movies to know how my story ends. The final scene to seal my love with Charlotte must center on overcoming my greatest fear. And sure enough, we had the perfect setup, given that we made plans to play guitar and compare Vitamix recipes (What did you expect? We live in LaLaland!). So you know what's coming. You see the look in her eye, how every bit of me oozes the certainty, clarity, compassion, and courage of an Alpha. Oh boy, this was getting good.

The day before our date, a text came through from Charlotte. Before cell phones, the old adage was that foreplay began at dinner. Nowadays it begins with a text. I opened it, smiling ear to ear, and singing at the top of my lungs. *"Hang a sign upon the door. Say, don't disturb this groove."*

This lyrical catastrophe came to a screeching halt when I read, "Hey Greg. I don't want to keep pushing this off. You're a really nice guy…"

Uh-oh.

You know from our discussion about language that what she *didn't* want to do (keep pushing this off) was the very thing she was doing. And you don't need to be a poker champ to realize that "really nice guy" is the kiss of death. A tear came to my eye as I struggled to read that she "only felt a platonic energy and didn't want to waste my time." Even in breaking a date, Charlotte was a class act. I paused, took a deep breath, and thanked her for her honesty.

I felt sad. I sat with it for a while. I grabbed my guitar and took a few more deep breaths. I thought about going to Jack in the Box, until another pause made me realize it wasn't what I was truly hungry for. I sat with it some more, and let the emptiness seep in. It hurt.

◉ ◉ ◉

In college, whenever Monte and I got blown off, which happened often, we would say, "She had one chance at greatness." We didn't believe it then, but at age 21, the "fake it till you make it" approach made us feel better. A couple of decades later, the thing that has changed the most for me and Monte is that we know who we are. And we love ourselves as we are.

Remember Abraham Maslow, creator of the *hierarchy of needs?* Maslow says that if you are a self-actualized person, no amount of praise can make you feel better and no amount of criticism can make you feel worse. Your internal state leaves you impervious to the moods and whims of others. This means that you don't give anyone or anything the power to affect how you feel. If a stranger cuts you off in traffic or a colleague cuts you off during a presentation, it rolls right off your back.

Imagine it having the exact same impact whether someone calls you arrogant or awesome, scumbag or scholar, dingleberry or dignified. Or if a woman you think is perfect for you can't keep her hands off you—or says she only feels a platonic energy.

If I claimed to be self-actualized, I would expect your BS meter to light up and fire back with "strong is weak." What I can tell you is that the day after Charlotte broke our date, I made my bed, played "The Gratitude Song," took my seven breaths, worked on my book, rode my bike at sunset, and made plans with the people I enjoy. Wash. Rinse. Repeat.

Knowing the power of belief systems, I reminded myself that it's better to want what you don't have than have what you don't want. Of course I, lucky number seven, believed it. I'm an enthusiast! To allow this belief to seep into my body, I grabbed my guitar and played *A Beautiful Day* by U2. "What you don't have you don't need it now. What you don't know you can feel somehow…"

It was a beautiful day.

Living the Ideal Day

My brother's simple, yet brilliant, question proved to be spot-on. Ask yourself what an ideal day looks like and live it. Once you realize how simple it is, it doesn't matter if you bought real estate at the peak or nadir, did or didn't get into the perfect college, or have been lucky or unlucky in love. When you see that all those stories are only stories, and that what you need to live your ideal day sits in between your ears—that you can, in fact, synthesize happiness—you let go and start living.

On Thanksgiving Day, 2013, I woke up, made my bed, played "The Gratitude Song," took seven breaths, made calls and sent notes to those for whom I'm thankful. Charles, who had fallen into a rut and had given up on his passion, replied with some big news, "Just got done interviewing two studios and producers. I'm going to do my own music with studio musicians. Finally. We'll talk!"

When you change the way you look at things, the things you look at change. Suddenly wherever I looked, I saw leading men breaking free. With thanks to Charles for his example on what it means to commence, I put the finishing touches on this manuscript.

I shipped! The first person I sent the finished manuscript to was the person to whom it was dedicated, my godson Reed.

Later, at a Thanksgiving feast with friends, I said with more conviction than ever: "In this food, I see clearly, the presence of the entire universe, supporting my existence."

One Final Nugget for the Leading Man

Before we get to your triumphant ending, I'll leave you with my most treasured bit of wisdom. You may, in fact, be waiting for me to turn into Curly from *City Slickers* and tell you the one thing that will change everything.

I've been down this road before. The speeches I give about using poker skills in business are often followed by a poker tournament. After emphasizing that the key to winning poker is to think critically rather than rely on rules, the group will still ask for a list of pointers.

I feel like they missed the point, especially after I detailed how experts make decisions based on each situation instead of memorizing lists. A part of me wants to go berserk. But rather than turn into Rasheed, I pause and remind myself to give the paying customers want they want. I'll list five tips, even using catchy phrases like "pump it or dump it" and "any two won't do" to make the checklist easier to remember.

If you're looking for that same kind of summary, if you want to know that one thing, it is simply this:

The only guidebook for a leading man is the one he writes himself.

No shortcuts. No secrets. No shoulds.

The Leading Man is about finding your own winning way. You do so by creating habits—with your thoughts, language, and actions—that cultivate the feelings you want as you live your ideal day. You know who you are and love yourself as you are.

You maintain the habit of asking questions and looking inward, rather than seeking answers outside of yourself. There's no checklist nor is there only "one" pearl of wisdom. There can be, however, a perfect Hollywood ending. The stronger the vision you hold for your life, the better chance it will lead you to the habits that create it.

Your imagination is reality. Tap into it and it will lead you to…

Well, don't look at me.

You want to know exactly what your movie looks like? You want to see yourself basking in the glory? You want that perfect Hollywood ending?

Then write it, hero.

Better yet…

Live it, leading man.

COMMENCEMENT
YOUR MOST POWERFUL QUESTION

1. What is your go-to question?

YOUR ANSWERS, YOUR MAP

CHAPTER ONE: WHY ASK?
More Empowering Questions

1. Is there a gap between the life you want and the life you have? If so, describe the emotions it creates in you.

2. What pain are you running away from? What pleasure are you running towards?

3. How will you know if you have been successful on your hero's journey? What is your leading man's ending?

4. What is your "Why"?

QUESTION TWO: WHAT IS MY IDEAL DAY?
More Empowering Questions

1. What is my ideal day? Be as specific as possible.

2. Describe how you want to feel as if it's already happening. Say it out loud and write it down. Be as specific as possible. Words like intellectually stimulated, fulfilled, loved, challenged, excited, and grateful might be applicable. Write in the affirmative.

I feel _____ because _____ .

QUESTION THREE: WHO AM I?
More Empowering Questions

1. Who are you?

2. What are you hungry for? What is your primary food?

3. What is the motto of the leading man in your movie?

QUESTION FOUR: WHERE AM I NOW?
More Empowering Questions

1. What's the one thing you can do right now to "look in the mirror" for a fresh vantage point?

2. What person do you trust the most to be honest with you? When is the last time you asked that person for an honest inventory of where you are now?

3. List one specific action you can take for each item on this list:
   a) Find a way to watch yourself.

   b) Consult a third party.

   c) De-construct technique and go back to the fundamentals.

   d) Slow down to become more aware.

   e) Personal development training.

4. List the love languages for at least two of the most important people in your life. Now write down what specific actions give love the best chance of landing on them. Also write down your love language(s).

QUESTION FIVE:
HOW DO THOUGHTS PROPEL ME?
More Empowering Questions

1. List belief systems that propel you using statements that you believe and that include the word because for:

   a. Money:

   b. Health:

   c. Purpose:

   d. Relationships:

2. List the five people you spend the most time with. Now list the five that most embody the life you want. How will you make them the same?

3. Rewrite your ideal day beyond your previous upper limits as if you are entitled, privileged, and delusional.

QUESTION SIX:
WHICH TOOLS UNIQUELY SUIT ME?
More Empowering Questions

1. What is the anchoring action that you can do daily, anywhere in the world, for the rest of your life? This may be the most important element of this book.

2. I put myself in the best state every day by starting my day with:

3. The best tools in the morning for me are:

4. The best tools in the evening for me are:

5. The best tools for me when I'm down in the dumps are:

QUESTION SEVEN:
WHAT HABITS PRODUCE EFFECTIVE RESULTS?
More Empowering Questions

1. Every day, I commit to the anchoring action that I listed in Chapter Six. Now I'm going to be even more specific about my anchoring action.

   Chosen Feeling:

   Awareness/Senses:

   Software:

   Tool:

   Tracking Device:

2. Once a week, I commit to _____ at _____ time because _____.

   I track this habit with _____.

3. Once a month, I commit to _____ at _____ time because _____.

   I track this habit with _____.

4. Once a quarter/year, I commit to _____ at _____ time because _____.

   I track this habit with _____.

5. Special dates for me are X and they coincide with these habits. List three:

   a.

   b.

   c.

COMMENCEMENT
YOUR MOST POWERFUL QUESTION

1. What is your go-to question?

ACKNOWLEDGMENTS AND TOOLS FOR LEADING WRITERS

I n keeping with the theme of focusing on you—and because so many people are interested in the craft of writing—I am going to combine my thanks with tools to become a successful writer.

Ray Bradbury said that the key to writing is to "Throw up, then clean up." The best advice I can offer is to write without judgment. Go, go, go, and get your information down. There will be plenty of time to revise later. When you decide in advance to let your friends and editors do their jobs, you have the freedom to write without inhibitions. Perfection is the enemy of the first draft. There will be plenty of time to pick nits later.

Moreover, when you share your material early, you are in a frame of mind to embrace feedback. When you wait until you think it's perfect to send to others, you want them to tell you how great it is and will be resistant to help. That's why I write quickly and send my work to others right away, with the instruction to be brutally honest and super specific.

My greatest strength as a writer should be no surprise to you. I *beg* for the gift of awareness and solicit feedback early and often. Even so, those who read my work are still hesitant to criticize. That's why I have learned to say, "Level with me, Sporto" a million different ways. Eventually, my readers figure out that I'm dying to know what they didn't like since it serves the purpose of making the book better.

If an author tells you how much his writing sucks, it's false modesty. If others say it, it really does suck. This book is about my friends telling me it sucked—for years—and me knowing that the book would be ready when *they* told me it was ready. Just as I wrote about how the audience lets a comedian know what is funny based on their laughter, I told myself over and over that this book would be finished not when I said so, but when my readers said so.

When someone like Adam Sakoonserksadee told me that the book was working, I believed him because he had told me several times before that it was not. Plus, he offered great ideas on how to make it better. Thanks, A15.

I could sense that my friend Sloane Miller, a brilliant author and editor, was holding back her feedback so as not to hurt my feelings. After insisting that she could not possibly offend me, she finally said, "I feel like you were clearing your throat." She was right that I often lead with a long preamble and take too long to get to my point. In fact, the very first line of the book, "Once upon a time I was fat, broke, lonely, and miserable," once required eight pages. Eight pages!

Sloane also told me that I seemed "bored" with my own stories. I told her that I was bored. She then offered up the wisdom that changed everything. She said great writing is about discovery, and readers must feel that they are discovering along with you. The 88 pages that she read more than three years ago were as much a memoir as a book about questions, and it helped me understand that I had no interest in writing a memoir. What I wanted to discover was how to put all the tools and knowledge I had accumulated into practice in my own life (and more importantly, give other men a structure to do so as well). This led me to start writing a book titled *The Complete Man*.

That shift gave the book the "discovery" component it sorely needed. The stories that had been boring me, like making the final table at the World Series of Poker, suddenly became stories that I was dying to tell because they fit with the principles I wanted to get across. When the book shifted from, "let me tell you what I did," to "let's figure out how to put all this together," I was on my way.

When I read *The Big Short* by Michael Lewis, it drove home Sloane's point about discovery. When Lewis tells the story, you actually "feel" as if he is as perplexed as we are. It's as if you can see him scratching his head as he writes,

"How the heck did a migrant worker making $14,000 a year get approved for a $700,000 mortgage?" Lewis' curiosity fuels the reader's curiosity, which makes his books so compelling.

◎ ◎ ◎

I met Hajjar Gibran on my first trip to Thailand in December 2006. The word "brother" doesn't do our relationship justice, but since I'm not the poet he is, it's the best one I've got. Hajjar was honest enough to tell me that he hated the title, *The Complete Man.* What started as a discussion about semantics (Are we ever complete?) turned into a discussion about what I really wanted to discover. Even though I already had elements of the movie metaphor in the manuscript, the shift to wanting to be a "leading" man rather than a "complete" man made me want to step up—not just in the book, but in my life.

Write what you need to learn. Write to dig deeper into your own questions, not rehash and preach your answers.

When I worked as a literary agent, I pitched books to Josh Behar, an editor at HarperCollins. Josh, who makes the brashest New Yorker seem timid, had no time for my lengthy preambles. As I would launch into my pitch, Josh would yell, "Enough already! What's the f&$king book?" When I sent him drafts of *The Leading Man,* he said the same thing. His *loud* voice in my ear (with the love that comes along with it) reminds me to focus, and his constant pleas to get clear on exactly what I want to say are priceless. His mom, Carol, wife, Lauren, and brother, Adam, have been equally supportive and have extended my "family of choice."

Josh, like my friend Jeremiah Rosenfels, is a school teacher. Both of them told me that no matter what they are teaching, they can never go too long without stopping and relating the material back to their students. Since the whole point of this book is for you to ask questions, whenever I found myself rambling, I heard Jeremiah in my ear saying, "How is this relevant to *their* lives?" It sounds so obvious, but for a guy who can get caught up telling stories, these words made a massive impact.

I am still humbled by how many generous people showed up for me in this process. My friend, Robert Campagna, read draft after draft and had no shortage of great feedback. In one of many amazing moments of kismet, he asked if he could send the manuscript to his dad. Like his son, Richard (author of *The Optimistic Existentialist*) offered outstanding feedback and furnished me with that fantastic quote in the introduction about "buying our way to death."

The Campagna's weren't the only great family duo in this process. Pete Fornatale was the editor of *The Poker MBA,* and twelve years later, I make sure his eyes find their way to anything I write. Not only did Pete offer astute edits, but on a lark, he sent the book to his cousin, Thomas Edward Harkins. I was only a week from my final deadline and was frustrated that Chapter One was scattered and unfocused. Tom didn't merely point out the problem. He gave me the clues to fix it, purely out of intellectual curiosity and the goodness of his heart.

Despite what he read in my manuscript about my attitude towards criticism, even Tom was surprised how open I was to feedback. I pride myself on being *impossible* to offend. Once I gave him free rein to remark without fear of hurting my feelings, and insisted that I pay him, his notes became even more poignant. Even his "asides" in the margins, suggesting a Bob Dylan quote or a reference to Münchausen syndrome (which I had never heard of), were so insightful that I said to Tom more than once, "You're bucking for a coauthor credit."

Speaking of coauthors/saviors, Jen Raphael saved me a thousand times. I posted on Facebook that I was looking to hire a copyeditor. Jen wrote to me saying that she had done a lot of writing and editing as an attorney and would like to take a crack at it. I ended up with not only the most detailed copy editor on the planet, but also a content editor, fact checker, and writer. I couldn't begin to name how many times she rewrote my sentences. Jen was so valuable that I hired her twice more. Because I was making so many changes near the final deadline, I asked her to edit the manuscript again. As I did with Tom, once I told her that I *wanted* her opinion, and that she had carte blanche to tell me which jokes and passages didn't work, she took the editing to an entirely new level. Given her level of detail, I told her that I would only be able to sleep at night if she agreed to read the final pages in layout form before I went to press. She somehow managed to exceed the sky-high expectations she created.

Chip Brookshaw was another godsend. He took what was a 33-page introduction and cut it down to 13 pages. When you are so deep into your own book, it's nearly impossible to have that kind of perspective. When Chip showed me what an intro with no fat looked like, I was able to see what was most important and arrived at what I thought was a solid 22 pages.

When I was close to the finish line, Jay Greenspan, a former literary client—who had been direct and honest with both praise and criticism in previous drafts—read the revised introduction. He said he liked the opening, but that it dragged at a certain point. That information helped a little. But when he was able to tell me where and why it dragged, I was able to cut a couple pages.

Jay's notes opened the door to more serendipity. My dear friend Monique Baron saved me from an awful joke that would have damaged the book's tone and told me that one section seemed "misplaced." Again, I was way too deep to see my own blind spot until she pointed it out. Even better, the very section that was misplaced in the introduction, fit perfectly in chapter one. Previous comments from Michael Friedland, another guy who was generous and insightful beyond belief, suddenly made even more sense and the pieces began to fit.

◎ ◎ ◎

I believe that the keys to writing are the same as the keys to being a leading man. It starts with asking questions, being open to criticism, having awareness, and displaying vulnerability. To that end, James Altucher is due a word of thanks for his advice to "bleed on the page" and constantly do just that.

Your ability to complete a project is influenced by belief systems. The reason I was able to take so many lumps is that the chorus in my head said that the book would be ready when my readers said so. My mom told me over and over as a kid that you're only finished looking for something when you find it. Thus, each "punch" of awareness gave me another clue on how to get there.

Alex Panelli threw one of those punches when he told me that I came across like Tom Cruise's character in *Magnolia*. "Douchey self-help guy" were his very words. Getting hit in the face hurt for only a second because I knew he was right. And because I fundamentally understand that rejection is redirection, I knew that his feedback would take the book another step closer to completion.

Author Tim Ferriss says to write for your five best friends. He says that most writers make the mistake of going too wide and not deep enough. I took Alex's feedback seriously not only because he is smart and honest, but also because he is at the heart of my target audience. If one of the people you are specifically writing for—who also happens to be one of your best friends—tells you he hates your book and can't stand you (as an author), it's time to go back to the drawing board. And when the same guy tells you, a year later, that the book is ready to go to press, you know those words come with credibility.

Mike Kelly is another buddy with a solid left hook. What I loved about Mike's feedback was the image of him in front of the book holding his pen, ready to work. I had gone overboard with the concepts of "I don't have any answers," and "a lot of guys don't actually want to do the work." Mike reminded me that many men want to do the work—and those are the guys I need to focus on by being more detailed in how I guide them through the questions.

My godson, Reed, didn't just turn into a man. He became a sage. I often call him when I'm looking for wisdom and he always delivers. I have all the confidence in the world that he can do whatever he feels like. Gosh! His mom, Michelle, who is like a sister to me, has developed a keen eye for the moments I make a fool out of myself. Lord knows she has had plenty of practice. Her comments in the manuscript such as, "Really?" and "Dear God" told me all I needed to hear. As for my goddaughter, my Booboolicious, she'll forever be one of my greatest teachers as I'm constantly in awe of the purity of her heart.

If you have read this far, you know all about my brother, Andy. He juggles a start-up business with a wife and two kids, and has a standard, sarcastic response whenever I ask about his day. "Just got back from two hours of hot yoga," he'll say. "I'm gonna' kick back with *War and Peace* after I research eco-resorts." Andy's greatest influence on the book was reminding me that I better shift my focus away from trying to get readers to *relate to me* to making sure *I relate to them.* His kids, Jayme Allison and Drew Harrison, light up my life.

The disdain Mike Wierzenski feels for the "throwaway" sentence was a remarkable blessing. I met Mike at Hajjar's retreat center in Thailand, hired him to design the book jacket (which he worked tirelessly on), and got way more than I could have bargained for as an editor. Each time I would come back with a new draft, he would tell me what worked, what didn't, and *why* it did or didn't. I have no idea where I'd be without him.

Andrew Feit said, "I don't want the CliffsNotes of all those other books. Tell me what you have to say." Many readers told me that I had way too many quotes, but something about Andrew's Long Island accent and cacophony of f-bombs made it hit home. Nat Wood told me the same thing, and pointed to several examples of *why* certain passages were ineffective. Mike Sandler was equally wise and taught me how thinking more like a journalist would better serve my readers.

From my former home by the beltway, I was also lucky to receive guidance from Bryan Blanken, Jackie Blanken, Barry Blanken, Lo-ee Blanken, Dan Bernard, Jimmy Haley, Joe Preston, Thom Loverro, Leslie Hillyer, Randy Goldman, Joe Kim, Wilbert Givens, Scottie Sussman, Josh Nasar, Andy McClellan, Keith Lemer, Jeremy London, Benjy London, and Robin London.

Lisa Carter built my first website 14 years ago and still manages to read my mind and make our work as efficient as it is enjoyable. Speaking of brilliant designers, I don't know how Katie Osborn created the diagram for "Dinkin's 7 Empowering Questions." She captured the inside-out path of the leading man and left me in awe of her talent. Book designer Gus Yoo helped me stay sane as I kept pushing against the deadline and asking him to oblige.

I've known Tim Simpson since college, but it wasn't until he volunteered to read the book that I *really* got to know him. His courage to be vulnerable and his insistence that this book was greatly needed was a constant motivation. Other college friends contributed in unique ways, including Ted VonHoene, Bob Hart, Lance Rosen, Ed Estrada, Doug Sundheim, Greg Knopp, Greg Greene, Mrs. Kendrick, Lorie Greene, Caitlin Nobile, Marc Bruno, Charlie Beard, Jon Gordon, Jim Meckley, Jack Gonzalez, Lance Sprinkle, Andy Hite, Brad Bosart, Shawn Fox, Bobert Cohen, Jeff Woodring, Nicole Woodring, Tim Barry, Butch Barry, Tony Tabasso, and Rich Owens (the clickety).

At the perfect time, Mark Meulenberg showed me just how wise he is. Darren Carpizo has a unique ability to kick me in the ass or give me a hug, sometimes in the same breath. He, along with Scott Weisenberg, kept urging me to stay in charge.

David Katz has never stopped pushing me to make information more accessible. He's one of the best networkers I know, and he led me to Victor Chi, who sharpened my skills as a columnist. Adam Fishman and Marc Recht were kind enough to read the manuscript and offer support. Carra Greenberg can keep the dime.

My friend Hemalayaa shed new light on the words "Alpha me, baby." I owe thanks to Gabriel Reyes for teaching me a lesson in embodying a leading man when he alpha'd me.

My former health coach, Amelia Catone, seems like she will forever be my coach and it's comforting to have such a wise soul in my corner. Joshua Rosenthal founded the Institute for Integrative Nutrition, and I'm grateful he helped me to see that most food problems are really life problems in disguise.

George and Tia Ghattas, as well as Mr. Skin, took turns wowing me with wisdom and support and somehow made a January trip to Chicago seem like a good idea.

Noah Sanders led me to add an entire new question to this book. Where would I be without his advice to "know who you are." For all his wonderful qualities, and he has many, the way Noah conveys how much he roots for others is most impressive.

For Yogi Nora, I'm out of words. We should all be so lucky to make this fabulous of a friend, after turning forty no less. There's no such thing as TMI with YN.

David London is a childhood buddy who not only offered detailed feedback on the manuscript, but he did it *three times.* I'm humbled. Scott McLinden spent hours on the phone walking me through his notes, and his "tuff" eye for nuanced detail was invaluable. Diane Anderson went far beyond any call of duty to offer detailed notes on the manuscript.

Mark England, both a friend and teacher, didn't get nearly the due he deserved in this book. I don't know anyone as curious and open to experimentation. Matt Cinderey is a constant source of comedy and support. Mattster! Anna Lovelight has a Supermac that just won't quit, and she insisted early drafts of this book were amazing when they were hardly legible. Thank you, Anna, for believing in my vision.

The friends I've met in Koh Samui continue to be some of my best teachers and always make me feel like they are rooting for me. Nadia Harper, Jo Rowkins, AnnMarie Woodall, San-bao Veith, Annabel Nichols, Gila Kuhlmann, Vanda Manprasert, Robbie Clapham, Ronnie Vee, Chaz Gaddie, Aree Bungalow, Maia "Google" Sutherland, Barrie Musgrave, LZ Glenda, Fearless Seeker, Raffaella Caiconti, William Evans, Simon Steam, Neal Beechwood, Jet Lie, Michael Choi, and Jennifer Thompson are as adventurous as they are amazing.

Ed Hudson constantly challenged my thoughts. If I told him I wanted to get a radio gig, I could count on him to say, "Why are you waiting for someone to tell you yes? Why don't you just buy the radio station?" He doesn't just mean it; he lives it.

This process brought me closer to family, who offered guidance and love. Jason Freeland, Jenny Freeland, Jenny Levy, Jeff Newman, Josh Klaff, Ira Rothman, Leslie Dinkin, Ed Gross, and Linda Gross, were generous with time and advice.

Jake Klisivitch, Dan Crissman, Aaron Makinen, and Jenifer Butler made this book better with their editing savvy and enthusiasm. Frank R. Scatoni remains on the Mount Rushmore of editors. Every time he goes to the racetrack, I still root for him to break even.

My mom and my dad read the manuscript and were generous with time and support. Perhaps they now have a better idea of why I am who I am. I'm grateful that they have provided the combination of guidance and freedom so I had the opportunity to find my own way.

Whether it was wise advice, a vote of support, or an insightful edit, the journey was enhanced by Jim Patterson, Perrin Patterson, Jessica Erler, Doug Kenney, Michael Parness, Doug Zeigler, Jeffrey Platts, Reid Mihalko, Michael Addis, Michael Roban, Daniel Negreanu, Phil Gordon, Nolan Dalla, Brian Balsbaugh, Lizette Acoba, Lauren Feinstein, Lici Rodriguez, Ingrid Rodriguez, Michael Greenwald, Alan Greenwald, Brian Davis, Melanie Lemay, Owais Ahmed, David Baron, Nicole Baron, Athena Baron, Jan Harkins, Ray Bonavida, John Bonaccolta, Sangjun Lee, Kevin Paris, #HeatherArcher, Adrienne Stevens, Aaron Smith, Scott Hoffman, Nikki Raiman, JL Stermer, and Jennifer Witt.

To the "dream team" that I referenced, especially Joe Ehrmann, thank you for inspiring me to think—and ask better questions.

To all you aspiring writers, it may seem obvious to write your acknowledgments last. It's actually best to write them as you go, so you don't forget anyone and are specific with your praise. What may surprise you is that sometimes you can't write the introduction until you finish the rest of the book. I heard that suggestion before, but it didn't sink in until I had written about 100 awful introductions. Only then did I realize that I could not make a "promise" to readers until I knew what I had actually delivered.

You thought that was long? Imagine if Sloane hadn't taught me not to clear my throat.

Good luck!

Greg Dinkin, April 17, 2014

CLARIFICATION OF CREATIVE LICENSE

A non-fiction book that touches on emotions, feelings, and real-life examples must be true in both spirit and intention. I believe *The Leading Man* passes that litmus test.

A Million Little Pieces turned into a controversy because readers (including Oprah) felt deceived that the author made up stories to sensationalize his life. That's why I want to be clear on the fact that parts of this book are fictionalized. I also want to explain to you why I made certain choices.

My "Why" is to make information accessible so you have the tools to live your best life. Stories are a big part of that strategy because they entertain and help you remember the lessons. I took creative license for the following reasons:

1. To protect the identity of people.
2. To improve the flow of the story.
3. To avoid confusion by minimizing the number of characters.
4. To serve the message by putting it in a form you can remember.

The first point of clarity is that Monte is a composite character. Early readers of the book told me that they couldn't keep track of all the people I mentioned. In order to reduce confusion and create a coherent flow to the story, many of these characters became Monte. For those who know me and are trying to guess who Monte is, he is many people.

It is accurate that I watched the Super Bowl right after returning from Thailand with a bunch of buddies who wanted to muzzle me. At a different event, I talked to my friends about *The 5 Love Languages,* and several of their wives bought the book. In other words, the events I described are true—they are just out of order and comprise a combination of characters. The part about Monte's fiancée throwing the book at him was exaggerated because it was the perfect segue to talk about hearing a wake-up call. I feel it passed the litmus test because the spirit of it is true. One of my friends read his wife's copy and said it made a huge impact on his communication with his wife and kids.

It's worth clarifying the story about my book deal for *The Poker MBA*. I did, in fact, partner with another author and his name and platform influenced our ability to get the deal with Random House. The publisher asked that we put my name first on the cover, and I refer to it as my book because I conceived it and wrote 98 percent of it. I believe that the spirit of the story is accurate since the change in my belief systems initiated the process and led me to the actions (including finding the coauthor) that secured a deal.

Intention is key. If someone makes up a story but calls it real to get pity or to convince you of something, I agree that it's not right. I based the entire chapter about your ideal day around a question my brother asked his friends. I based another chapter on Noah's advice to "know who you are." Those events had to have happened, and of course they did. When Andy surveyed his friends, he got a combination of blank stares and material explanations. Neither of us remembers the exact responses, just as Andy can't remember the exact words Mack Brown said to him in 1988, though these exchanges are true to the spirit of what was said.

The email from Reed with the picture of the superfoods was 100 percent accurate. Anything recent with a direct quote, as you should expect, happened as described. A friend sent that exact email about coming to Spa Samui after cashing out (which was attributed to Monte) and Charles sent that exact text on Thanksgiving Day.

In short, this book is an accurate reflection of events. If you want further clarification about anything, please email me at gregdinkin@gmail.com.

LEADING MOVIES, SHOWS, AND BOOKS

My desire to be a "portal" for information has led me to furnish you with abundant resources and tools to find your own winning way. What follows is a list of movies, TV shows, and books mentioned in *The Leading Man.*

Movies and TV Shows

1. The Answer Man
2. Austin Powers
3. The Big Lebowski
4. Caddyshack
5. Celebrity Poker Showdown
6. City Slickers
7. Dumb and Dumber
8. Entourage
9. Fast Times at Ridgemont High
10. Fight Club
11. Good Will Hunting
12. I Love You, Man
13. Kung Fu
14. Rounders
15. Tin Men
16. Tommy Boy
17. Trading Places

Books

The books are in alphabetical order, by title. You will find most of the authors of these books, categorized by area of expertise, also listed on page 255 with our "Dream Team."

1. *The 4-Hour Body* and *The 4-Hour Workweek,* Timothy Ferriss
2. *The 5 Love Languages,* Gary Chapman
3. *The 7 Habits of Highly Effective People,* Stephen Covey
4. *Amarillo Slim in a World Full of Fat People,* Amarillo Slim Preston with Greg Dinkin
5. *The Artist's Way,* Julie Cameron
6. *Be Excellent at Anything,* Tony Schwartz
7. *The Big Leap,* Gay Hendricks
8. *The Big Short,* Michael Lewis
9. *The Biology of Belief,* Bruce Lipton
10. *The Blood Sugar Solution 10-Day Detox Diet,* Mark Hyman
11. *The Book of Basketball,* Bill Simmons
12. *Caro's Book of Poker Tells,* Mike Caro
13. *Catching the Big Fish,* David Lynch
14. *The China Study,* T. Colin Campbell & Thomas M. Campbell II
15. *Choose Yourself,* James Altucher
16. *Eat to Live,* Joel Fuhrman
17. *Eat Pray Love,* Elizabeth Gilbert
18. *Eleven Rings* and *Sacred Hoops,* Phil Jackson
19. *Emotional Intelligence,* Daniel Goleman
20. *The Farther Reaches of Human Nature,* Abraham Maslow
21. *Fifty Shades of Grey,* E.L. James
22. *Fight Club,* Chuck Palahniuk
23. *The Finance Doctor,* Greg Dinkin
24. *The Four Agreements,* Don Miguel Ruiz
25. *The Game,* Neil Strauss
26. *How to Win at the Sport of Business,* Mark Cuban

27. *How to Win Friends and Influence People,* Dale Carnegie

28. *Influence: The Psychology of Persuasion,* Robert Cialdini

29. *InSideOut Coaching,* Joe Ehrmann

30. *Iron John,* Robert Bly

31. *Lean In,* Sheryl Sandberg

32. *Learned Optimism,* Martin Seligman

33. *Linchpin* and *Tribes,* Seth Godin

34. *The Little Engine That Could,* Watty Piper

35. *Loving What Is,* Byron Katie

36. *Man 2.0: Engineering the Alpha,* John Romaniello & Adam Bornstein

37. *Man's Search for Meaning,* Viktor E. Frankl

38. *Men Are from Mars, Women Are from Venus,* John Gray

39. *A Million Little Pieces,* James Frey

40. *The Miracle of St. Anthony,* Adrian Wojnarowski

41. *The Monk and the Riddle,* Randy Komisar

42. *Now, Discover Your Strengths,* Marcus Buckingham & Donald O. Clifton

43. *The Omnivore's Dilemma,* Michael Pollan

44. *The One Thing,* Gary Keller with Jay Papasan

45. *One of a Kind,* Nolan Dalla and Peter Alson

46. *The Optimistic Existentialist,* Richard V. Campagna

47. *Outliers,* Malcolm Gladwell

48. *Phil Gordon's Little Blue Book,* Phil Gordon

49. *Phil Hellmuth Presents Read 'Em and Reap,* Joe Navarro

50. *The Poker MBA,* Greg Dinkin

51. *The Power of Habit,* Charles Duhigg

52. *The Power of Intention,* Wayne Dyer

53. *The Power of Negative Thinking,* Bob Knight

54. *The Power of Positive Thinking,* Norman Vincent Peale

55. *The Primal Blueprint,* Mark Sisson

56. *The Prophet,* Kahlil Gibran

57. *The Return of the Prophet,* Hajjar Gibran

58. *Save the Cat,* Blake Snyder

59. *Season Of Life*, Jeffrey Marx
60. *The Secret*, Rhonda Byrne
61. *Sex at Dawn*, Christopher Ryan & Cacilda Ryan
62. *Start with Why*, Simon Sinek
63. *Steve Jobs*, Walter Isaacson
64. *Stumbling on Happiness*, Daniel Gilbert
65. *The Trick to Money Is Having Some*, Stuart Wilde
66. *The Way of the Peaceful Warrior*, Dan Millman
67. *The Way of the Superior Man*, David Deida
68. *What Are You Hungry For?*, Deepak Chopra
69. *Wheat Belly*, William Davis
70. *When Food is Love*, Geneen Roth
71. *The Wisdom of the Enneagram*, Don Richard Riso & Russ Hudson

THE DREAM TEAM

Here is a list of people who were either directly referenced or whose work added value to the questions in *The Leading Man.*

Actors, Comedians, and Filmmakers

1. Woody Allen
2. Jeff Bridges
3. George Carlin
4. Louis C.K.
5. Jeff Daniels
6. Ellen DeGeneres
7. Leonardo DiCaprio
8. Nora Ephron
9. Brian Koppelman
10. David Lynch
11. Michael Parness
12. Todd Phillips
13. Braxton Pope
14. Chris Rock
15. Katie Rubin
16. Martin Scorsese
17. Jerry Seinfeld
18. Bill "The Sports Guy" Simmons
19. Mr. Skin
20. Will Smith
21. Blake Snyder
22. Howard Stern
23. Oprah Winfrey
24. Steven Wright

Athletes and Coaches

1. Jim Abbott
2. Roger Bannister
3. Charles Barkley
4. Tyrone "Muggsy" Bogues
5. Mack Brown
6. Rick Carlisle
7. Julius "Dr. J" Erving
8. Reggie Evans
9. Wilbert Givens
10. Wayne Gretzky
11. Bob Hurley, Sr.
12. Phil Jackson
13. LeBron James
14. Michael Jordan
15. Mark Mason
16. O.J. Mayo
17. Al McGuire

18. Dirk Nowitzki
19. Pat Riley
20. Nick Saban
21. Noah Sanders
22. Fred Shepherd
23. Tim Tebow
24. Rasheed Wallace
25. Bill Walton
26. Wes Welker
27. Russell Wilson

Business and/or Efficiency Experts

1. Dave Asprey
2. Marcus Buckingham
3. Warren Buffett
4. Dale Carnegie
5. Stephen Covey
6. Mark Cuban
7. Ray Dalio
8. Michael Dell
9. Larry Ellison
10. Timothy Ferriss
11. Bill Gates
12. Seth Godin
13. Daniel Goleman
14. Steve Jobs
15. Randy Komisar
16. Michael Lewis
17. Chris Morton
18. Elon Musk
19. Blake Mycoskie
20. Paul O'Neill

21. Sheryl Sandberg
22. Tony Schwartz
23. Russell Simmons
24. Simon Sinek
25. Neil Strauss
26. Doug Sundheim
27. Mark Zuckerberg

Health and Wellness Mavens

1. Heather Archer
2. Xochitl Ashe
3. Yonnus Becker
4. Adam Bornstein
5. T. Colin Campbell
6. Thomas M. Campbell II
7. Amelia Catone
8. Deepak Chopra
9. Peter D'Adamo
10. William Davis
11. Joel Fuhrman
12. Leo Galland
13. Donna Gates
14. Vaughn Gray
15. Nadia Harper
16. Hemalayaa
17. Mark Hyman
18. Mary Beth LaRue
19. Frank Lipman
20. Bruce Lipton
21. Anna Lovelight
22. Joseph Mercola
23. Sloane Miller

24. Michael Noonan
25. Yogi Nora
26. Dr. Oz
27. Michael Pollan
28. Weston Price
29. James Prochaska
30. John Romaniello
31. Geneen Roth
32. Joshua Rosenthal
33. Joe Rowkins
34. Mark Sisson
35. Zoe Soleil
36. Jennifer Thompson
37. Andrew Weil

Musicians

1. India.Aire
2. Bono
3. Bob Dylan
4. Michael Franti
5. Art Garfunkel
6. M.C. Hammer
7. Anthony Kiedis
8. Bob Marley
9. Tom Petty
10. Keith Richards
11. Paul Simon
12. Aaron Smith
13. Bruce Springsteen
14. Cat Stevens
15. Tom Waits
16. Scott Weisenberg

Mystics, Poets, and Philosophers

1. Robert Bly
2. Ray Bradbury
3. Richard Campagna
4. Joseph Campbell
5. Andy Dinkin
6. Hajjar Gibran
7. Khalil Gibran
8. Thich Nhat Hahn
9. Jimmy Haley
10. Thomas Jefferson
11. The Dudely Lama
12. Martin Luther King, Jr.
13. Wang Yang Ming
14. Earl Nightingale
15. The Peace Pilgrim
16. Joe Preston
17. Don Miguel Ruiz
18. Rumi
19. Socrates
20. Henry David Thoreau
21. Mark Twain
22. Ronnie "Woo-Woo" Wickers

Psychology, Sociology, and/or Spirituality Leaders

1. James Altucher
2. Shelley Bullard
3. Rhonda Byrne
4. Gary Chapman
5. Robert Cialdini

6. David Deida
7. Joe Ehrmann
8. Mark England
9. Mike Gervais
10. Daniel Gilbert
11. Malcolm Gladwell
12. John Gray
13. Gay Hendricks
14. Alexander Heyne
15. Russ Hudson
16. Arianna Huffington
17. Byron Katie
18. George L. Kelling
19. E. L. James
20. Abraham Maslow
21. Reid Mihalko
22. Dan Millman
23. Anaïs Nin
24. Alexander Peyne
25. Don Richard Riso
26. Tony Robbins
27. Jim Rohn
28. Martin Seligman
29. Stuart Wilde
30. Marianne Williamson
31. James Q. Wilson
32. Doug Zeigler

Poker Players

1. Nick Binger
2. Jim Boyd
3. Mike Caro
4. Roy Cooke
5. Nolan Dalla
6. Antonio Esfandiari
7. Phil Gordon
8. Phil Hellmuth, Jr.
9. Jeff Madsen
10. Chris Moneymaker
11. Joe Navarro
12. Daniel Negreanu
13. Pat Poels
14. Amarillo Slim Preston
15. Stuey Ungar

DINKIN'S
7 EMPOWERING QUESTIONS

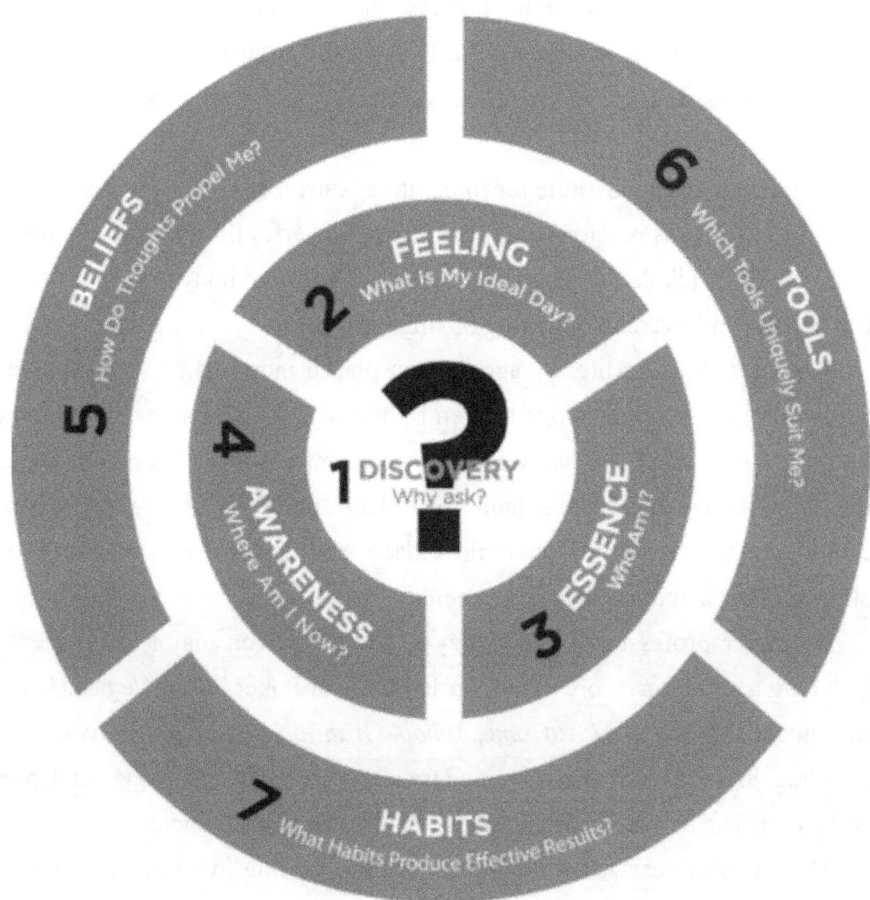

5 BELIEFS — How Do Thoughts Propel Me?

6 TOOLS — Which Tools Uniquely Suit Me?

2 FEELING — What is My Ideal Day?

1 DISCOVERY — Why ask?

4 AWARENESS — Where Am I Now?

3 ESSENCE — Who Am I?

7 HABITS — What Habits Produce Effective Results?

ABOUT THE AUTHOR

Greg Dinkin is a coach for men, professional speaker, and TV host.

In addition to *The Leading Man,* Greg is the author of *The Poker MBA* (Random House), *The Finance Doctor* (Vital), and Amarillo Slim's memoir (HarperCollins).

A graduate of the Institute for Integrative Nutrition, Greg, who also has an MBA in Finance, is passionate about making powerful life tools accessible to men. His TEDTalk detailed how he combined mind and body practices to lose 100 pounds and overcome his fear of singing.

Greg cofounded a literary agency that placed more than 130 books with major publishers and developed several films with Academy Award–winning actors and producers. He has served as a corporate spy for Inter-Continental Hotels, a management consultant for PricewaterhouseCoopers, a housing coordinator for the Atlanta Olympic Village, and has sold portrait packages, office products, and home improvements.

A former professional poker player, Greg has won major tournaments, including a six-figure score at the World Series of Poker in Las Vegas. He has written columns for *ThePostGame, Yahoo, Grantland,* and *Card Player.*

Greg loves to play guitar, sing, travel, read, write, do yoga, and play basketball. The native Washingtonian calls Los Angeles home.

He wants to hear about how questions are leading to your winning way and can be reached at www.gregdinkin.com.

www.ingramcontent.com/pod-product-compliance
Lightning Source LLC
La Vergne TN
LVHW051254080426
835509LV00020B/2965